C0-AJZ-940

SWIFT AS NEMESIS

FRANK BOYLE

Swift as Nemesis

MODERNITY AND ITS SATIRIST

STANFORD UNIVERSITY PRESS
STANFORD, CALIFORNIA 2000

Stanford University Press
Stanford, California

Printed in the United States of America

CIP data appear at the end of the book

for

LEE,

KATHERINE, AND ISAAC

ACKNOWLEDGMENTS

> of making many books there is no end . . .
>
> —Ecclesiastes

The making of this book has buried whatever misanthropic pretensions its author may once have harbored under the weight of an unacknowledgable accumulation of generosity from family, friends, colleagues, students, and even strangers at reference desks and in rare book rooms, coffee houses, and on electronic mailing lists. Misanthropy, too, is vanity.

Ian Campbell Ross of Trinity College, Dublin, began guiding me in my work on Swift before I had more than an inkling of where the work would take me. More than a decade ago when I was his student, he made me behave as a colleague and, throughout the development of the current project, he has offered a model of collegial friendship I study with little hope of ever equaling. I am indebted to Ken Craven for his time and great kindness, but most especially for his constantly original insights. William Park and Ann Cline Kelly have been the kind of patient, supportive, creative readers one might in a reckless moment hope for, but never expect to find. I owe considerable thanks to Tom Biegacki, Patrick Boyle, Adam Bresnick, Mary Ellen Carroll, James Gill, Hugh Ormsby-Lennon, Leland Peterson, Hermann Real, Michael Seidel, and Patricia Spacks, each of whom offered me encouragement at important moments. Ruth Mathewson's editorial skill and authority were decisive in convincing me that this work could be finished.

Colleagues and students at Fordham have supported me in this work in so many ways I could never fully acknowledge the debt, much less acquit it. Among those who contributed directly to the thinking and rethinking of this work, I must mention Babette Babich, Yvette Christiansë, Anne Hoffman, Chris GoGwilt, Eva Stadler, and the students of a graduate seminar called *Swift as Nemesis*, where many of the ideas presented in the following pages began to fall into place. Leonard Cassuto and Susan Greenfield have been great friends and great readers every step of the way.

I am extremely grateful to Helen Tartar of Stanford University Press for her advice and encouragement and to Kate Warne of the Press for her patience and professionalism guiding the manuscript to print. I am indebted to Ellen Browning for copyediting with a sensitive and exacting pen.

My father abandoned me and this work just before it was finished, along with the whole of the temporal world, but not without bequeathing a set of convictions that refute despair. My mother, my brothers, and my sister are constant—sources of comfort and happiness. My dear wife, Lee Riffaterre, and my impossibly wondrous children, Kate and Isaac, have borne the day-in and day-out costs of making this work, returning only joy.

CONTENTS

PREFACE

The earliest citation for the term *modernism* in the *Oxford English Dictionary* is from a letter Jonathan Swift wrote to Alexander Pope in 1737. He used the term to refer pejoratively to the proliferating invention of words accompanying the rise of modernness as a positive intellectual value. Swift invented a word to censure the invention of words. He then immediately reflected on his own here and now: "I now am daily expecting an end of life." Approaching his end, Swift bequeathed Modernity a name that circumscribed it with perfect linguistic irony: the value that is modern—what is just now—will ever be in conflict with its articulation—the *-ism* or state or condition the new words attempt to recognize. Inherent to Swift's notion of modernism is a web of linguistic paradox by which Modernity makes obsolescent whatever it claims by naming. "Was ever anything so modern," Swift had Aesop ask long before in *The Battle of the Books*, "as the Spider in his air, his turns, and his paradoxes?"

For Swift, the Modern can be located historically, culturally, and geographically. Rather than a culminating step in human history, the Modern is a phenomenon limited (in his time) to a particular part of the globe and further limited within the West to those who seek to extend human dominion via "the lines and measures" of human reason. Although Swift attacked Modern thinking in politics, religion, social mores, poetry, and art, he located the foundations of Modernity in philosophy, and he identified its most formidable cultural representation as the New Science that began its move to the center of Western thought in the seventeenth century. Throughout his satiric work, I argue here, Swift presented Modern readers with what he understood to be the contradictions—dangerous, and potentially antihuman—inherent to Modernity.

The question of the relation of Swift's *Modern* to our *Modern*, hangs in the critical air of this book. I approach this question via Stephen Toulmin's remarkable work, *Cosmopolis: The Hidden Agenda of Modernity*. Though Toulmin has only an intuitive understanding of Swift's role in the formation of the Modern,[1] he bases his rereading of the Modern on the works of authors who are central to Swift's reading of the Modern: Montaigne, Descartes, Bacon, Hobbes, Boyle, Newton, and such others. And like Swift, Toulmin discovers a hidden "politico-theological" agenda that gives ideological shape and direction to a new-scientific view of the world that its adherents insist is nonideological.

What Toulmin identifies as the general problem of the received history of Modernity has specific application to Swift. Toulmin argues:

> Little of our revised account [of the reception of the new science in the early seventeenth century] . . . was recognized or understood by historians of science or philosophy before the 1960's. . . . Committed to a rationalist view of science, they saw all empirical data as "supporting," "failing to support," or "lending partial support to" new hypotheses, as measured by numerical and probabilistic indices. (132)

In an analogous way, "rationalist" readings of Modernity caused the best work on Swift and science from the 1950s and 1960s to declare its own irrelevancy. For example, Miriam Starkman's groundbreaking study of *Swift's Satire on Learning in* A Tale of a Tub (1950) apologizes for the antiquated ideas of its subject: "To a modern reader Swift's satire [on the new science] is scarcely just or perceptive. We can see the universality and utility of seventeenth century science."[2] The great Swiftian, Herbert Davis, is also compelled to apologize: "I am afraid it is necessary to admit that Swift did not realize that he was privileged to be living in the bright dawn of the scientific era; he did not realize that some of his contemporaries were leading mankind across the threshold of the modern world" (207).

This scholarly line reached its fitting comico-tragic terminus in the work of Isaac Asimov who, rather than apologizing for Swift, attacked him while annotating *Gulliver's Travels.* The method of Asimov's attack is to show how the experiments Swift ridicules in the third book of the *Travels* have turned out to serve science and humanity. But Asimov happens unluckily upon the projector's treatise on the "Malleability of Fire": "Uranium and plutonium are metals, and malleable, and each is the source of a radiation, a nuclear fire more deadly than anything Swift knew or could imagine. Do not these metals then represent malleable fire?" (170).

The critical line on Swift and science, like progressive readings of the Modern itself, founders on the triumph of scientific knowledge in destructive powers beyond anything even our most sepulchral visionary "knew or could imagine." Three centuries of science, as I. I. Rabi noted in initially refusing to work on the atomic bomb project, end with a weapon of mass destruction.[3] This ghastly reality challenges the modern idea of its own progressive goodness and opens a discourse after the Modern—a postmodern discourse, which here simply means a place from which the assumptions of the Modern can be examined. The point is decidedly not that Swift's Modern is our Modern, but that the Modernity we have been reassessing during the last several decades is rooted in the New Philosophical work that is at the center of Swift's major satires.

~

The question of Modernity in Swift's work is approached here from the perspective of a theory of satire that identifies vengeful destructiveness as an ethical end of a satiric undertaking. This theory helps illuminate the nature of Swift's various attacks on Modernity and contextualizes various critical "explanations" of Swift's work within their modern contexts.

In *Travels into Several Remote Nations*, Swift attacks modern culture while aiming directly at individual modern readers. Novelistic identification with Gulliver's individual narcissism (beginning with masturbation and encompassing his various "scatological" observations) implicates readers in the larger cultural critique in which

Gulliver, paralleling Narcissus, successively rejects cultures he encounters until he attempts to embrace a cultural image that destroys him. The extent and importance of Swift's cultural critique is seen in his use of travel as a metaphor. Swift's primary critique of orientalism links the inhuman consequences of European colonial ambitions with new-scientific notions of discovery.

That Swift associates the Modern most directly with the New Science and the Royal Society is evident in his first published work. In his early poetry he represents Modernity as a particular pernicious strain of narcissism that devalues poetry and humanistic discourse generally. In his early satires he compiles a profane history of the Modern in which the New Philosophy is an extension of a methodology shared by alchemists, the debased Roman Catholic Church, and the various Puritan sects. This history culminates in the ridicule in *A Tale of a Tub* of the intellectual basis of the most formidable of all modern works, Newton's *Principia.*

Finally, critical readings of Swift that have appeared to be opposed to one another are shown to be instances of critics ensnared by narcissistic projections in the mirror of a satiric nemesis. Recognizing that Narcissus and Echo have become important to the critique of the Modern, I argue that contemporary critical discourse may find it useful now to turn to the contextualizing role of Nemesis. She emerges from Swift's critically irreducible satire with an ironic claim on Modernity itself. For in the satiric mirror the Modern's integral expectations of epic greatness are realized, but in work that traces its lineage, not from Milton back to the *Iliad* or the *Odyssey*, but from Rabelais back to Homer's lost work, the *Margites.*

I have upset what otherwise might be a nearly chronological (in terms of Swift's work) presentation here by having the discussion of Swift's *Travels* (Chapters 2 and 3) directly follow the opening chapter. The theoretical propositions set out in Chapter 1 are, I believe, most clearly explicated in relation to the *Travels.* After this, I work more nearly chronologically to historicize the theory in relation to Swift's emergent understanding of the Modern. A reader inclined to the chronological might, without major dislocations I think, read the Gulliver chapters (2 and 3) after having read Chapters 4, 5, and 6.

ABBREVIATIONS

Corr.	*The Correspondence of Jonathan Swift.* Ed. Harold Williams. 5 vols. Oxford: Clarendon Press, 1963–65.
OAS	*The Oxford Authors Swift.* Ed. Angus Ross and David Woolley. Oxford: Oxford University Press, 1984.
Poems	*The Complete Poems.* Ed. Pat Rogers. New York: Penguin Books, 1983.
PW	*The Prose Works of Jonathan Swift.* Ed. Herbert Davis, et al. 16 vols. (various reimpressions, sometimes corrected), Oxford: Basil Blackwell, 1939–69.

SWIFT AS NEMESIS

Chapter One

NEMESISTIC SATIRE

He saw himself in the true point of ridicule. . . .
—*Tristram Shandy*

In Ovid's telling, Echo is a nymph who acquired her imitative way of speaking as punishment from a furious Juno: Echo had used her naturally chattering voice to stall the great goddess's determined pursuit of Jove's relentless infidelities. No longer an intermediary in the sexual politics of the gods, Echo attempts to use her repeating voice to express her own amorous desires for the incomparably beautiful youth Narcissus. Separated one day from his companions while hunting, Narcissus calls out to a presence he senses near him in the woods, "*Huc coeamus*" (Let us come together here). Echo, still corporeal, responds verbally and physically, presenting herself before him with the word "*coeamus*," (Let us come together), drawing out the sexual sense of his words by illustrating—

with arms all ready
To fling around his neck—

the sexual possibilities of their meeting.[1] Ovid does not give Echo the opportunity to respond to Narcissus's rejection, "Fly from me and do not touch me," but she is allowed to participate in his unwitting statement of his own impending mortality. To his scornful dismissal, "I would die before I give you power over me," Echo returns, "I give you power over me." She too will die as a consequence of their defining failure to come together.

In no love story is the body more problematic. Echo and the other nymphs will not find Narcissus's body for the funeral pyre they have built for him, and Echo fades from flesh to a mere returning voice whose source in nature can no longer be found.

Integral to this story is a goddess who is often omitted from the telling of it. Nemesis answers the vindictive wish of a male suitor Narcissus rejects after Echo:

> "May Narcissus
> Love one day, so, himself, and not win over
> The creature whom he loves!" Nemesis heard him,
> Goddess of Vengeance, and judged the plea was righteous.
> (III, 405–8)

A judge of righteousness, Nemesis administers vengeance measured to the narcissistic crime:

> There was a pool, silver with shining water,
> To which no shepherds came, no goats, no cattle,
> Whose glass no bird, no beast, no falling leaf
> Had ever troubled. (III, 409–12)

Beyond natural pools, which return reflections textured by—and so contextualized with—the activity of human, animal, and vegetable life, lies the untroubled glass of Nemesis, an artifice of mortal vengeance.

Nemesis renders destruction that gives meaning to the separate experiences of Echo and Narcissus. Echo's repeating speech had made her a nearly perfect aural reflection of Narcissus; he rejects her because she remained conspicuously other to him. Nemesis's mirror matches the punishment to this crime, returning to Narcissus the untroubled reflection that entraps him with the love of "that unbodied hope," and deludes him with the discovery of "a substance / In what was only shadow." When this delusion gives way to self-recognition in the mirror of vengeance, the end is not reform but righteous destruction. The flower Narcissus becomes at the end of Ovid's tale is not a softening of Nemesis's ruinous intentions, but an ethically beautiful echoing: the flower's narcotic essence is linguistically linked with blind and destructive self-involvement.[2]

Echo, too, becomes a natural phenomenon mediated by language. Already a disembodied but "living voice" when Narcissus discovers the pool, Echo is with Narcissus in the stones and woods even as she is being avenged, answering his sighs and repeating his final words, "Beloved in vain." Nemesis does not seek to alleviate her pain or restore her hope. But by way of administering vengeance, the goddess gives Echo the opportunity to remember, to be angry, to pity, and to mourn, even as her voice, now of nature, still fails to convey intended meanings. It is the destructive action of Nemesis that transforms the stories of the tragic lovers into a mythic representation of the limited possibilities of human communication.

SWIFT AND NEMESIS

Jonathan Swift's identification with Nemesis may be discerned from his defining statements about himself and his art. Swift's satiric writings begin, in the preface to *The Battle of the Books*, with a definition that misdirects:

> Satire is a sort of glass, wherein beholders do generally discover everybody's face but their own; which is the chief reason for that kind of reception it meets in the world, and that so very few are offended with it. (*OAS*, 1)

The reader is here encouraged to focus on the gentle humor of Swift's definition: the folly of the human condition, like an amusing self-deprecating remark, is a tonic that keeps us in balance. Swift feeds this reading by telling us there is no real danger in the satiric enterprise:

> But if it should happen otherwise [i.e., that a Beholder does recognize him- or herself] the danger is not great; and, I have learned from long experience never to apprehend mischief from those understandings I have been able to provoke; for anger and fury, though they add strength to the sinews of the body, yet are found to relax those of the mind, and to render all its efforts feeble and impotent. (*OAS*, 1–2)

The "gentle reader" finds here a kind of homespun wisdom that says we need not worry about the mischief done to those foolish enough to be provoked to anger by being told the truth. But the destabilizing glass of the myth of Narcissus suggests an entirely different reading. The glass that Narcissus searches, not initially discovering his own face, is far from gentle or innocuous. The ridiculousness of his mistaken identification of the image in the glass gives way to anger and fury: the perfectly desirable body is awakened and inflamed, but rendered useless except as an ironic symbol of feeble impotence. Seen through the lens of the myth of Narcissus, Swift's misdirection—both the seemingly gentle humor and the claim that there is no danger—straightens into a kind of focus. The burlesque of Narcissus's attempts to apprehend his image is not ultimately comic but tragic. The danger of the narcissistic recognition brought about by the satirist is, precisely as Swift suggests, no danger at all for Nemesis or the satirist, but potentially fatal for the entrapped beholder. That critical rejections based on confusion or revulsion dominate the history of Swift criticism may be considered a first indication of the efficaciousness of the nemesistic lens. To be like the reflecting pool of Nemesis, Swift's satiric glass must be initially misleading. It must somehow entrap the beholder.[3]

If Swift's definition of satire, from the preface to the earliest of his satires, encourages us to consider his work in connection with the myth of Narcissus, it is his final words that confirm the link between Swift and Nemesis. In the epitaph he composed, Swift places himself in the tomb where "*saeva indignatio*"—fierce indignation—can no longer lacerate his breast:

Hic depositum est Corpus
IONATHAN SWIFT S.T.D.
Hujus Ecclesiae Cathedralis
Decani
Ubi saeva Indignatio
Ulterius
Cor lacerare nequit.
Abi Viator
Et imitare, si poteris,
Strenuum pro virili
Libertatis Vindicatorem.

> [Here is laid the body of Jonathan Swift, Doctor of Sacrosanct Theology, Dean of this cathedral church, where savage indignation can no longer tear his heart. Depart, wayfarer, and imitate if you can a man who to his utmost strenuously championed liberty.[4]]

A mortal, Swift imagines an escape through death from the justified resentment, the fierce indignation that Nemesis personifies. If Swift had referred to his death as a release from the torment of self-love, we would refer to his narcissistic description of himself;[5] his "*saeva indignatio*" allows us to speak reasonably of his nemesistic identity. But it is literally with his final word, *Vindicatorem*, that he speaks of vengeance, a term he uses elsewhere to refer specifically to Nemesis.[6] Typically, not even his final word is without misdirection: "*Vindicatorem*, is not classical. Polished Latinity, and Swift was practised, demands *vindex* for 'vindicator' or 'defender.' *Vindicator* is found only in late, ecclesiastical Latin, meaning 'avenger'" (*OAS*, editors' note, 694). Having defined his art in terms of Nemesis's technique—the glass that destroys through an initially misleading process of recognition—Swift defines his life in terms of the defining characteristics of Nemesis, fierce indignation and vengeance.

RETHINKING THE RIDICULOUS

In *The Dialogic Imagination*, Mikhail Bakhtin suggests (not without ironic awareness) that the only useful work remaining for literary theorists corresponds to the lost second book of Aristotle's *Poetics*, which concerned comedy. Bakhtin's argument is based in large part on his assertion that "theory dealing with . . . already completed genres," particularly tragedy, "can add almost nothing to Aristotle's formulations" (8). For genres defined by the surviving book of the *Poetics*, Aristotle's theory has remained largely sufficient and essentially unimprovable. But for genres not treated in the *Poetics*, which Aristotle grouped under the term *comedy* and Bakhtin refers to as the *novel*, everything remains to be done: "The existence of novelized genres leads theory into a blind alley." Swift, who relished sending theoreticians of all types down blind alleys, worked from an adaptation of Aristotelian literary theory he understood in terms of the Nemesis myth.

From what Aristotle says of the genres he will treat "hereafter," we know satire was fundamental because he offers Homer's *Margites*, also lost, as the generic equivalent to the *Iliad* and *Odyssey*. In a parallel argument, Bakhtin traces the origins of his evolving genre, the novel, to Socrates, who is "almost a *Margit*," and whose dialogues are ironic and full of laughter, and to menippean satire including the *Satyricon*. Bakhtin concludes that a new theoretical language (a veritable theoretical heteroglossia) is needed to map the expanding literary universe he calls the *novel*. But reading Swift in the context of the Nemesis myth suggests a theory of satire that is at once less radical than Bakhtin's theory in its departures from Aristotle, and more clearly expressive of the reasons for the incomplete, or open, or polyphonic, nature of satiric forms.

The Nemesis myth may in fact be taken as the paradigmatic foundation of a new theoretical approach to satire, one that construes satire as Bakhtin construes the novel—a form ever engaged in a process of definition. The myth shares metaphors of reversal and recognition with the surviving book of the *Poetics*. In particular, Narcissus's recognition of himself ("He is myself") may be understood in terms of Aristotle's notion of reversal (*peripeteia*) and discovery (*anagnorisis*). But this link does not necessitate associating the myth with tragedy. The limiting definition of tragedy in Aristotle depends on the link between its object—a serious and complete action—and its effect—a catharsis involving fear and pity. Even without the second book of the *Poetics*, it is clear that comedy and tragedy may each employ some of the same quantitative parts, or elements, and qualitative parts, including plot. It is, therefore, an open possibility that reversal and recognition, which are features of plot, may have figured in Aristotle's discussion of comedy. The Nemesis myth provides a structure for discovering in this open possibility a reading of satire that is grounded in the surviving *Poetics* and intrinsic to "the ridiculous," the object of the genre Aristotle calls comedy.

Comedy, according to Aristotle, has its roots in invectives or lampoons. But in the way tragedy developed from hymns, so comedy developed from a nondramatic to a fully dramatic form. It follows that Aristotle's definition of comedy would, like that of tragedy, have relied on the object comedy represents and the emotions it aims to arouse in an audience. Of the object, Aristotle says, comedy is: "an imitation of men worse than the average; worse, however, not as regards any and every sort of fault, but only as regards one particular kind, the ridiculous, which is a species of the ugly" (2319). Aristotle goes on to define the ridiculous in a way that has circumscribed commentary on the cathartic possibilities of comedy: "The ridiculous may be defined as a mistake or deformity not productive of pain or harm to others; the mask, for instance, that excites laughter, is something ugly and distorted without causing pain" (2319).

Recognizing that for Aristotle laughter is an emotion, commentators have generally read laughter as the comic equivalent of the tragic catharsis. The evident logic of this equation has obscured how incomplete it is. The emphasis on laughter as a "pleasant" emotion has in many ways divorced Aristotle's idea of comedy from its satiric origins. If comedy is the genre that aims to produce laughter without causing pain, what is its relation to the early invectives and to developed satires like Homer's *Margites*?

Answering this question involves noticing that Aristotle himself recognized that comedy aims at emotions other than pleasant forms of laughter. In *Rhetoric II*, Aristotle's discussion of the primary emotion associated with tragedy—fear—leads directly to a discussion of shame, an emotion he links directly to comedy. Shame is "the imagination of a disgrace, in which we shrink from the disgrace itself and not from its consequences." We feel it before various categories of people including, "those whose main occupation is with their neighbours' failings—people like satirists and writers of comedy; these are really a kind of evil-speakers and tell-tales" (2206). Aristotle sees no contradiction in associating the writers of comedy with the painful emotion of shame, and, in fact, the philosopher is in essence defining such writers by the painful consequences of the work they do.

In this context it is no accident that the second emotion associated with tragedy—pity—similarly leads in *Rhetoric II* directly to a discussion of indignation: "Most directly opposed to pity is the feeling called indignation. Pain at unmerited good fortune is, in one sense, opposite to pain at unmerited bad fortune" (2209). So the cathartic emotions of tragedy, fear, and pity have counterparts in shame and indignation. From Swift's perspective the logic of these parallel cathartic possibilities would have been underscored by the Philosopher's mythic reference. Aristotle associates indignation directly with Nemesis, saying "Whatever is undeserved is unjust, and that is why we ascribe indignation even to the gods" (2209).[7]

If recourse to the *Rhetoric* establishes other or additional aspects to catharsis in comedy, it does not resolve the question of the relationship of laughter to such painful emotions as shame and indignation. But a practitioner/critic of the eighteenth century can help to illustrate how one, writing while Swift was still alive, considered the problem. Noting in the preface to *Joseph Andrews* that Aristotle's definition of the term *ridiculous* wants explication, Henry Fielding introduces the term *affectation*, making the ridiculous a representation of actions caused by either hypocrisy or vanity. While all human faults, including those that doom tragic characters, might ultimately be traced to vanity and/or hypocrisy, Fielding's comments tie the ridiculous to the Aristotelian notion of discovery or recognition. Once beyond the spectacle or burlesque, comedy concerns itself with uncovering or exposing affectations that are ridiculous. Fielding's argument that the ridiculous implies discovery is buoyed by Aristotle's choice of a mask to illustrate the ridiculous. Unmasking is inherent in an imitation of the ridiculous. The laughter the mask provokes belies the fact that "people like satirists and writers of comedy" are for Aristotle "really a kind of evil-speakers and tell-tales." In this context, catharsis in the representation of the ridiculous involves a kind of Bakhtinian laughter—the laughter "without which it would be impossible to approach the world realistically" (23). Comedy is the construction of ridiculous masks; catharsis in the experience of comedy involves a kind of laughter that makes possible discoveries arousing shame or indignation.

Fielding's prefatory remarks on the ridiculous suggest that comedy shares with tragedy one of its "most powerful elements," the discoveries or recognitions. But it is later in the text of *Joseph Andrews* that Fielding echoes Swift's understanding of the nature of satiric recognition. For Fielding, a satirist may be distinguished from a writer of invective or lampoons because a satire "hold[s] the glass to thousands in their closets, that they may contemplate their deformity, and endeavour to reduce it, and thus by suffering private mortification may avoid public shame" (148).

For Swift as well, "satire is a sort of glass." It is particularly important to notice that for both Swift and Fielding, the satiric glass reflects upon the reader: satiric recognition for these eighteenth-century practitioners of satire was not a part of mimetic representation, but rather a part of the experience of seeing or reading the satiric work. Swift and Fielding understand the move Aristotle describes from lampoons to comic or satiric representation as a development from abusive direct attacks on recognizable individuals to recognizable "universal statements" that redound, upon reflection, on individual readers.

Although we cannot know specifically how Aristotle understood discovery in relation to comedy, Swift and Fielding locate discovery in the experience of reading or viewing the text. In tragedy a character discovers a mortifying aspect of identity, and an audience feels fear or pity as a direct consequence of that discovery. So Oedipus's discovery that he has killed his father and slept with his mother arouses fear and pity in an audience, not because we think we may make the same discovery, but because it makes us aware of how tenuous each of our identities is. In comedy a character's discovery is ridiculous, laughable. The mortifying discovery is a beholder's recognition that the ridiculous mask is a representation of *me*. So Strepsiades' recognition scene in *The Clouds* is laughable. Having forced a sophist's education on his son, the old fool finds himself forced to accept his son's argument that it is right and just for a son to beat his parents. But the work's power derives from the discoveries a viewer may make. Strepsiades has looked to education for a quick fix to financial problems. In doing so he has turned his child from an irresponsible luxuriant into a scorner of the gods and violent abuser of his parents. Readers will find themselves in various places in the comic mirror, but only the proudest reader will not see some recognizable reflection. Who has not at least at some point looked to education with venal ends in mind? Who has not used learning or wit to cover some self-serving action with respectability? How many parents can say that their child-rearing decisions are always in the interest of the child?

My own recognition in reading *The Clouds* corresponds exactly to the emotions Aristotle associates with the comic catharsis. I first laugh with pleasure at the wonderfully ridiculous predicament Strepsiades tirelessly works himself into. But I am also metaphorically struck by the blows he receives from his son. I am shamed by the recognition that I, as a teacher, am analogous to the representation of Socrates in the play. I am a participant in a game in which educators (particularly in higher education) position ourselves rhetorically above mundane concerns (Socrates' basket) and at the same time serve commercial culture in direct and often shameless ways. The financial arrangement between Strepsiades and Socrates—the "Think Shop" tuition is worth paying because it will allow him to prosper dishonestly in the wider commercial culture—is so recognizable, that its product—a child without respect for anyone or anything—is frightening. I am also indignant. As a teacher I am indignant that Strepsiades comes to me demanding an education with narrow commercial ends in mind. As a parent I am indignant that Socrates is willing to debase me, my child, and himself.

An idiosyncratic example of comic recognition is necessary because the dramatic discovery is outside the text. Authors of comedy represent ridiculous but recognizable masks but do not and cannot represent the significant discoveries such works engender. As such, comedies are inherently less stable, more multivocal works than tragedies. One can imagine the reader who will recognize himself or herself in the context of Strepsiades' lamentable marriage or in the context of the child who has used a parent's faults as an excuse for a disreputable life. With the discovery residing in the experience of reading, or viewing, or reflecting upon the comic work, the action of comedy is open or incomplete in ways the action of tragic works is not.

Comedy, in fact, reverses the relationship of tragic recognition and catharsis. Tragic recognition scenes give rise to fear and pity, and to the cathartic sense of relief and pleasure that viewers of tragedy often experience. Comedy on the other hand, may give rise to pleasurable laughter from an opening scene, but discomforting resemblances arise later in the drama or upon reflection through the cathartic laughter.

It is the metaphor of reflection that links the theory of comedy derived from Aristotle with Ovid's myth of Nemesis. The primary features of comedy from Aristotle are the representation of the ridiculous and the arousing of shame and/or indignation. The myth combines these features in a narrative that emphasizes how necessarily closely allied the ridiculous and tragic must always be in the human comedy. In both Aristotle and Ovid, Nemesis is a divinely sanctioned principle of indignation. A "foolish boy" who "wants himself," Narcissus personifies the ridiculous, which Aristotle terms "a species of the ugly." In this context Narcissus is a perfectly ironic emblem: the draw of his incomparable physical beauty makes him metaphysically ugly. And Ovid's description of his repeated attempts to apprehend his image in the pool underscores the laughable: Narcissus is so unreflective he cannot understand reflection at all.

Shame resides with Echo. Rejected by Narcissus, she is filled with shame (*pudibunda*). If seeking approval in sexual relations is a universal, the source of her shame is fundamental. She has made a specifically sexual overture to Narcissus, and now she is a nymph who has been rejected by a mortal man. Echo's importance to an understanding of comedy depends both on the sexual source of her shame and on her response to it. When she withers from a being who can be seen, she becomes nothing but voice, which Aristotle calls "the most imitative of our faculties" (*Rhetoric III*, 2239). "Shame dwells in the eyes," Aristotle says, citing a proverb, so Echo becomes the mimetic faculty that cannot be seen. She is the voice of comedy itself, which represents us in precise but incomplete ways and which illustrates the necessarily polyphonic nature of the art form. Read in this Aristotelian context, the myth suggests that beyond narcissism and shame is the voice that speaks deceptively of the mortification inherent in the human comedy.

Making satire a glass in which beholders fail to recognize themselves, Swift refers to the open nature of the experience of satire. Unlike the writer of tragedy, whose work involves bringing a character who is somehow "like us" through an experience of recognition, the author of satire constructs a mask that engages us. The mask must be ridiculous enough to disarm us with laughter and enough like us to be recognizable upon reflection.[8] And in such recognition is shame, indignation, and—"Alas, poor YORICK!"—the mortifying levity of the human condition itself.

However much my reconstruction of a pre-Enlightenment theory of satire may draw from Aristotle's fragmentary comments on comedy and from Bakhtin's vision of a dialogic, and unfinishable, genre, nothing in their works allows a reader to comprehend the intellectual violence and diseased flesh of satire associated with Nemesis. Two relatively recent post-Bakhtinian studies of satire map a path to a philosophical *terra incognita* of literary and cultural satire—a critical place corresponding, not to the lost second book of the *Poetics*, but to the dangerous extrarational place the *Poetics* was written to contain. Scott Blanchard's *Scholar's Bedlam: Menippean Satire in the Renaissance* begins by quoting a sixteenth-century student of Petronius who warns of the vanity of attempting to "reduce all such works to the standard of poetics." And it is Blanchard's project to show how menippean satire was revived in the Renaissance as a prodigiously learned and "paradoxically anti-intellectual" critique of the "immense program that humanism represents" (14–15). The menippean satire of the Renaissance used the instruments of the massive program of humanism against the program itself. In terms of the theory of satire I am advancing here, Blanchard's study suggests that the destructive power of the nemesistic mirror is proportionate to the power of the cultural program it reflects. Though Swift's work is beyond the range of the works he studies in detail, Blanchard looks ahead to make the claim that the "antigenre" (25) of the Renaissance "reaches its most anarchic and destructive potential in Swift's *A Tale of a Tub*" (28). As the immense program of humanism gives way to the "universal" (and arguably antihumanistic[9]) project of Enlightenment, so Swift, as the inheritor of the Renaissance "antigenre," has not merely massive, but "universally" destructive instruments at his disposal.

As in *A Tale*'s own claim on its title page—"Written for the Universal Improvement of Mankind"—the term *universal* is ironic in a manner that is at once ridiculous (laughable) and terror inducing. Blanchard's reading revises Bakhtin's carnivalesque by illustrating the intellectual violence of the form, and Blanchard does so for the historical period that is, at least with respect to Rabelais, Bakhtin's period. Universalizing the violence of the carnivalesque, Michael André Bernstein's *Bitter Carnival: Ressentiment and the Abject Hero* is a work that, it seems likely, will emerge as the most significant twentieth-century statement on the relationship between satire—what Bernstein refers to as the "Saturnalian dialogue"—and modern culture. Hearing a "distinctly melancholy undertone," Bernstein finds that Bakhtin's "typology of laughter . . . is haunted from its inception by a nostalgic longing for a realm of pure spontaneity" (17). In place of the nostalgia, Bernstein uncovers "abjection and *ressentiment*," which find their expression in violence in literature and in society.

More specifically, Bernstein's work is a study of the literary and cultural transformation of the Saturnalian, from the ancient practice in which *ressentiment* was given a carnivalesque moment for expression, to the bitter modern carnival in which: "The voices of abject rage ceased even pretending to the status of outside or marginalized positions, and fed by increasingly powerful injections of *ressentiment*, they sought to present themselves as enunciators of the 'sole truth' on which both society as a whole and the consciousness of its most gifted members rested" (173).

Some readers will no doubt be distracted by the way Bernstein ends his study with a highly principled polemic that positions pop culture and Charles Manson as successors to literary culture and its "abject" heroes. What gives his contemporary argument weight is the astonishingly compelling line he draws from the dark side of the Enlightenment, particularly in a study of Diderot's *Neveu de Rameau*, through to a discussion of the way "Dostoevsky's novels raise the stakes of the Enlightenment's conception of human nature by dramatizing the consequences when abstract theories become the ideological justification for, and psychological goad to, immediate action" (158).

My own study extends Bernstein's line to the formation of the Enlightenment in the works of Swift. This is not to say Swift's characters are abject heroes equivalent to those of Dostoevsky's or to the gruesome idols of popular culture. But as Bernstein's abject heroes move from "pathetic failure" through violence to "messianic destiny" (175), so too do Swift's greatest characters: the report of the starving Hack of *A Tale* on seeing a "woman flayed" informs his "universal" and "divine" treatise; Gulliver is an epic failure who offers the recipe for gunpowder to the Brobdingnagian king, fashions a sail from the skins of human babies, and expects his book to reform all human vices in six months' time; and the proposer of *A Modest Proposal* redirects the bitterness of the failure of more measured reform schemes into one simple, perfectly inhuman, model of Enlightenment systematizing. The "bitter carnival" in Swift's nemesistic mirror is in direct relation to the violence inherent in the collective narcissism of the Enlightenment project.

NEMESIS NEXUS

Unlike the figures of Narcissus and Echo, Nemesis has played only a minor role in contemporary criticism.[10]

Narcissus has maintained an important and highly visible place, especially in contemporary cultural criticism, due in large part to Freud (*Civilization and Its Discontents* being even more important in this context than "On Narcissism") and to Christopher Lasch's *The Culture of Narcissism*. These influential works call on the myth to illustrate explanations for evident destructive tendencies in societies that are almost godlike (Freud's "prosthetic god") in their physical transformations of the natural world. These works and the many works they have given rise to have created a cultural discourse in which the awesome material power of modern systems has been linked to the individual's narcissistic desire for omnipotence. Critical recourse to narcissism is generally etiologic, reflective not only of assumptions about a disorder in the culture of society but of the conviction that successful reordering depends, in Freud's words, on "unsparing criticism . . . to uncover the roots of [civilization's] imperfection" (*Civ.*, 74). Contemporary thinkers who invoke the myth of Narcissus tend, like Freud and Lasch, to be scientific rationalists trying to determine why, despite enormous material progress, modern society seems an increasingly lonely, only fleetingly illusional, pool of unhappiness, violence, and death.[11]

In response, ironically, to the high profile of the work on cultural narcissism, Echo has emerged from the critical woods to interest critics who distrust the medical and scientific assumptions of traditional modern rationalism. One recent role for Echo has been as a powerful if necessarily fragmented emblem for feminist discourse: even the woman who asserts herself and makes known her desires, as Echo does, becomes ancillary to the dominant discourse of the self-loving male and the cultural devastation he engenders. Gayatri Chakravorty Spivak has challenged this interpretation by reading Ovid's Echo as unintentionally powerful—powerful beyond the intentions of her Roman author and beyond her own intentions. Attempting "to 'give woman' to Echo" (17), Spivak finds the perception underlying Ovid's portrayal of Echo in his failure to allow Echo to say what she must say to Narcissus when he rejects her: she has no choice but to echo the command "Fly from me," thereby, however unintentionally, rejecting the other she desires.[12] In Spivak's deconstructive reading of the *Metamorphoses*, Echo speaks truths about female power that Ovid could not.

The greatest significance of Spivak's Echo is in the nymph's indirect and unintentional role in the story of Narcissus's destruction. Here Spivak finds Echo representative of the "insufficiency that is the name not of the limits of self-knowledge but of the possibility of deconstruction" (25). Spivak's important, if necessarily elusive, suggestion is that Echo is a figure of a voice beyond Derridian deconstruction. An unintentionally truth-telling, ultimately reflective voice that does more than attack the systemizing European philosophy that is Derrida's dragon, it reflects in revealing and devastating ways the monstrous human consequences of male positivism. Echo's role, like that of the entrapping pool, presents women as *essentially* deconstructive. Ethical attempts to communicate in a world constructed of male narcissism will expose, in necessarily unpredictable and dangerous ways, the fragmentary and mortal nature of existence.

In considering Echo to be an ethical voice beyond deconstruction and beyond feminism, Spivak has located her in a place that resonates, oddly and unintentionally, with the poet John Hollander's search for Echo: "Ovid's poetic device in telling her story becomes in later poetry a way of deconstructing words, often of love, into their hidden but operative *ultimae*" (12). Hollander speaks of the satiric Echo in Ovid to distinguish her from an older Echo associated with Pan and hence with nature and lyric poetry. He is particularly interested in the poetic Echo and an aural allusiveness he identifies as her legacy in poetry since Milton. Nevertheless, his history of Echo suggests the deconstructive possibilities of unintended meaning. It is in fact Nietzsche's Echo, whom Hollander characterizes as "complex and insidious," who mocks assumptions about the relationship between voice and text in a way that opens or reopens language for poetic consideration. Nietzsche's Echo, Hollander points out, as

> a trope of the trope that purports to be literal, is an epistemological mocker and deceiver: Nietzsche characterizes the literalist, the scientist, as a seeker who without knowing it "contemplates the whole world as related to man, as the infinitely protracted echo of an original sound: man; as the multiplied copy of an arch-type: man." Echo is here the metaphor that is misread as the literal, even as an image of voice is mistaken for a vocal presence. And yet, as both voice and echo are sound, the literal dimension—whose possibility Nietzsche denies in this essay on "Truth and Falsity in an Ultramoral Sense"—and the figurative one are both language.
>
> Language answering language, then . . . characterizes the later phase of the transubstantiation of echoed voice. It is inevitable that the trope of echo should come to stand for crucial questions about poetic language itself. (20–21)

The questions Hollander proceeds to consider involve the way Echo—the disembodied voice or sound—"haunts" poetic texts. While Nietzsche's Echo represents the devastating reverberations of literal modern discourse, Hollander's Echo represents the possibility for voice and sound "in texts where more is heard than meets the eye" (22). Nietzsche, Spivak, and Hollander each turn to Echo for a figure who represents the voice whose meaning extends beyond the echoing words available to it.

Whereas Narcissus has become a trope for the destructive human consequences of a measurably powerful cultural monologue on the material world, Echo has become a trope for the immeasurable dialogue through which humans may approach an ultimately unfathomable relationship with the natural world. Echo and Narcissus find a critical nexus in the figure of Nemesis, whose brief but decisive intervention in the mythical narrative provides context, a kind of meaning, for their tragic encounter. It is the vengeful artifice of Nemesis—a mechanically reflective pool derivative of Echo's aural reflectiveness—that transforms Narcissus's otherwise idiosyncratic self-destructive self-obsession into an ethical emblem of cultural narcosis. It is the artifice of Nemesis that metamorphoses the one avenged, transforming her from failed lover into a naturally sanctioned emblem of the indeterminacy inherent in human attempts to communicate—Spivak's postfeminist, postdeconstructive critical discourse and Hollander's poetry.

Swift's satires identify Modern cultural referents for the mythical emblems. Not entirely unlike Freud and Lasch, Swift represents the materialist discourse of modern science in ways that expose its narcissistic cultural implications, and not unlike Spivak, Nietzsche, and Hollander, Swift, by the nature of his art, is tied to the echoing voice that is the affirmation of nonlinear or poetic discourses. By identifying himself with Nemesis, however, Swift aligned his discourse—his satires—with the echoing art that destroys. Following his vengeful muse, Swift creates a mimetic artifice for the Modern, not to reform or heal or rebuke, but to destroy and avenge. Critics like F. R. Leavis who have correctly identified the destructive nature of Swift's work have invariably assumed it was informed by a perverse Iago-like malice in Swift's character. But the identification of Swift with Nemesis provides the context that reveals the satirist working to undermine the foundations of Modernity by representing the Modern as a singularly dangerous and inhuman manifestation of cultural narcissism.

MODERNITY AND THE CRITICS

A work that is among the most brilliant and durable of twentieth-century Swift studies and one that has had a particular influence on the present study, is also a work that dismisses the possibility that Swift's satires attack Modernity, a central argument of this study. Edward Rosenheim's *Swift and the Satirist's Art*, first published in 1963, begins with a lucid theory for reading satire that requires readers to pursue and employ historical information in disciplined ways. Critical reappraisals of Modernity in the time since Rosenheim wrote help explain why certain of the lines of Rosenheim's reading of Swift can now be extended.

In an exceptionally clear and persuasive reading of Swift's *Argument Against Abolishing Christianity*, Rosenheim comes to the conclusion that the work ridicules its audience. *An Argument*'s readers, therefore, are represented in the self-avowed "nominal Christian" whose debased argument epitomizes the actions and perhaps the thought of those for whom Swift wrote. Similarly, Rosenheim comes to the conclusion that the readers of *A Modest Proposal* are its main satiric target: "The central satiric victim in this tract, as in the *Argument Against Abolishing Christianity*, is the audience for whom the work is primarily intended" (49). For Rosenheim satire may be distinguished from other genres because it aims to wound or kill what it represents, and, in the case of these two short satires, the victims are readers. Without recourse to the Nemesis myth, Rosenheim identifies an essential dynamic of the satiric theory articulated here.

Rosenheim does not, however, carry this theoretical insight to Swift's major works, *A Tale of a Tub* or *Travels into Several Remote Nations*:

> The quest for particular satiric victims may produce results precisely the opposite of those yielded by his procedure in our scrutiny of the *Argument* and *A Modest Proposal*. Instead of a sustained principle of order and wholeness, we are likely to discover greater diffuseness, fragmentation, and even contradictions than the *Tale* presents at first sight. Our search for particulars may illuminate crannies and corners but leave the great structure of the *Tale* in relative darkness. (55–56)

Rather than following the major satires in what Rosenheim recognized was "precisely the opposite" direction of the shorter satires, the present essay turns this reading back to Rosenheim's original direction by seeing the specific satiric victims among the readers who are linked by their modernity. But rather than attempting to reveal a "sustained principle of order and wholeness," this study understands "diffuseness" and "fragmentation" as intrinsic to the satiric critique of Modernity.

When Rosenheim briefly considered and dismissed the idea that Swift's targets in *A Tale* could be identified "as Moderns," he was responding to the critical moment in which he wrote. The most brilliant explication of Modernity as a target of Swift's satire in *A Tale*, Miriam Starkman's *Swift's Satire on Learning in* A Tale of a Tub (1950), made recognition of the attack on Modernity a prelude to critical oblivion. For Starkman and other critics of the time, Modernity had won. *A Tale*, for Starkman, was written as a rearguard action in a "lost cause," and so Swift's attacks on science are "of antiquarian interest" (86). Rosenheim avoids this reductive trap by concentrating on historical particulars and drawing his reader's attention to the ways the satire continues to resonate:

> The conception of truth as readily mastered, neatly formulated, and delightfully communicated is the error with which this section, for all its diversity, recurrently taxes its satiric victims. . . . We, in our day, may view such phenomena as *Life* or *Reader's Digest*, the novels of Ayn Rand, or the palliative pieties of Norman Vincent Peale as manifestations of disturbing public tendencies. A courageous satirist, however, will leave the tendencies to the social scientists and attack the writings themselves. (88–89)

Whereas references to "us" or "the modern reader" in Starkman embody exactly what Swift satirizes—the quintessentially modern arrogance of understanding better because we live later—the modern "we" in Rosenheim signals a discussion of satiric resonance. Rosenheim here suggests the fundamental opposition of satire, which works deconstructively with language, and the Modern, which debases *scientia* by equating quantification (perhaps the grossest form of generalization) with knowledge.

If Rosenheim is implicitly skeptical of certain scientific premises of the Modern, the voluminous critical discourse on the end of the Modern over the last three or four decades has made every aspect of such skepticism explicit. My revised understanding of Modernity is of course indebted to Thomas Kuhn's *The Structure of Scientific Revolutions*, and certain of the many works it has inspired, as well as to Stephen Toulmin's *Cosmopolis: The Hidden Agenda of Modernity.* Kuhn, as the preface of his landmark book relates, was (adapting his own terminology) a "normal" scientist before he participated in teaching a course on the history of science, which took him back (for the first time) to the works of Boyle and Newton and of other New Philosophers. The radical debate that continues to engage contemporary science stems from Kuhn's return to the works of Swift's contemporaries, many of whom are targets of Swift's satires. In a similar way, Stephen Toulmin's "modern" philosophical perceptions were fundamentally altered when he taught a course that took him back to the sixteenth- and seventeenth-century origins of Modernity. Toulmin recognizes in retrospect what Swift anticipates, that the Modern is defined by the general application of the ideologically conditioned methods of the New Philosophy to all areas of human experience. It is in part because of the work of Kuhn and Toulmin and writers like Richard Rorty, Paul Feyerabend, Alasdair MacIntyre, and, from a related feminist perspective, Carolyn Merchant and Londa Schiebinger, who trace the Modern back to its formative moments in the sixteenth and seventeenth centuries, that a plausible argument can now be made that the Modern describes a worldview coherent enough to be satirically attacked in its particular manifestations.

Relating Swift's Modern to our modern takes this literary historical study into the realm of what is now called *cultural studies.* It is helpful in this regard that Edward Said, whose work is in evidence throughout this study, derives his own considerable critical power from his reading of Swift. In *The World, the Text, and the Critic,*[13] Said argues for a recognition of context, not in the old sense of naive reconstruction of objective historical settings or biography, but of a critic's awareness of the world beyond the border of a text. With a traditional, modern view of history, one would read Said as saying that a critic must be aware of the world in which the text was composed as well as the world in which the criticism is written, and Said, in his own criticism, demands just such knowledge from himself. But Said's discussion of "the world" also transcends traditional literary historical categories. His argument is not so much for placing a text in its historical context, but for recognizing a text in the place it has claimed in the world as we now know it. Here history is not objective fact that can be reclaimed, but a part of a collective memory that changes in the telling and re-telling, and literary texts are immortals only in the sense that, while each came into the world at a particular time, they remake and retell themselves in the world that now exists:

> Moreover, critics are not merely the alchemical translators of texts into the circumstantial reality or worldliness; for they too are subject to and producers of circumstances, which are felt regardless of whatever objectivity the critic's methods possess. The point is that the texts have ways of existing that even in their most rarefied form are always enmeshed in circumstance, time, place, and society—in short, they are in the world, and hence worldly. Whether a text is preserved or put aside for a period, whether it is on a library shelf or not, whether it is considered dangerous or not: these matters have to do with a text's being in the world, which is a more complicated matter than the private process of reading. The same implications are undoubtedly true of critics in their capacities as readers and writers in the world. (*World*, 35)

While the "same implications" are said to be true of critics, it is texts that provide the interesting illustration. For the argument that a critic or an author lives in a particular world and is influenced by it is less controversial than Said's assertion that what many would consider a finished text is only and always a developing text that will mean something more or less—something different—in the different places and times in which it exists.

Swift said when he read a book "whether wise or silly, it seems to me to be alive and talking to me." It is no coincidence that Said was listening to Swift when developing his critical stance:

> He [Swift] stands so far outside the world of contemporary critical discourse as to serve as one of its best critics, methodologically unarmed though he may have been. In its energy and unparalleled verbal wit, its restlessness, its agitational and unacademic designs on its political and social context, Swift's writing supplies modern criticism with what it has sorely needed since Arnold covered critical writing with the mantle of cultural authority and reactionary political quietism. (*World*, 28)

To illustrate the "otherness" of what Said is doing here, it is useful to contrast his approach with George Orwell's essay on *Gulliver's Travels*. Orwell began his essay wondering why the *Travels* is a book he seemed unable "to grow tired of" (182). In the course of examining this question, Orwell labeled Swift a "reactionary," an "anarchist," an opponent of liberty, whose political ideal was "a static, incurious civilization," an impotent man, probably incapable of happiness, and a "diseased writer," who expressed "a palpably false view of life." Orwell finally decided he admired Swift so much because Swift clearly had such conviction of his diseased beliefs that this allowed him to make isolated prescient observations, and because Swift had the talent "to produce a great work of art" (185). Orwell was a modernist,[14] relegating Swift (despite protests to the contrary) to an academic, aesthetic realm, while excluding him from any real part in twentieth-century intellectual discourse. Said, by contrast, recognizes that Swift writes in his own "social and political context," that Swift's discourse exists "far outside the world of contemporary critical discourse." Said is acutely aware, moreover, that Swift held political beliefs, such as a hostility to freedom of the press, that would push the limits of conventional contemporary definitions of conservatism. But Said keeps listening to the agitation and energy, to the wit and restlessness, and this listening leads, not to simpleminded judgments on Swift's personality or to anachronistic labels for his politics, but to profound questions about *current* critical responsibility. The voice of the text from "far outside the world of contemporary critical discourse" begins to take on the lines and definition of our "best" critic.

What Said gains from turning to Swift for the tools to deconstruct the "mantle of cultural authority" that cloaks insidious assumptions of the Modern is not yet another fraudulent modern methodology, nor an arsenal of negations, but a critical voice. While much poststructural discourse moves further into an "alchemical" criticism[15] distinguishable from the modernist criticism only by the assertion that there is no philosopher's stone, no progress, Swift's restless, agitated deconstruction is one that points us back to the "political and social context" in which we live. If this is, as Said suggests, because Swift has the voice of an other—one "far outside" the discourse that we know—it is also because Swift was able to construct in literature the image of the world that we know. While Swift's Hack is the true Modern, "a most devoted servant of all modern forms," who writes a "divine" treatise "for the Universal Improvement of Mankind," he is also a postmodern who claims his writing "is true," only for the very minute in which he writes. Inherent in the modern project is the postmodern crisis: the quest for certainty and material progress leads in Swift's construction to a world of pervasive uncertainty in which existence itself is dependent on increasingly desperate assertions of the ego. Said's claim, and perhaps his hope, is that Swift can "serve" us, not by opposing the Modern with some premodern model, but by showing us an engaged deconstructive discourse. That is, Swift's engaged criticism is one that suggests construction is not only possible, but inevitable, and that an intellectual's role in society is to expose the tyranny toward which social, political, and intellectual constructions tend.

It in no way detracts from Said's accomplishment to observe that he chose to focus on certain occasional, political pieces by Swift. Writing for other critics, Said pointed a way with respect to Swift criticism, leaving the work on the major satires for those who would follow.

A work that undertakes something very like what Said calls for, Kenneth Craven's *The Millennium of Madness*, may come to be counted among the most original and significant works on Swift in the twentieth century. Craven finds in Swift's *A Tale of a Tub* a profound and unrelentingly censorious critique of the world in which we live. This claim may sound strange, particularly when Craven has chapters on figures like Paracelsus, Milton, and Shaftesbury. But what Craven shares with both Said and Swift is a profound conviction that history is a continuum, not in a linear, progressive sense, but as each new child embodies characteristics—glorious, mediocre, or evil—of his or her progenitors. As Swift seems to have relished representing the degradations that the Moderns were making their inheritance, Craven seems to relish the role of cataloguing the monstrous births that are the issue of modern times. Along the way he offers powerful arguments for understanding Swift as one who unsettles modern intellectual history. He sees Swift disrupting the givens of an age that offers slavery under an illusion of liberation—an illusion maintained by way of powerful information technologies. It is perhaps only as a student of Swift that one could write a work of such unprecedented critical malevolence so well grounded in scholarship.

While the rigor of Craven's study serves a reading that locates Craven on Swift's side in assailing common or at least contingent enemies, an enormous scholarly rigor allows Carol Houlihan Flynn to assail Swift himself in the interest of elucidating "the materiality that consumed the eighteenth-century imagination" (224).[16] In *The Body in Swift and Defoe*, Flynn represents Swift as one who used language to keep the world at bay, to recreate the narcissistic conditions of the nursery, and thereby to manipulate and abuse people, particularly the women who were close to him. Though she is not working with the Narcissus myth, she negotiates a critical path from Swift's biographical narcissism through satire that "punishes rather than corrects, and it punishes through pain" (196) and out into representations of a culture consumed with its own materiality. Though I am less interested here in Swift's biography, I map a parallel path between the narcissism of Swift's literary characters and satire that draws readers into potentially mortifying awareness of personal and cultural vacuity.

Some of the harder edges of my reading of Swift are also explored in *Cutting Edges*, a fascinating volume of essays that "see eighteenth-century satire . . . within the framework of postmodern critical approaches" (ix). Brian A. Connery's "Persona As Pretender and Reader As Subject" gives a political framework to the "indeterminacy" of meaning in Swift's *Tale*, arguing that readers are satirized by an author "we have constructed and authorized to do so" (177). In the terms of this study, Connery has precisely identified the destructive reflective characteristics of nemesistic satire. In the same volume, James E. Gill draws on theories of Girard and of Derrida in associating Swift's satire with the *pharmakon*—cure/poison—and Swift with the *pharmakos*—the outsider/scapegoat physician, finding that Swift opposes "'modern' productions" by presenting readers with "a complex intellectual exercise consisting of self-deconstructing allegories" (198). It is directly germane to the current study that "postmodern" strategies point to representations of the Modern in Swift's work where the attack/assault/poison is located not in the text itself, but in the modern expectations of the satire's readers.

Of especially direct significance here are those critics who have been revising critical assessments of Swift's satires on science. Ann Cline Kelly has shown that the seventeenth-century search for a universal language, an important subject of most historically grounded reassessments of the Modern, is central to attacks on the New Philosophers.[17] Picking up where Starkman and Marjorie Nicolson left off decades ago, Frederik Smith has shown that the language of the new science pervades Swift's satiric works, underscoring the consistency of his satiric focus on the Modern.[18] And Douglas Lane Patey has published an invaluable reconsideration of Swift's satire on science in which he shows why Swift's oppositions to the claims of the New Philosophy need not determine him a benighted Luddite.

In reading Swift as the Nemesis of Modernity, I build upon these and other works in tracing Swift's concern about human implications of the rise of the New Philosophy. Swift recognized that narcissism is fundamental to all human experience. But to identify this as a great psychological insight is to diminish it, to circumscribe it within precisely the sort of scientific category Swift attacks. In Swift's works, Modernity is defined less by narcissism itself (for what human construct is not at bottom narcissistic?) than by the ridiculous (in the Aristotelian sense of the word) attempts to deny the tragic consequences of systemic narcissism. Whether it is the scientifically trained traveler measuring the globe for the intellectual and commercial improvement of mankind (Chapters 2 and 3), the Royal Society naming Francis Bacon the new Moses (Chapter 4), literary and religious hacks claiming transformative alchemical powers (Chapter 5), or Newtonians finally (save just a few experiments) offering a unified mechanical explanation of all nature and its creator (Chapter 6), Swift's representations work as mirrors in which readers almost invariably identify the faces of others. Professional readers are not exempt from this critical paradigm (Chapter 7). With the "hidden agenda" of Modernity now an open subject of contemporary critical discourse, we may discover, "after the usual Proceeding of Mankind, because it is too late" (*PW*, 18: 89) reflections of the unrelenting violence of the modern project itself.

Chapter Two

GULLIVERIAN NARCISSISM

These body fluids, this defilement, this shit are what life withstands, hardly and with difficulty, on the part of death.

—Kristeva, *Powers of Horror*

Narcissus is an incomparably beautiful youth beside an idyllic pool, staring at his reflection. Narcissism is a meeting of libidinal and egoistical drives, essential in the development of children, and common in varying degrees in adults both healthy and ill. Gulliver is an intrepid narcissistic traveler in an intellectual world that exists between the pastoral abstractions of the myth and the technical abstractions derived from the medical study of the mentally ill.

It is difficult to discuss Gulliver's relationship to the myth of Narcissus without being directed by a vocabulary that encourages analysis of the (diseased) psyches of Gulliver and Swift rather than the work's representation of a diseased Modern world. After Freud, we tend to read as psychoanalysts, moving back through a narrative of abnormal behavior to a diagnosis, narcissism. In this context, narcissism is an answer to such questions as, Why does Gulliver end up reviling contact with his family and talking to his ponies? For the satirist, however, individual narcissism is a universal. The discovery that a particular individual is directed by self-love has all the interpretive value of noticing that he or she eats, sleeps, defecates, and copulates. To the extent Gulliver represents a human individual, he will be motivated by self-love, and this, together with his carefully elucidated bodily demands, links him to individual readers.

The clinical or quasi-clinical vortex of much of psychoanalytic discourse "after Freud" is usefully distinguished from the work of the theorist himself.[1] Freud was particularly aware that instruments he derived from the myths were at once drawn from, and significant within, the larger cultural framework that myth and literature delineate. For Freud the story of Narcissus is not merely a tool for discussing aspects of psychological development or for illustrating a particular category of mental illness. It is a story that links a range of individual behaviors to overarching cultural behaviors including organized religion and genocide. Like Freud, Swift was an extraordinarily perceptive reader of myth. From the myth of Narcissus, Swift derived a perspective that enabled him to draw connections between the primacy of self-love in human development and the delusional self-destructiveness that dominates human history. Gulliver's individual narcissism, therefore, is essential to linking him to each reader. But what makes Gulliver interesting as a satiric figure, and what positions Swift as Nemesis, is that Gulliver is constructed of a specific strain of narcissism—the cultural narcissism of Modernity. Rather than a pious or general condemnation of individual narcissism, Swift's *Travels* exposes what Freud refers to as the "special case" of narcissism, when the "delusional remoulding of reality is made by a considerable number of people in common" (*Civ.*, 32). While Freud illustrates his notion of collective narcissism by reference to world religions, Swift draws his examples from apparently secular political and scientific ideologies.

TOWARD THE SPECIAL CASE

Gulliver is identified as a narcissist from the opening pages of his *Travels into Several Remote Nations*. As Christopher Fox has skillfully shown, Gulliver's apprenticeship to his "good Master *Bates*" is not in any sense a Freudian slip, but an intentional and significant word play that signals an extensive use of the myth of Narcissus in the *Travels*.[2] This apprenticeship positions Gulliver as the very type of the narcissist, the type, in fact, Freud takes as his point of departure in the opening of "On Narcissism": "[Narcissism denotes] the attitude of a person who treats his own body in the same way in which the body of a sexual object is ordinarily treated—who looks at it, that is to say, strokes it and fondles it till he obtains complete satisfaction through these activities" (73). But the joke that makes Gulliver a narcissist based on his masturbatory apprenticeship is not without complicating resonances. While still under the direction of Master Bates, Gulliver is "advised to alter his condition," and so marries Mary Burton. After this alteration, Master Bates dies, and soon Gulliver becomes a parent.[3] In this context Gulliver's apprenticeship may be read as an allegorical guide to typical male sexuality: Gulliver's masturbatory practice gives way in due course to a healthy and generative heterosexual relationship.[4]

A reading that sees Gulliver's sexual development through narcissism as "normal" is consistent with what is one of Swift's favorite themes, expressed succinctly in *Cadenus and Vanessa*:

> Self-love, in nature rooted fast
> Attends us first, and leaves us last.
> (ll. 692–93)

That narcissism is fundamental in human development is a satiric commonplace. Self-love is not merely a stage "normal" people pass through, while the ill degenerate into narcissism. Self-love is universal and fundamental, the motivating factor in all human behavior. Writing to console a friend who had lost a child, Swift said, "Self-love, as it is the motive to all our actions, so it is the sole cause of our grief"(*Corr.*, 3: 245). Swift is acutely aware that this view of human nature contains the sort of paradox associated with Greek tragedy: any action taken to avoid the grief inherent to narcissism will necessarily be motivated by narcissism itself. Behind the joke of Gulliver's masturbatory education stands a wily student of the human condition. Readers laugh at Gulliver only by ignoring the paths of their own apprenticeships in self-love.

But if self-love is the most fundamental of natural human motives, Swift's allegorical treatment of it adds a level of complexity. Gulliver's "good Master Bates" is also James Bates, a surgeon who directs Gulliver along his professional path. Gulliver's narcissism is not merely psycho-sexual, but professional and specifically commercial. Gulliver's desires are materially determined. In his second sentence he complains about the "scanty allowance" his father allowed him at Cambridge, and that a "narrow Fortune" forced him from Emmanuel College Cambridge into his apprenticeship and his career as a physician. Each of these autobiographical details expands the context in which Gulliver's narcissism needs to be considered. Swift constructs the biography of his character from elements of an emergent modern culture.

In addition to his apprenticeship, there are at least four aspects of Gulliver's early biography that inform his identity as a representative of Modernity: his birth in 1660; his repetition of the word Fortune; his aborted stay at Emmanuel College Cambridge; and his study at Leiden.

Born in the year of the Restoration of Charles II, Gulliver is raised in the intellectual and social compromises of the Restoration period. When his father's land cannot support him through his university studies, he turns or is directed to the New Philosophy's most practical discipline, medicine, and to sea as a ship's surgeon. Swift is not merely representing a path that a young man born in Nottinghamshire in 1660 might have taken; he is creating a character whose experience illustrates the cultural path by which the traditional aristocratic order is first altered and finally determined by a new and powerful commercial order.[5] Gulliver begins his travels in 1699, the date underscoring the ways the social, political, and economic discoveries of Gulliver's eighteenth-century enterprise are forged in the cultural accommodations that followed the Puritan revolution. That Gulliver's biography, from birth until he begins the voyage to Lilliput, links the Cromwellian period to the eighteenth century is crucial to the allegorical significance of the *Travels*. A premise of the *Travels* is that the messianic character of the Revolutionary period is not so much replaced in the Restoration period as displaced onto an emerging materialistic culture. Gulliver comes to embody the secular messianism of Modernity, expecting that his book, with its report of the existence of a land "governed by reason," should nearly instantaneously reform "every Vice and Folly" of the European Yahoos.

This overview of the significance of Gulliver's biography from 1660 to 1699 has significant nuances. Gulliver uses the term *fortune* no fewer than six times in his opening five paragraphs, sometimes to mean chance or luck, but most often to refer to his financial condition. Gulliver is driven from Cambridge, to an apprenticeship in medicine, to Leiden, to marriage, and to sea by financial necessity. As a "third of five sons" studying at Cambridge, Gulliver would most likely have been considering a career in the Church. That Emmanuel College was earlier known for fervent Puritanism and that it is named for the Messiah underscore the religious context of the education Gulliver would have received whether he joined the clergy or not. Removed of necessity from this religious context, he undertakes a materially motivated study of the material body. And this takes him to the city and the university, which was becoming, in the 1680s when Gulliver is there, a symbol of new mechanistic ways of looking at the world: "Leiden became the undisputed center—in our modern sense—for the study of the *sciences of man*: not merely man medically considered, but man in his crucial postures as an anatomical, physiological, and chemical animal" (Rousseau, 199). Moving Gulliver from Emmanuel College, with its Puritan past, to Leiden, Swift is exploiting the rich irony that the New Science is emerging on the ground of the old home of (mad) Jack of Leiden. Gulliver's first trip abroad is to the geographical locus of the debasing religious fanaticism of Jack in *A Tale of a Tub*. Gulliver emerges from Leiden studied in the vocabulary, transformative and dehumanizing, of the New Science.

The point is not that Gulliver would somehow have been better off had he been able to stay with his vaguely messianic studies at Cambridge. It is rather that Gulliver becomes the intellectual compromise that develops out of the passing from Puritanism to the new rationality associated with the New Philosophy and, eventually, the Enlightenment. Gulliver speaks, as Frederik Smith has conclusively demonstrated, with a vocabulary drawn from the Royal Society,[6] and he seems to have no personal interest in religious matters. But the influence of the Puritan view of the world is evident in Gulliver's expectation that "seven Months were a sufficient Time to correct every Vice and Folly to which the *Yahoos* are subject; if their Natures had been capable of the least Disposition to Virtue or Wisdom"

(*PW*, 11: 7). Either one is among the elect and recognizes the Houyhnhnm's good rational news, or one is not. Swift's satiric charge in *A Tale of a Tub*, that Puritanism and the New Philosophy share a common Modern methodology,[7] is carried forward into the *Travels*. But he changes the focus from the cultural equivalence of these two Modern phenomena to make the more far-reaching charge that the eighteenth-century travels (beginning with Gulliver in 1699) an ostensibly secular path toward a strain of messianism more subtle, more radical, and more dangerous to human welfare than the overtly revolutionary ideology that first emerged from Leiden.

Gulliver's narcissism is just that: the self-love that is the motivation for all our actions. The *Travels into Several Remote Nations* is the account of how that universal satiric insight works in the context of a culture that, rather than restraining individual narcissism, encourages it.

The modern medical profession is the crucial nexus of individual and cultural narcissism because of the significance of the body as the narcissistic object, whether personally or culturally defined. The move at this time from the barber surgeon or the midwife to the scientifically educated physician signals a cultural concern with the body that first parallels and then surpasses in cultural value the work of doctors in various learned fields.[8] Later, in *Tristram Shandy*, Sterne will write large the great comedy of this continuing conflict. But Swift's *Travels* imagines that the conflict is already resolved. Gulliver, though he expects in the end to effect the greatest changes in human behavior ever conceived, is never a metaphysician. He is rather a traveling physician who, in the course of his travels, identifies the world's disease and discovers its antidote. Gulliver embodies the cultural narcissism inherent in the modern dialectic that sees the human condition as a curable illness.

THE NARCISSISTIC PATH

The story of Narcissus is a story of successive rejections and of one destructive acceptance of an impossible other. Though initially attracted to the various peoples he meets, Gulliver ends up scorning and rejecting the Lilliputians, the Brobdingnagians, and the various peoples of the third book. He accepts, at nothing less than the cost of his human identity, the cultural beliefs of the horses of Houyhnhnmland. The encounters of the first three voyages echo aspects of Gulliver's (English/European) cultural identity, while his initially happy discovery in Houyhnhnmland emerges as an unanswerable reflection on the very identity that has allowed Gulliver his continuing sense of superiority. As Narcissus's failure to obtain his "unbodied hope" uncovers the source of his recurring refusals, so Gulliver's disastrous experience of Western culture's realized ideal—a land governed by rational philosophers—forces him to acknowledge that, of all the things of nature, only humans do not belong in a place where reason governs. Inherent in the specifically narcissistic Modernity that Gulliver embodies are both a persistent and overwhelming arrogance and a dangerously unhinging recognition that the cultural arrogance has had no basis, that the image that informed the arrogance was a delusion.

The ways in which the first three books echo Gulliver's home culture have received a great deal of attention in the critical consideration of these voyages. But it is not the echoes themselves that are most significant but the material they provide for linking personal and cultural narcissism. Critics often play the *Travels* as a conventional game of chess in which there is a historical black piece for every fictional white: Walpole, for example, is represented and opposed in the character of Flimnap. Not a little scholarly effort has gone into attempting to tie Gulliver to Bolingbroke, or Temple, or Swift himself. But the Narcissus myth adds a critical dimension. Lilliputian politics with its direct and indirect European analogues is a part of a narrative punctuated by bodily functions, avowed and alleged. All but one of the potential readers of the *Travels* look at Walpole at a significant remove. Even Walpole or someone like him may be able to laugh with pleasure at political satire general enough to expose the irony of going to war to enforce religious doctrine (Big-Endians and Little-Endians). But Gulliver's defensiveness and shame about what he imagines others are saying about his bodily functions ground the cultural satire in the first three books in personal experience and individual narcissism. Consider, in this context, Gulliver's first discussion of defecation:

> I had been for some Hours extremely pressed by the Necessities of Nature; which was no Wonder, it being almost two Days since I had last disburthened myself. I was under great Difficulties between Urgency and Shame. The best Expedient I could think on, was to creep into my House, which I accordingly did; and shutting the Gate after me, I went as far as the Length of my Chain would suffer; and discharged my Body of that uneasy Load. But this was the only Time I was ever guilty of so uncleanly an Action; for which I cannot but hope the candid Reader will give some Allowance, after he hath maturely and impartially considered my Case, and the Distress I was in. From this Time my constant Practice was, as soon as I rose, to perform that Business in open Air, at the full Extent of my Chain; and due Care was taken every Morning before Company came, that the offensive Matter should be carried off in Wheel-barrows, by two Servants appointed for that Purpose. I would not have dwelt so long upon a Circumstance, that perhaps at first Sight may appear not very momentous; if I had not thought it necessary to justify my Character in Point of Cleanliness to the World; which I am told, some of my Maligners have been pleased, upon this and other Occasions, to call in Question. (*PW*, 11: 29)

Who are these "Maligners"? One can construct an argument that points to Gulliver's enemies among the Lilliputians. In this context Gulliver's appeal to the "candid Reader" would seem an attempt to answer intelligence that European readers might one day receive from Lilliput. Virtually every reader beyond grammar school will now have a psychoanalytic term for this: Gulliver is paranoid. Emboldened by the hermeneutic power of this vocabulary, few readers resist extending such readings to the person who created Gulliver. Arguably the most settled commonplace of Swift criticism at all levels is that Swift was "obsessed" with the body and bodily functions.

The commonplace may even in some context be true, but it usually has a powerful, reductive effect. Protected by a rationalist vocabulary that gives us access to nothing less than the writer's subconscious, we redirect the hilariously unsettling insight of this narrative construction back to character and author without ever acknowledging the irony of our role as "candid" readers. However "mature" and "impartial" we may think ourselves, we understand precisely Gulliver's embarrassment at having to defecate in a manner he thinks reflects on the perception of his cleanliness. The shame Gulliver refers to is not a fear of literally being seen in the act: Gulliver is proud that hereafter he defecates in the open air. He fears, rather, the sullied image of himself that he imagines forming in the minds of others. Huge industries (mouthwash, deodorant, etc.) exist to defend us from just the sort of "maligners" Gulliver fears. Shame, which Aristotle defines as the "imagination" of a disgrace, is fundamental to self-love. In this context, our psychoanalytic explanations of Gulliver's concern with bodily functions are precisely analogous to his own delusional apology. Character and reader put at a distance the immediate and embarrassing truth that as narcissists we often find ourselves "between urgency and shame," somatic realities threatening idealized images of self. Swift's text mocks readers, not for sharing Gulliver's embarrassing concerns, but for working as hard as Gulliver does to "maturely and impartially" remove ourselves from them.

Such personal or novelistic episodes mediate the social and political satire of the first three books of the *Travels*. Like Pope, who sings "What mighty Contests rise from trivial Things," Swift links the great events Gulliver encounters in his travels to ostensibly trivial matters related to the body and bodily functions. This is illustrated clearly enough in the first book, which is traditionally read as a satire on English politics and the relations between England and France. The emperor of Lilliput is taller by "almost the Breadth" of Gulliver's nail than any of his court, "which alone is enough to strike an Awe into the Beholders" (*PW*, 11: 30). The irresolvable and bloody "Big-Endians/Little-Endians" controversy begins when a prince cuts his finger breaking an egg. Gulliver is made a Nardac because of the services his prodigious size (his body "must contain at least 1728" Lilliputian bodies) allows him to perform. His size, moreover, serves a symbolic political function when he stands a Colossus above the emperor's troops exposing his enormous member through torn breeches. Gulliver is sentenced to be blinded because he used this emblem of the emperor's martial power to urinate on and so defile the palace of the empress. And finally Gulliver's great enemy among the emperor's chief ministers believes Gulliver has had an affair with his wife, leading Gulliver to appeal to the candid reader in a manner analogous to his apology for having defecated in his temporary home.

Lest we think these connections between individual bodies and the great social or political bodies are coincidental to Gulliver's experience, Swift in the third book allows Gulliver access to "true" accounts of history where he discovers "How great a Share in the Motions and Events of Courts, Councils, and Senates might be challenged by Bawds, Whores, Pimps, Parasites, and Buffoons." Those remembered for their elevated stations confess "they owed their Greatness and Wealth to Sodomy or Incest; others to the prostituting of their own Wives or Daughters" (*PW*, 11: 199–200). This historical perspective confirms the evidence from Gulliver's own experience, that what is momentous in the affairs of the world (prior to Book 4) is always directly linked to what is common enough to link each of us to the narrative—bodily waste, sexual desire, shame, and the idiosyncratic exercise of narcissistic wills. Virtually every time we laugh reading the *Travels*, we are being asked to consider that the impetus for the things in human affairs we consider most elevated may be traced (like the vapors in the *Digression on Madness*) to the groin, the bowels, or to narcissistic anxieties arising from these "lower parts."

If Gulliver's penis is important in Lilliput as a symbol of martial power, an instrument of defilement through micturition, and a stimulus for life-threatening personal jealousy, in Brobdingnag, Gulliver becomes a sort of toy phallus, the sexual plaything of adolescent girls: "They would often strip me naked from Top to Toe, and lay me at full Length in their Bosoms; wherewith I was much disgusted; because, to say the Truth, a very offensive Smell came from their Skins" (*PW*, 11: 118). He is particularly upset that he is treated as a "Creature who had no Sort of Consequence": "They would strip themselves to the Skin, and put on their Smocks in my Presence, while I was placed on their Toylet directly before their naked Bodies; which, I am sure, to me was very far from being a tempting Sight, or from giving me any other Motions than those of Horror and Disgust" (*PW*, 11: 119). Recalling how he had been set "astride" one of the maid's nipples, Gulliver finally asks to be excused "for not being over particular" about other ways she had used him. Readings of these passages tend to focus on Gulliver's disgust with the bodies of the nubile maids, but there is more here than an entry in a catalogue of Swift's "neurotic" comments on the flesh. Gulliver juxtaposes sexual arousal ("a tempting sight") with the motions or arousal of feelings of horror and disgust. Even if Gulliver were to become aroused by the naked giants, his penis, potent and generative at home and awe-inspiring in Lilliput, would be hardly detectable in Brobdingnag. As in the *Digression on Madness*, which articulates the "principle" by which frustrated sexual energy is redirected to violence, Gulliver's impotence in Brobdingnag gives rise to horror and disgust. This principle of redirection, which we now understand in Freudian terms,[9] is essential to the myth of Narcissus, who tears his garments and beats himself in response to his inability to possess his lover and satisfy his desire.

Swift's investigation of the consequences of frustrated desire in Brobdingnag go beyond a critique of individual narcissism. The narcissism of Gulliver's experience with the maids is in fact linked with cultural practice in the celebrated episode in which Gulliver offers the king of Brobdingnag the recipe for gunpowder. This link becomes palpable when the context in which Gulliver presents and interprets his story is given as much attention as the searing critique of modern warfare at the center of this episode.[10] Personally humiliated in his encounters with various animals, a baby, a dwarf, the Brobdingnagian maids, and a pile of cow dung, Gulliver offers a social and political review of European culture to the Brobdingnagian king, only to find himself denounced as one of "the most pernicious Race of little odious vermin that Nature ever suffered to crawl upon the Surface of the Earth." Gulliver opens the gunpowder episode by saying he has learned: "It was in vain to discover my Resentments, which were always turned into Ridicule" (*PW*, 11: 133). He offers gunpowder when he can think of no other way to assert his sense of his own dignity. It is no accident that Gulliver describes his secret as a way he knows to give potency to great iron shafts and balls:

> That, a proper Quantity of this Powder rammed into an hollow Tube of Brass or Iron, according to its Bigness, would drive a Ball of

> Iron or Lead with such Violence and Speed, as nothing was able to sustain its Force. That, the largest Balls thus discharged, would not only Destroy whole Ranks of an Army at once; but batter the strongest Walls to the Ground. . . . That we often put this Powder into large hollow Balls of Iron, and discharged them by an Engine into some City we were besieging. . . . That I knew the Ingredients very well, which were Cheap, and common; I understood the Manner of compounding them, and could direct his Workmen how to make Tubes of a Size proportionable to all other Things in his Majesty's Kingdom; and the largest need not be above two hundred Foot long. (*PW*, 11: 134)

The ellipses in this quotation correspond to the sensationally graphic description of the violent effects of gunpowder. Omitting them here draws attention to the mechanical means of the gory scenes Gulliver describes, as well as to the accelerating rhetorical effect of repeating "That" at the beginning of each sentence. The report of these devastating machines culminates in the news that Gulliver's knowledge is the essential ingredient to providing the king with a potent two-hundred-foot-long phallus that would make him the "absolute Master of the Lives, the Liberties, and the Fortunes of his People" (*PW*, 11: 135). In Lilliput Gulliver was restrained and high minded in the exercise of the martial power he embodied there. As a person of "no Sort of Consequence" in Brobdingnag, Gulliver attempts "to ingratiate" himself with the king in the most graphically murderous way imaginable.

Swift has made Gulliver's narcissism an instance of precise and exacting irony: the desperate attempt to claim potency and stature with the Brobdingnagian king brings Gulliver condemnation as "impotent and groveling." But the king's description of Gulliver as an insect with "inhuman Ideas" also begins to delineate the lines of the larger structure Swift rests upon individual narcissism. It is specifically Gulliver's detachment—"to appear wholly unmoved at all the Scenes of Blood and Destruction"—that amazes and appalls the king. Few students of Swift will read of the king's amazement without being reminded of the Hack's account in *A Tale of a Tub* of having seen a "woman *flayed*" (*OAS*, 145). In *A Tale* the Hack's detachment is tied to the experimental technique he learns from the

New Philosophy. In the *Travels* the influence of New Philosophical ways of understanding the world has permeated European culture. It is, therefore, the king's failure to detach himself that allows Gulliver to feel sure his readers will agree that the gunpowder episode has demonstrated the king's gross ignorance. The "Defect," Gulliver explains, that causes the king to refuse gunpowder is traceable to the fact that the Brobdingnagians have not "hitherto reduced *Politicks* into a *Science*" (*PW*, 11: 135). The reduction of politics to science involves stripping the body politic, like the woman on the laboratory table, of human qualities.

The satiric charge is ultimately straightforward. Individual narcissism, the motive for all our actions, inevitably leads to moments when the frustration of the narcissistic will detaches us from a sense of human sympathy. Affable Gulliver becomes the purveyor of tools of mass destruction. The "special case" of Modern narcissism is the case in which inhuman detachment is collectively sanctioned. Reducing *scientia* to science, like the specific case of reducing politics to a science, involves privileging a method or approach to knowledge that is premised on detachment or objectivity.

Nemesis emerges with the recognition that Gulliver accurately reflects the Modern reader. We recognize, that is, that Gulliver is a pathetic creature in the gunpowder episode. Gulliver's dismissal of the king as a product of a "*confined Education*" initially serves to make us laugh at Gulliver's despicable self-importance and his apparent inability to see the enormity of what he has offered the king. But Gulliver's sense of complicity with the reader is brought home by the charge that the Brobdingnagians, unlike Europeans, have not reduced politics to a science. Swift has presented us with a question that, should we attempt to answer it, ties us directly to Gulliver. What is a Modern approach to Gulliver's offer? This question has now been answered innumerable times. There is a reasonable probability that Gulliver was not the only survivor of the wreck that brought him to Brobdingnag, and yet he is the only one known to the king. Even if Gulliver were the only survivor, the very fact that he made it to Brobdingnag suggests the likelihood that others will one day arrive. The material possibility that one of Gulliver's kind could end up among the king's enemies dictates the king's actions with respect to Gulliver's offer: he must take the recipe for gunpowder to be prepared in the event that this knowledge falls into the hands of his enemies. With the history of Modern politics largely determined by just such reasoning, at least with respect to technological "advancements," it is the truly exceptional reader who can positively distinguish him- or herself from the ridiculous, violent image of Gulliver in this part of the satiric mirror.

SCIENCE AND SEX

As Swift links apparently disjointed sections of *A Tale* by carrying images (e.g., the tailor) and themes (transmutations) throughout, so in the *Travels* apparent breaks are opportunities for sustained satiric assault. The overt political nature of the first two books culminates in an episode that sees Modern political theory as a specifically inhuman science. In the futuristic third book, Gulliver travels to a land where science and technology govern, only to discover that the Modern pursuit of knowledge is an astonishingly dangerous political affair. This voyage also provides Gulliver with a final opportunity to reflect on his identity in a specifically human context.

In the third voyage Swift bifurcates scientific discourse, giving the speculative philosophers the flying island and the technologists the mainland that figuratively and physically supports the island as its magnetic counterforce. This metaphorical bifurcation would seem to identify an abiding political tension between the "pure" and practical sciences. But Swift's categories of scientific inquiry do not easily correspond to our current muddy distinctions between abstract and applied sciences. Instead, Swift has imagined that in a culture where the New Science gains intellectual ascendancy, a power elite will emerge to determine the aesthetic parameters of the discourse and to monopolize its most potent practical applications. So the men of Laputa are addicted to mathematics and music as complementary abstractions (e.g., the musical chord informing an understanding of the geometric chord, and vice versa). On the other side, this elite rigorously controls the loadstone technology that gives them (or should give them) dictatorial power over the majority who live below.

Down below, the sciences work largely as delusional diversions. The more practically minded projectors of Balnibari are, ironically, unable to effect anything. While the elite are able to use the sciences for enjoyment and extortion, the men of Balnibari are continually hatching wild scientific schemes that bring them nothing but confusion and misery, engendering more wild schemes. Significantly, the Royal Society is associated with the latter:

> About Forty Years ago, certain Persons went up to *Laputa*, either upon Business or Diversion; and after five Months Continuance, came back with a very little Smattering in Mathematicks, but full of Volatile Spirits acquired in that Airy Region. That these Persons upon their Return, began to dislike the Management of every Thing below; and fell into Schemes of putting all Arts, Sciences, Languages, and Mechanicks upon a new Foot. To this End they procured a Royal Patent for erecting an Academy of PROJECTORS at *Lagado*. (*PW*, 11: 176)

Visiting "the whore" on business or diversion, the Balnibarians pick up a sort of communicable disease, so that there is now "not a Town of any Consequence in the Kingdom without such an Academy" (*PW*, 11: 177). While the Laputan men understand the nature of intellectual prostitution—science serves their pleasure and preserves their power—the Balnibarians are sincere about the possibilities of the new science:

> In these Colleges, the Professors contrive new Rules and Methods of Agriculture and Building, and new Instruments and Tools for all Trades and Manufactures, whereby, as they undertake, one Man shall do the Work of Ten; a Palace may be built in a Week, of Materials so durable as to last for ever without repairing. All the fruits of the Earth shall come to Maturity at whatever Season we think fit to chuse, and increase an Hundred Fold more than they do at present; with innumerable other Happy Proposals. The only Inconvenience is, that none of these Projects are yet brought to Perfection; and in the mean time, the whole Country lies miserably waste, the Houses in Ruins, and the People without Food or Cloaths. By all which, instead of being discouraged, they are Fifty Times more violently bent upon prosecuting their Schemes, driven equally on by Hope and Despair. (*PW*, 11: 177)

Swift's representation of the emerging scientific world retains the most fundamental elements of the world from time immemorial: wealth and power will gravitate to knaves in a constellation where the vast majority are fools. The Royal Society in this context is the vehicle of scientific delusion. If a machine will enable one man to do the work of ten, the fool reasons, surely I will one day be a person of leisure. If a palace can be built in a week, I will one day live in a palace, and with food production increasing a hundred-fold, I will never go hungry. The point is decidedly not the technical likelihood of any particular project; rather, the satire depicts the new science as a system built on fraudulent promises of material transformation. The Royal Society plays the part of democratizing the delusion, spreading to every town both the hope and despair inherent in the promise that the material world can be altered to permanently serve human needs and desires.

Gulliver is an observer more than a participant in Book 3, more so than he is in any other part of the *Travels*. This would seem to limit the role of his narcissism in the satiric representation of the ascendancy of the new science, but Swift has given Gulliver a position with respect to scientific culture that corresponds to that of the general reader in such a culture: Gulliver is "contemptible" to the power elite, and interesting to the projectors only where he has relevant specialized knowledge. It is in this alienated position that Gulliver begins to lose his sense of himself as a human being.[11]

Though Gulliver will studiously miss opportunities to see it, alienation is related to the role of gender in a scientific culture. The meaning of the red light at the door, the name Laputa, is explained by the position of "honest" women in the society: "The Wives and Daughters lament their Confinement to the Island, although I think it the most delicious Spot of Ground in the World; and although they live here in the greatest Plenty and Magnificence, and are allowed to do whatever they please" (*PW*, 11: 165). The freedom women enjoy on the Island extends to taking lovers from among the strangers who visit from below: "The Vexation is, that they act with too much Ease and Security; for the Husband is always so rapt in Speculation, that the Mistress and Lover may proceed to the greatest Familiarities before his Face" (*PW*, 11: 165). The desperation of the Women on Laputa to leave the Island arises from their sense of their own irrelevance to the society in which they live. Women are excluded from the scientific and musical discourse that dominates the attention of "People of Quality" on the Island. So complete is the influence of the speculative "whore" that the women of the island are neither regular sexual partners nor even sexual objects of their male masters.

Swift uses the principle of redirection of sexual energy in Laputa to link an emerging scientific culture with the primary joke of Western speculative knowledge. The story about Thales, so lost in abstract thought that he falls in a ditch, is given a specifically sexual turn at the conclusion of *The Mechanical Operation of the Spirit*:

> Lovers, for the sake of celestial converse, are but another sort of *Platonics* who pretend to see stars and heaven in ladies' eyes, and to look or think no lower; but the same *pit* is provided for both; and they seem a perfect moral to the story of that philosopher who, while his thoughts and eyes were fixed upon the *constellations*, found himself seduced by his *lower parts* into a *ditch*. (*OAS*, 180)

The Mechanical Operation makes speculative philosophy a fraud that, like fanatic spirituality, serves bodily desires: the lower parts are, in a sense, always getting the upper hand.

The voyage to Laputa considers Thales's fall from the perspective of the scientist "married" to his work (often a stereotype in Grade B movies). The Laputan men each have one eye turned inward and one turned to the zenith, so, like Thales, they may be wholly absorbed in their considerations of the cosmos. Improving on Thales, they are fitted out with servant "flappers" who keep them from "falling down every Precipice." Never ending up in a ditch, and rarely in bed with their wives, the Laputan men fully embrace speculative knowledge, "the whore" to whom all their vitality is directed. It follows that they become the vilest of companions. Swift's vicious turn on the original Thales jest is that the successful descendants of Thales—those who could give themselves wholly to their speculative work—would, like persons wholly engaged in dehumanizing carnality, lose touch with what it means to be human.

Gulliver's narcissism draws the reader to an encounter with the modern Thales. Gulliver illustrates his comments on the Laputan women with the story of the wife of the prime minister, who despite having every material comfort and every available mark of social status, escapes to the land below:

> She was found in an obscure Eating-House all in Rags, having pawned her Cloths to maintain an old deformed Footman, who beat her every Day, and in whose Company she was taken much against her Will. And although her Husband received her with all possible Kindness, and without the least Reproach; she soon after contrived to steal down again with all her Jewels, to the same Gallant, and hath not been heard of since. (*PW*, 11: 166)

What does it mean that this woman would rather be beaten every day than live in material and social splendor on Laputa? Gulliver offers his own sort of answer: "This may perhaps pass with the Reader rather for an *European* or *English* Story, than for one of a Country so remote. But he may please to consider, that the Caprices of Womankind are not limited by any Climate or Nation; and that they are much more uniform than can be easily imagined" (*PW*, 11: 166). For the misogynist reader, Gulliver has simply and naturally recalled the question made famous in recent times by Freud, "What do women want?" A superficial feminist reading will project Gulliver's misogyny onto Swift and dismiss the episode as typical of male views of women at the time. But such readings are comfortable misidentifications of images in the nemesistic mirror. Gulliver, though scientifically trained and mathematically inclined, cannot communicate in any satisfactory way with the men of Laputa: "I conversed only with Women, Tradesmen, *Flappers*, and Court-Pages, during two Months of my Abode there; by which at last I rendered my self extremely contemptible; yet these were the only People from whom I could ever receive a reasonable Answer" (*PW*, 11: 173).

After only two months in the land where speculative philosophy reigns, Gulliver is "very desirous to leave." He is "heartily weary" of the Laputan men, having "never met with such disagreeable Companions." After only two months, that is, Gulliver is faced with the very situation that dominates the lives of the Laputan women. Gulliver's condemnation of the capriciousness of women in general and his failure to see his own situation reflected in theirs is closely analogous to gendered readings of Gulliver in this episode. A conventional male reader participates with Gulliver in condemning women for not appreciating their well-furnished lives. An angry female reader accurately condemns Gulliver as a bigoted male without recognizing he has been feminized by the same scientific discourse that has excluded and terrorized the women of Laputa. With Gulliver, readers protect themselves from the implication, writ large in the fourth voyage, that human beings would be or are miserably alienated in a culture governed by the rationalist discourse originating with Thales.

Significantly, Gulliver finds some relief from his experience on Laputa in the company of Lord Munodi, who is himself ostracized and alienated in his own land. Failure to understand the role of the outsider leads to the common mistake of seeing Gulliver as a mere mouthpiece of Swift's negative view of the new science in the visit to the Academy of Lagado. Though he had been "a Sort of Projector" in his younger days (*PW*, 11: 178), Gulliver's unhappy experience on Laputa, his kind treatment by the reviled Munodi, and his position as observer, all work to undermine Gulliver's naturally "easy Belief." As one brought up in the methods of the new science, Gulliver is predisposed to embrace its cultural ascendancy, but his extraordinary experience with this culture's elite has a destabilizing effect. Munodi's understated claim that none of the "happy Proposals" of the projectors "are yet brought to Perfection," follows Gulliver throughout his tour of the academy. Gulliver is like a well-meaning religious adherent (imagine a Gulliver who completed his studies at Emmanuel College) who, having been forced to witness a self-interested and self-serving church government, is guided by an honest, ostracized priest to look critically at the more general practice of the religion. Forced to the outside of the scientific culture on Laputa and Balnibari, Gulliver's "easy belief" and core identity are shaken.

The role of the new science in Gulliver's mental deterioration is crucial. From the time he leaves Cambridge, Gulliver pursues a profession that conditions his identity as a man of modern sensibilities. His training at Leiden equips him with the intellectual tools of the new sciences of man. The centrality of modernness to his identity is illustrated in the way Gulliver uses his superior scientific perspective to protect himself from the crushing humiliation before the Brobdingnagian king. But the narcissistic protection that science afforded him in Brobdingnag comes under direct assault in the third voyage. The extent to which the modern Gulliver has become unhinged by his experiences on Laputa and Balnibari may be discerned in the dramatic return of his "easy belief" in a land of conjurers. The assault on his "happy" beliefs in the scientific lands leaves him ready to believe without question the shockingly evil report of every spirit magically brought before him. From this nadir he travels to Luggnagg where he momentarily reaches a new zenith of optimism on learning of the existence of the immortal Struldbruggs:

> I cryed out as in a Rapture; Happy Nation, where every Child hath at least a Chance for being immortal! Happy People who enjoy so many living Examples of antient Virtue, and have Masters ready to instruct them in the Wisdom of all former Ages! But, happiest beyond all Comparison are those excellent *Struldbruggs*, who being born exempt from that universal Calamity of human Nature, have their Minds free and disingaged, without the Weight and Depression of Spirits caused by the continual Apprehension of Death. (*PW*, 11: 208)

For a moment Gulliver's own deepening depression lifts as he sees an image of what lies beneath all his happy modern expectations, the ultimate narcissistic fantasy of the incorruptible, undying body.

Munodi's characterization of the projectors as "driven equally on by Hope and Despair" perfectly describes Gulliver at the end of the third voyage, and describes as well Swift's representation of the alienating path of scientific modernism. The happy expectation that something permanent can be done about the "universal Calamity of human Nature" is a formula (the mathematical sense of the word resonating) for desperate, debilitating alienation. The human consequences of the path Gulliver has traveled, which are considered at length in the fourth voyage, are signaled at the end of the third. Just before hearing of the existence of the Struldbruggs, Gulliver is planning to leave Luggnagg, claiming "Prudence and Justice" call him "to pass the Remainder of my Days with my Wife and Family" (*PW*, 11: 206). A page later, having learned of the immortals, Gulliver is determined to accept a Royal offer to stay permanently so he can "pass my Life here in the Conversation of those superiour Beings" (*PW*, 11: 208). Marrying Mary Burton signaled Gulliver's intention to "alter [his] Condition," to leave off his apprenticeship with his good Master Bates, to make his own generative way in the world. But the path Gulliver has traveled brings him back to the modern "la puta" who schooled him, to the now desperate hope that the calamitous human condition can be altered, to the ultimate narcissistic belief that he can participate in the conversation of material immortality. With the wives and families of the Laputan men, Gulliver's wife and family, as well as Gulliver himself, represent human casualties along the *via moderna*.

THROUGH THE SATIRIC GLASS

Gulliver opens the voyage to Houyhnhnmland reflecting on his relationship with his family: "I continued at home with my Wife and Children about five Months in a very happy Condition, if I could have learned the Lesson of knowing when I was well" (*PW*, 11: 221). So the fourth voyage begins with a dangling, contrary-to-fact conditional that grounds Gulliver's final voyage on the shoals of Eden. Is the "happy [human] Condition" necessarily a part of a contrary-to-reality statement, as the Hack affirms in *A Tale*? Will the conditional that describes the path to human happiness ever be distinguishable from a description of the path not taken? As Milton vainly warns Adam and Eve to know—for the sake of happiness—"to know no more," so Gulliver's opening sentence invokes a prevailing sense of dissatisfaction that drives him from what in retrospect seems "a very happy Condition" to a condition of unwellness many times more lamentable. With Swift as Nemesis there will be no fortunate Fall: even the grammar of the first sentence of the final voyage speaks of the futility of articulating a happy return.

The discontent of Gulliver's opening sentences suggests a partial awareness of the choices that have brought him to a state of profound misanthropy. The five months between Gulliver's third and fourth voyages is the most time he has spent with his family since he left for Lilliput. In fact he will spend less than twelve months at home in the more than fifteen years between 1699 and his return from Houyhnhnmland. That he sets out on this final voyage with his "poor Wife big with Child" is a particularly important indication that the "alter[ed] . . . condition" Gulliver achieved in his relations with his wife, Mary, remains a generative and potentially "happy Condition." In the first book, Gulliver's relationship with his wife is a counterpoint to his masturbatory apprenticeship; the fourth book begins with his generative home life as counterpoint to his sexually solitary travels. And it is finally sexuality—Gulliver is attacked by a "libidinous" female Yahoo—that confirms him as a self-loathing, misanthropic narcissist.

The path of Gulliver's personal narcissism in Book 4 begins with his famous misidentification of the Yahoos. While reports of animals that resemble humans were a staple of travel accounts, a literature Gulliver claims to have read widely, he not only fails to recognize any human likeness in his detailed description of the Yahoos, he expresses an immediate and extraordinary revulsion for them: "Upon the whole I never beheld in all my Travels so disagreeable an Animal, or one against which I naturally conceived so strong an Antipathy" (*PW*, 11: 223–24). Ironically, Gulliver's antipathy for the Yahoos and his failure to identify them as human establish his kinship with them. For, as Gulliver's Houyhnhnm master will later tell him, the "*Yahoos* were known to hate one another more than they did any different Species of Animals; and the Reason usually assigned, was, the Odiousness of their own Shapes, which all could see in the rest, but not in themselves" (*PW*, 11: 260). This passage at once links Gulliver's nature to that of the Yahoos and invokes Swift's definition of satire. Like a beholder of the satiric glass, a Yahoo recognizes every odious face but his own. That Gulliver is determined a Yahoo for just such a failure puts the reader in a troubling position with respect to Gulliver. The failure to discover one's face in the glass of Book 4 would seem to confirm one a Yahoo like Gulliver, which is, of course, the same result as recognizing the resemblance immediately. Is there an escape from this satiric trap?

Gulliver himself travels the darkly comic escape route. He begins with denial based on superficial differences. Though forced to acknowledge, with indescribable horror and astonishment, that a Yahoo to whom he is compared possesses "a perfect human Figure,"

Gulliver is "obliged" to his clothes for preventing the Houyhnhnms from seeing this. But eventually he is seen naked and examined in his natural state by his master: "He then stroaked my Body very gently, and looked round me several Times; after which he said, it was plain I must be a perfect *Yahoo*" (*PW*, 11: 237). Gulliver nevertheless persists in denying his link with the Yahoos until the incident with the female Yahoo forces him to acknowledge a more fundamental connection:

> I immediately stripped myself stark naked, and went down softly into the Stream. It happened that a young Female *Yahoo* standing behind a Bank, saw the whole Proceeding; and inflamed by Desire, as the Nag and I conjectured, came running with all Speed, and leaped into the Water within five Yards of the Place where I bathed. I was never in my Life so terribly frighted; the Nag was grazing at some Distance, not suspecting any Harm: She embraced me after a most fulsome Manner; I roared as loud as I could. (*PW*, 11: 266–67)

Bringing together the satiric glass and the Narcissistic pool, Swift has Gulliver meet his Echo (she was, Gulliver concedes, not "so Hideous as the rest") in a passionate and mortifying sexual embrace. Like Narcissus, Gulliver drives the reluctant female away with a roar that, though unspecified, carries precisely the sense of Narcissus's cry:

> Do not touch me!
> I would die before I gave you power over me.

Gulliver has gone to great lengths to distinguish himself from the Yahoos, but the consequences of his encounter in the narcissistic pool are immediate: "Now I could no longer deny, that I was a real *Yahoo* in every Limb and Feature, since the Females had a natural Propensity to me as one of their own Species" (*PW*, 11: 267). Like Narcissus, whom Tiresias says will live so long as he does not know himself, Gulliver would seem to be destroyed by the discovery he makes in the pool. He finds himself an object of ridicule—the incident is a "Matter of Diversion to my Master and his Family." And this ridicule informs his description of the encounter as a matter "of Mortification to my self."

But unlike Narcissus, who is metamorphosed once he knows

himself, Gulliver continues on his way. It is in this afterlife of mortifying humiliation that Gulliver comes to represent for individual readers an alternative to seeing our reflections in the odious faces of the Yahoos. Prior to his tutelage in Houyhnhnmland, Gulliver had not acknowledged a personal "master" since the death of his "good Master Bates" in the opening pages of the book. While Master Bates trained Gulliver in the business of the material body, his Houyhnhnm master teaches him to abhor the body and to emulate "the Voice and manner of the Houyhnhnms." Gulliver suffers ridicule for these affectations without "the least Mortification." But, he says, "When I happened to behold the Reflection of my own Form in a Lake or Fountain, I turned away my Face in Horror and detestation of my self; and could better endure the Sight of a common *Yahoo*, than of my own Person" (*PW*, 11: 278).

Gulliver becomes a representation of the figure that has passed through the satiric glass, one whom the mortifying power of laughter can no longer reach. As Narcissus becomes a common and powerful narcotic flower, dangerous to human welfare, so Gulliver is metamorphosed into a common emblem of narcissism, the inhuman human being. Swift underscores the extent to which Gulliver has become a being whose humanity is fully mortified by having Gulliver, the father of a Yahoo under three years of age, report that he makes the sail for his boat from the skins "of the youngest" Yahoos he can find. Swift has left us with the option of seeing our reflection in the ridiculous Gulliver who tries to deny or disguise his Yahoo nature, or in the monster Gulliver whose misanthropy extends beyond the hatred endemic to the species, to thoroughly dispassionate murder.

The explication of Gulliver's narcissism adds crucial specificity to readings of Swift's critique of reason. Considerations of reason have with rare exception dominated critical discussions of the fourth book of the *Travels*. Swift's contention in his correspondence that he "got materials toward a treatise proving the falsity of that definition *animal rationale*," has been read in the context of the Houyhnhnm master's belief that Gulliver and his kind had been endowed with "some small pittance of reason," which is used only to aggravate "natural corruptions." In these readings, Swift's skepticism about human reason is understood as analogous to, and perhaps informed by, the formidable rational skepticism of Montaigne, as expressed in the *Apology for Raymond Sebond.*[12] Indeed Montaigne's intention to "trample" on human arrogance by ridiculing "puny weapons of . . . reason" suggests the evident sense of reading Swift's fictional representation of the link between reason and narcissism in the light of Montaigne's skepticism.

But Swift's linking of narcissism and rationalism suggests a still more specific reading of his representation of reason. As the term that would come to identify the age in which the *Travels* appeared, reason is very directly implicated in the critique of modern narcissism. It is no coincidence that Gulliver's Houyhnhnm master, like Descartes, understands human reason by way of a paradigm of reflection. Unlike Descartes, however, he uses the evidence of human experience to distinguish reflective human reason from reason itself—reason, that is, as it would exist in a land of rational beings: "He seemed therefore confident, that instead of Reason, we were only possessed of some Quality fitted to increase our natural Vices; as the Reflection from a troubled Stream returns the Image of an ill-shapen Body, not only *larger* but more *distorted*" (*PW*, 11: 248). The Houyhnhnm has not here disputed the Modern sense that reason is inextricably linked with a metaphor of mirroring: the untroubled stream, presumably, "returns the [true] Image." He has instead disputed the Cartesian assumption that a human mind can in any sense correspond to an untroubled stream. Swift is suggesting that Modernity has drawn its optimistic paradigm of rational reflection from Narcissus at the nemesistic pool.

If modern rational reflexivity, with its claims on certainty and truth, were a misidentification of narcissistic reflection, then Modernity itself would be one of Freud's "special cases" of narcissism when the "delusional remoulding of reality is made by a considerable number of people in common." This is an irony only a Brobdingnagian satirist would attempt to expose: Modernity built on delusional rationality. If the whirling dialectic of an oxymoron like *delusional rationality* is suggestive of postmodern discourse, it is important to recognize that Swift's interest in the *Travels* lies less in intellectual contradictions *per se*, than in the "larger and more distorted" human consequences of narcissism passing for reason. Gulliver's dispassionate, murderous identity at the end of the *Travels* echoes back to the dream of the flying island as a machine of "universal destruction," to the "inhuman" account of gunpowder in Brobdingnag, and beyond to the Hack's matter-of-fact description of a "woman *flayed*" in *A Tale of a Tub*. Gulliver's use of baby Yahoo skins also looks forward to the monster who offers *A Modest Proposal* for the children of Ireland. Whereas *A Tale* mocks the intellectual violence of the process by which *scientia* becomes science, the *Travels* mordantly figures the human implications of politics—in Swift's words—"reduced to a science."

Swift is Nemesis because his satiric pool reflects the cold and bloody implications of the Modern identity. There is striking confirmation of the precision of Swift's instrument and of the power of the myth of Narcissus in the respective visions of mass extermination in the *Travels* and in *Civilization and Its Discontents*. Writing near the beginning of the Modern project, Swift represents Modernity as a journey through an emergent scientific culture to a place where humans live between slavery and "exterminat[ion] from the Face of the Earth." Well along the course of the Modern project, Freud finds himself wondering why the awesome technical power of Modernity has failed to bring a corresponding advance in the level of human happiness. His conclusion, that despite having come "very close to the attainment of [our] ideal," we remain subject to our instincts and appetites, ties Freud directly to Swift: the further we move on a scientific level from our Yahoo nature, the greater danger we become to ourselves. But Freud, of course, is not Nemesis. His retrospective cultural reading leaves the possibility of closure in an open question: Who knows if we will "exterminat[e] one another to the last man"? Nemesis reflects Modernity as unending: once we have seen who we are in the satiric mirror or the death camps, we go on, stitching together human skins, writing salvific books, and loathing the Yahoos we live among.

Chapter Three

TRAVELING METAPHOR

For in *writing* it is as in traveling.
—*A Tale of a Tub*

Introducing a libelous catalogue of Calvinist religious notions near the end of *A Tale of a Tub*, the Hack is confident that "They will furnish plenty of noble matter for such whose converting imaginations dispose them to reduce all things into *types*; who can make *shadows*, no thanks to the sun, and then mould them into substances, no thanks to philosophy; whose peculiar talent lies in fixing tropes and allegories to the *letter*, and refining what is literal into figure and mystery" (*OAS*, 153).

The Modern in *A Tale* is defined by the reductions of such "converting imaginations." When the mysterious presence of the flesh of Christ in bread is literalized by way of an Aristotelian critical method, the salvific bread of the lamb is reduced to a commercial product, mutton, and a fraudulent one at that (it is only bread). Vapor rising from the earth to the clouds is, in the work of New Philosophers from Descartes to Hobbes to Boyle to Newton, the empirical base for an ethereal vapor that remains (now in other metaphorical guises) the evasive final stuff of a unified material explanation of the universe. The metaphors of *A Tale* are those Swift appropriates to represent a reeling Modern world, but the "chief thread" (*OAS*, 98) of his tale is the fluid transport (*metaphorein*) of meaning by way of language between the literal and figurative, between what is measurable and what is mysterious. The metaphor for the *Tale*—what is "within the compass of the pen"—the metaphor for metaphorizing, is travel: "After so wide a compass as I [the Hack] have wandered, I do now gladly overtake and close in with my subject, and shall henceforth hold on with it an even pace to the end of my journey" (*OAS*, 152).

In *Travels into Several Remote Nations*, Swift simplifies his representation of the Modern to a book of travel, a supposedly literal journey brought within the compass of the pen and made text. Travel emerges, in Swift's ironically accessible satire, as the governing metaphor of a nemesistic assault on the Modern.

Not coincidentally, recent critical theory related to travel is rooted in Swift's own historical period. The work of the theorist Georges Van Den Abbeele is initially useful here because he shows the singularity of the role of the travel trope in Western intellectual discourse. His work is also useful here because his basic argument—that travel tropes provide unintended critical paths back through texts that claim to work in a particular direction—informs Swift's own notion of the circularity of modern textual travel. In a more direct way, Edward Said's work on orientalism helps illustrate cultural manifestations of Swift's own extensive use of "oriental" travel accounts in his *Travels*. Recognizing how the distinct theoretical ideas of Van Den Abbeele and Said are historically contextualized by the uses of travel in Swift's own time helps explicate Swift's representation of the modern as a debased metaphor of travel—the metaphor that does not travel; the journey that goes nowhere.

TRAVELING THEORY

"What if," Van Den Abbeele asks in *Travel as Metaphor*, "the critique of a system were itself encoded as an institutionalized part of the system?" (intro., xiv). His answer is that travel tropes, "the most common of commonplaces" in Western philosophical and literary discourse, provide such an encoded critique, and as such, a focal point for critical consideration of textual possibilities and limitations. Pervasive and banal, travel tropes paradoxically signal exciting and innovative textual "paths," marked most often by clichés: new ground, steps forward, new horizons, uncharted territory, progress, etc. Van Den Abbeele understands this paradox as inherent to the textual economy of travel as the metaphor for an intellectual journey, the adventurous quest outward serving to enrich with information or experience a fixed point of return or a home to which the text of the journey is necessarily tied: as a European traveler to China writes for a European audience, so the text of the intellectual journey tells a tale conditioned by and for a home audience.

The authors Van Den Abbeele chooses to consider, Montaigne, Descartes, Montesquieu, and Rousseau, root his theoretical discussion in an age called by the travel trope, *discovery*, and in geographic space that provided much of the intellectual capital for the construction of the Modern:

> It is appropriate that this study [*Travel as Metaphor*] should take place on the terrain of early modern French thought, since in that historical period there occurs a remarkable conjunction between the vogue of exoticism and the imaginary voyages, on the one hand, and the philosophical trends of skepticism, relativism, and *libertinage*, on the other. So if ever the motif of travel inhabited the critical spirit or *esprit critique*, it would have been in the Classical age. (xxiii–xxiv)

Although Van Den Abbeele does not explain this "remarkable conjunction," we can infer that the two hands he refers to belong to the great body of the historical moment: "The so-called age of discovery (roughly spanning the fourteenth through the nineteenth centuries) is also the era during which 'economics' itself is discovered by European society and formulated progressively into a discernible object of knowledge and discipline of thought" (xxvii). The critical spirit, inherent in the use of travel as a metaphor for an intellectual journey, is mediated in "early Modern" thought by the literal expansion of travel and by the commercial systems of thought invented (not discovered) to harness within a "science of wealth" the power derived from military conquest and economic exploitation. Travel metaphors may always, as Van Den Abbeele argues, have held the potential to inform "ethnocentrism and imperialism" (xxv), but the historical period he concerns himself with is one in which the service of home is constructed of a remarkable conjunction of commercial travel and systematic thought dependent on travel tropes.

Van Den Abbeele's theoretical aims deflect him from fully acknowledging the importance of the historical transformation of the travel trope.[1] Mediated by the literal discoveries of an age of travel, the travel metaphor negotiated a treacherously slippery path between the intellectual critique of home and the literally new—what has been arrived at abroad. Whereas writers like Montaigne (and Donne across the Channel) see the new as humbling evidence of deficiencies in what we (Europeans) think we know, writers like Descartes see these same deficiencies as possibilities for additional forward movement, a movement from the figurative trip, which is always a circle, to the literal trip, which is linear and will take us somewhere new. As the intellectual journey of the past informed an insular world of economic circularity, so the dynamic economy of an expanding world demands a new and better intellectual model, one that moves minds forward, that progresses.

In the England of the New Philosophy, the accounts of travel informed the radical rethinking of intellectual activity that explains the move from an "Age of Discovery" to an "Age of Reason." The alchemist Thomas Vaughan may be described, ironically, as mired in figurative language when he laments the pernicious influence of old ways of thinking: "It is in Nature, as it is in *Religion*; we are still hammering *of old elements*, but seek not the *America* that lyes *beyond them*" (51). But the Royal Society refined the notion, even as it refined alchemists' experimental methods, to take from travel the data that will allow it to make tangible and reasonable the alchemists' romantic fantasies. Bacon had suggested the importance of travel in the *New Atlantis* by having the representatives of Salomon's House collect and catalogue information from secret envoys sent all around the world: "Every twelve years there should be set forth out of this kingdom two ships, appointed to several voyages; That in either of these ships there should be a mission of three of the Fellows or Brethren of Salomon's House; whose errand was only to give us knowledge of the affairs and state of those countries to which they were designed, and especially of the sciences, arts, manufactures, and inventions of all the world" (3: 146). Adapting Bacon's fiction to the practical terms of a proposal for an academy for the natural sciences, Abraham Cowley provides that "Four Professors Itinerant be assigned to the four parts of the World, *Europe*, *Asia*, *Africa*, and *America*, there to reside three years at least, and to give a constant account of all things that belong to the Learning, and especially Natural Experimental Philosophy of those parts" (2: 288).[2] While the designers of the Royal Society hoped to systemize the collection of data from around the world by placing their own observers in strategic places, the market of the emerging imperial order was already delivering information that could be put to immediate use: "Travel literature was one of Locke's special interests; it has been suggested that such reading seems a rather trivial occupation for a philosopher, but, of course, travel accounts were to him what the laboratory and experiments were to men in the Royal Society. Travel accounts gave experimental knowledge of human nature and behavior, including language" (Aarsleff, 45).

Locke's philosophical project was, of course, carried on in the service of the New Philosophy. His study of language, measured against the evidence from reports from around the world, was intended to help the New Philosophers understand and communicate more precisely. In the formation of modern rationalism is the idea that not travel itself but the texts (reports) of travel, like the supposedly literal records of other types of observations of the world, provide empirical evidence contributing to the explanation of "human understanding."

If the New Philosophy sought information for new modes of literal expression along the notoriously unreliable roads of the travel narrative, the New Philosophy gained considerable support and direction from the political transformation of travel itself. Thomas Sprat in his *History of the Royal Society* celebrates London as the most propitious location for the society because as the "head of a *mighty Empire*, the greatest that ever commanded the *Ocean*," it is the logical locus for "that *Knowledg*, which is to be made up of all the Reports, and Intelligence of all Countreys" (87–88). Sprat's political agenda in this first history of the Royal Society informs his choice of images: the society will benefit from its correspondence to the rapidly emerging empire. The implication of his description makes the society a nascent empire of its own; its position at the center of information collected from "all Countreys" gives it command of the economy of empirical knowledge about the world. In the ode *To the Royal Society* prefaced to Sprat's *History*, Cowley adapts the travel metaphor to the interests of new science. Addressing the members of the Royal Society, the poet says:

> From you, great champions, we expect to get
> These spacious countries but discovered yet;
> Countries where yet instead of Nature, we
> Her images and idols worship'd see:
> These large and wealthy regions to subdue,
> Though learning has whole armies at command,
> Quarter'd about in every land,
> A better troop she ne'er together drew.
> (ll. 109–16)

Beyond the imperial nation is the greater empire the members of the society have already begun to conquer, and the conquest is a journey from the observation of nature, to the heavens, to the voyeuristic penetration of nature's (female) private parts,[3] to text and literal truth:

> Already your victorious lights appear;
> New scenes of Heav'n already we espy,
> And crowds of golden worlds on high;
> Which from the spacious plains of earth and sea
> Could never yet discover'd be
> By sailor's or Chaldaean's watchful eye.
> Nature's great works no distance can obscure,
> No smallness her near objects can secure;
> Y' have taught the curious sight to press
> Into the privatest recess
> Of her imperceptible littleness.
> Y' have learn'd to read her smallest hand,
> And well begun her deepest sense to understand.
> (ll. 135–50)

The most common of rhetorical commonplaces, the travel trope travels with the age of discovery from its function of signaling the importance of critical distance to signaling the importance of literal distance. The "America that lies beyond" the circularity of the ancient and medieval worlds is not the place that allows one to reconsider assumptions about home, but the object of conquest, the space for an endless projection of material power. The journey is, in fact, not about discovery at all, but about invasion, consumption, and mastery.

PRIMARY ORIENTALISM

In considering this line of inquiry about travel in the formation of the Modern, it is reasonable to ask if it is a coincidence that the most prominent literary critic to write on Western cultural imperialism is the same critic who thinks Swift may "serve as one of . . . [the] best critics" of the "world of contemporary critical discourse." Said is not directly concerned with Swift in *Orientalism* or in *Culture and Imperialism*, but Said's work identifies a highly developed instance of the systematizing travel that Swift makes the hallmark of the Modern. It is no coincidence that Said must, to tell the story of how the West fashioned the East into a quasi-scientific discipline, look back to the seventeenth century and the ideas of Bacon and Newton.

Dominant in the history of the Western construction of the Orient, Said says at the outset of *Orientalism*, are "knowledge and power, the Baconian themes" (32); "Knowledge of subject races or Orientals gives power, more power requires more knowledge, and so on in an increasingly profitable dialectic of information and control" (36). The "enlightened" Baconian project of "enlarging the bounds of the Human empire" has its application in the relations between those gathering knowledge and exercising power and the rest of humanity. Said calls on the work of Henry Kissinger to illustrate how persistent is the assumption that access to knowledge and power distinguishes "the developed" from "the developing" peoples along the lines of acceptance of the methods of the New Philosophy. Quoting Kissinger, Said observes:

> The first half, which is the West, "is deeply committed to the notion that the real world is external to the observer, that knowledge con-

> sists of recording and classifying data—the more accurately the better." Kissinger's proof for this is the Newtonian revolution, which has taken place in the developing world: "Cultures which escaped the early impact of Newtonian thinking have retained the essentially pre-Newtonian view that the real world is almost completely *internal* to the observer." (46–47)

Both those who endorse the legitimacy of the categories (Kissinger) and those who dispute them (Said) turn to the seventeenth century and work of the New Philosophers as the formative moment in the political identity of the Modern. One need not agree with Kissinger's conclusions about the impact of the Newtonian revolution to understand the political utility of using it as a marker between those who are able to recognize and measure objective reality and those for whom reality is profoundly subjective: the developed world's access to the truth via science gives it a responsibility for ordering the world for those who cannot.

Said recognizes that the sense of destiny to order the world has roots in the imperial designs of early modern Europe, but his insight—perhaps the great insight of *Orientalism*—is that the Modern conditions imperial conquest with scientific systems:

> To say simply that Orientalism was a rationalization of colonial rule is to ignore the extent to which colonial rule was justified in advance by Orientalism, rather than after the fact. Men have always divided the world up into regions having either real or imagined distinction from each other. The absolute demarcation between East and West, which Balfour and Cromer accept with such complacency, had been years, even centuries in the making. There were of course innumerable voyages of discovery; there were contacts through trade and war. But more than this, since the middle of the eighteenth century there had been two principal elements in the relation between East and West. One was a growing systematic knowledge in Europe about the Orient, knowledge reinforced by the colonial encounter as well as by the widespread interest in the alien and unusual, exploited by the developing sciences of ethnology, comparative anatomy, philology, and history; furthermore, to this systematic knowledge was added a sizable body of literature produced by novelists, poets, translators, and gifted travelers. (39–40)

From the middle of the eighteenth century, the Western narrative of the East complemented the scientific ordering of the East, which was itself informed by voyages of discovery, trade, and war. All the things "men have always" done are present in the history of the Western construction of the Orient, except that the conquest was institutionalized not only on a political level but as a rational or a scientific system that put the Oriental perpetually in the role of the subject of study. It is in particular this claim to scientific or systematic study that institutionalized Western superiority, and this confident distinction feeds the Western narrative that keeps the two from sharing a common humanity: "The Orientalist reality is both antihuman and persistent. Its scope, as much as its institutions and all-pervasive influence, lasts up to the present" (44). Baconian themes of knowledge and power establish dominion; the Newtonian revolution is a paradigm shift that allows distinctions between more and less powerful people. Said sees that the exercise of systematic power, at least in relations between people, is necessarily at the expense of humanity. Inherent in the New Philosophy's demand for an objectified subject, is a rejection of what Kissinger refers to as the "internal" real world—the individuated worlds of human beings.

The objectivity of the West's scientific study of the Orient should not be confused, as it is in Kissinger's work, with a notion of objective reality. Making something an object of one's study does not make one's conclusions objective. Said points out that in fact the West has, in studying the East, continually uncovered degraded reflections of itself:

> It is as if, having settled on the Orient as a locale suitable for incarnating the infinite in a finite shape, Europe could not stop the practice; the Orient and the Oriental, Arab, Islamic, Indian, Chinese, or whatever, become repetitious pseudo-incarnations of some great original (Christ, Europe, the West) they were supposed to have been imitating. Only the source of these rather narcissistic Western ideas about the Orient changed in time, not their character. (62)

Said traces the knowledge the West gains from study of the East—the discipline of orientalism—to cultural narcissism: having traveled the world round, Western observers found data that served to confirm the West's ideas of its centrality and superiority. In other words, objectifying the Oriental for scientific study did not assure objective data. On the contrary, the systematic study of the Orient confirmed assumptions that justified the narcissistic exercise of power. The assurance of an independent reality, derived from the Newtonian revolution, allows those employing the "scientific method" the illusion of objectivity; the necessarily idiosyncratic internal worlds of the observed seemed irrelevant to those who imagined themselves operating what Bacon himself described as his "machine."

Fundamental to Said's critical dismantling of orientalism is Swift's representation of Modernity as a narcissistic journey that ends in madness and misanthropy. Swift sends Gulliver on an oriental journey to a modern reality that is, in Said's words, "anti-human and persistent."

Unlike Europe's encounters with nations it dismissed as barbarous, Europe heard echoes of itself in the highly developed civilization of the culturally distinct Chinese. But like Narcissus and Echo, the European encounter with China was destroyed by a delusional European requirement that its Other be Europe's own fantasy of itself. The failure of this discovery informs the failure of Modern discoveries generally. In Swift, Cartesian, Baconian, or Newtonian methods, not to mention the disciplines such as orientalism that arise from them, are constructed of narcissistic projections.

GULLIVER IN THE ORIENTAL POOL

As improbable as it may seem, even to many specialists, there is a literature that says Swift sent Gulliver to China.[4] If this has been a decidedly marginal discourse, usually admittedly speculative and occasionally bizarre, it has nevertheless turned up an elaborate array of references in the *Travels* to China. Read in the context of Swift's use of the myth of Narcissus, these references reveal how Swift used the materials of contemporary travel literature on the East to construct an image of Modernity set on an inherently misanthropic course.

Swift's use of China in the *Travels* was germinated in *A Tale* where the Hack advertises to "the most reverend Fathers the Eastern Missionaries, that I have, purely for their sakes, made use of such words and phrases as will best admit an easy turn into any of the oriental languages, especially the Chinese" (*OAS*, 111–12). As "a most devoted servant of all *modern* forms," the Hack is tapping into a delusional modern strain of truly monumental proportions. An idealized European picture of the Chinese, which can be traced back to medieval travel accounts, was cultivated by the Eastern missionaries, particularly the Jesuits, who argued that the Confucian Chinese were a people ready to embrace Christian doctrine. From the early articulation of what the Jesuit Valignano termed the "Admiranda Sinarum,"[5] the European Jesuit's extraordinary attempt to "become Chinese" developed over the course of the seventeenth century into a controversy that Voltaire would say, sardonically of course, was as well known in Europe as "La guerre de Troie."[6]

The controversy that erupted within the Roman Church had less to do with the Chinese than it had to do with political warfare among religious orders. But the fight spilled well beyond Rome and drew the attention of intellectuals throughout Europe to the Chinese. Prior to the late eighteenth-century aesthetic fascination in things Chinese, there was an intellectual *goût chinois* that involved many of Europe's leading savants, including La Mothe Le Vayer, Nicolas Malebranche, Gottfried Wilhelm Leibniz, Pierre Bayle, Isaac Vossius, Voltaire, and, in England, Sir William Temple and the Viscount Bolingbroke.[7] Although the Jesuits were to a large extent able to control the news Europeans received of China, they were not able to guide the interpretations these and other intellectuals were giving to reports from the Middle Kingdom. An unintended effect of the Jesuits' lionizing of the Chinese and their rationalist sage Confucius was that China was transformed into an emblematic mainstay of European religious skeptics: the Chinese were the proof that people can live by simple rational precepts in unequaled peace, prosperity, and harmony, and without religion. Swift's Hack is adapting his treatise, "Written for the Universal Improvement of Mankind," for "easy" communication with a people particularly ready for his free-thinking doctrine.

China's significance as cultural emblem within the European intellectual world explains why the Scriblerians[8] were planning to send their Gulliver, Martin Scriblerus, on a "Voyage upon *Cunturs*, to *China*." Their advertised intention to give "an account of all the *hidden Doctrines* of Religion, and the *refined Policy*" of China and certain other remote nations indicates that Swift, a creative power of the Scriblerians, was thinking about the satiric possibilities of a voyage to China in the decade or so prior to the composition of his *Travels*.[9]

But rather than sending Gulliver directly to China, as was the plan for Scriblerus, Swift mined the materials of the European view of China for what they offered a satirist considering the delusion of Modern travel. In effect Swift turned frequently to a most remarkable instance of the fraud of modern discovery in developing his representation of the paradigm of modern discovery, first articulated in his *Ode to the Athenian Society*—

> We often search contentedly the whole world round,
> To make some great discovery,
> And scorn it when 'tis found. (ll. 142–44)

China was indeed an instance of "a great discovery" for Europeans of a world that Montaigne said, thinking specifically of China, was "plus ample et plus divers" than either the Europeans or the Western Ancients had known. But Europe's narcissistic treatment of its discovery—either the Confucian Chinese are uniquely prepared for Christ, or the Confucian Chinese demonstrate the benefits and viability of rational deism or atheism—led to the eventual scorn of the Chinese. In fact the central features of the utopian view of China near the turn of the seventeenth century—incorruptible justice, learned officials, rational morality, powerful pacifism—form the basis for the later European view of the Chinese as uniquely corrupt, ignorant, immoral, and effeminate.

The first indication of the importance of China in the *Travels* is the recognition that the Chinese language is mentioned in three of the four books,[10] and is an important reference in the Voyage to Laputa, where it is not named. Ann Cline Kelly argues that Swift's metaphorical use of language in the *Travels* is consistently related to attempts in the seventeenth and eighteenth centuries to discover the original and hence universal language. She points out that China, acknowledged to be the oldest nation in the world, was often thought to have the oldest and, therefore, most primitive language.

The reason the Chinese language is a particularly important reference for Swift is that Chinese is a nexus for scientific and travel discoveries. The project of the "School of Languages," which would replace words with things, is a satire on the European search for a "real character." In the *Advancement of Learning*, Francis Bacon observed that the Chinese "write in characters real, which express neither letter nor words in gross, but things or notions" (131). Bacon's influence was such that speculation about Chinese became a central aspect of the European search for a universal or pre-Babel language (Cornelius, 31), eventually making Chinese the point of departure for those interested in the subject. In the episode in the School of Languages, Swift had in mind writers like John Wilkins (1614–72), a founder of the Royal Society, who considered the Chinese language before offering his own scheme for a universal language.[11] Recognizing that the Chinese language is more complex than Bacon had hoped, Wilkins dismisses it in favor of an invented scheme, which was, however, never brought to perfection. The "great discovery" of the Chinese language is scorned, but this is no occasion for self-reflection; instead, Moderns, like Wilkins, staggered on under the ever-growing weight of their fantastic expectations. From the search for a universal language, Swift drew the figure of the Modern as so many professors of a School of Languages who think that "discovery" means finding in the world or the laboratory what we wish we could find—in this case a means of perfect communication.

The first references to the Chinese language in the *Travels* point up the source for a great number of references to China throughout. In the late 1950s Mackie L. Jarrell noticed that Gulliver's report on the handwriting of the Lilliputians—"Their Manner of Writing is very peculiar; being neither from the Left to the Right, like the *Europeans*; nor from the Right to the Left, like the *Arabians*; nor from up to down, like the *Chinese*; nor from down to up, like the *Cascagians*; but aslant from one Corner of the Paper to the other, like our Ladies in *England*" (*PW*, 11: 57)—was taken in large part from Sir William Temple's description of handwriting in China: "Writing is neither from the left-hand to the right like the European, nor from right to left like the Asiatic languages, but from top to bottom of the paper in one straight line, and then beginning again at the top till the side be full" (3: 335). Jarrell removed any doubt about this source by pointing to another borrowing by Swift from the same section of the same Temple essay. Temple observed that in China, "The two great hinges of all governments, reward and punishment, are no where turned with greater care, nor exercised with more bounty and severity" (3: 341). And Gulliver reports that: "Although we usually call Reward and Punishment the two Hinges upon which all Government turns; yet I could never observe this Maxim to be put in Practice by any Nation, except that of *Lilliput*" (*PW*, 11: 59). The metaphor Temple uses to describe the exemplary administration of justice in China is borrowed by Gulliver for his description of the Lilliputian system of government. Jarrell reasonably concludes that Swift was writing with Temple's essay, *Of Heroic Virtue*, "open before him or with a remarkably exact memory" (Jarrell, 117).

In *Of Heroic Virtue*, Temple looks, with varying degrees of success, for evidence of past or present heroic virtue in four regions—the extremes of north, south, east, and west. His work, therefore, is largely an interpretive summary of travel reports on nations in those regions. China, Temple finds, is the largest, most populous, best-governed, most enlightened nation on earth. While he finds heroic virtue in the form of courage and martial prowess in the other regions, in China he finds heroic virtue in the very fabric of the society: citizens respect the authority of leaders who earn their positions by becoming educated; the ruler—the most absolute in the world—governs through the advice of elite statesmen who come to their positions by distinguishing themselves in learning and patriotism. The incomparable "felicity" (3: 328) of the Chinese state is explained by Temple in terms of the extraordinary genius of their great rational philosopher, Confucius. Through the study of the sage's rational philosophy, the learned of China have come to happily govern the greatest nation on earth "without temples, idols, or Priests" (3: 344). Temple's summary pronouncement on the virtues of the Chinese is as unrestrained as one is likely to find in any work claiming to be nonfiction:

> Upon these foundations and institutions, by such methods and orders, the kingdom of China seems to be framed and policed with the utmost force and reach of human wisdom, reason, and contrivance; and in practice to excel the very speculations of other men, and all those imaginary schemes of the European wits, the institutions of Xenophon, the republic of Plato, the Utopias, or Oceanas, of our modern writers. (3: 342)

It is not, Temple says, that the Chinese have merely realized utopia, but that they live "in practice" a life salutary beyond the happiest utopian imaginings of Western thinkers.

Swift had before him in microcosm what the literature represented in the Modern scheme of things. Temple's enthusiastic embrace of the Chinese is best understood in terms of a kind of autobiographical wish fulfillment. After successfully negotiating the Triple Alliance and arranging the marriage of William and Mary, Temple became disillusioned with Charles II's tortuous reversals and secret agreements, particularly with Louis XIV, and so retired to his library at Moor Park where he wrote learned essays, advised King William when called upon to do so, and refused the office of foreign secretary as many times as it was offered to him. Temple's advice on good government centered on the idea of a privy council. He imagined a council of learned men, like himself, who would disinterestedly advise the king, and he imagined a king who would bow to the advice of such a group. If his concepts of political practice matched his perceptions of how China was governed, his political philosophy was even more in line with his understanding of the teachings of Confucius. For, as he read the Jesuits' translation of the works of Confucius, Temple saw a rational philosophy more rooted in the experience of everyday life than that of the Greeks and devoid of the mysticism of Christianity and other religions. Confucius was indeed the "Socrates of China" in Temple's estimation, but with this immense qualification: Confucius's rational philosophy had been put into practice while Socrates' philosophy, never practiced, had been all but extinguished under the weight of Christian superstitions (3: 456). In China a simple but profound rational philosophy enabled a benevolent, all-powerful ruler to govern a happy, healthy, incomparably prosperous people under the felicitous direction of learned men like Temple. China was a demonstration for Temple of the soundness and viability of his own political views and advice.

It would be a mistake to think Swift was turning to *Of Heroick Virtue* only to mock Temple's narcissistic reading of the Chinese. Even considering Temple's prominence and noting the excessiveness of his claims for the Chinese will not make his sinophilism singular. Like Temple, Leibniz came to the conclusion that the Chinese offered a model Europe should learn from, arguing that: "The condition of our affairs, slipping as we are into ever greater corruption, seems to me such that we need missionaries from the Chinese who might teach us the use and practice of natural religion" (*Preface*, 75). And Gulliver echoes him, recommending that Houyhnhnm missionaries be sent "For civilizing *Europe*, by teaching us the first Principles of Honour, Justice, Truth, Temperance, publick Spirit, Fortitude, Chastity, Friendship, Benevolence, and Fidelity" (*PW*, 11: 294).

Long after Temple, sinophilism marked the work of influential Europeans. Voltaire had a portrait of Confucius above his desk, presumably to inspire him in his rationalist discourses (Rowbotham, "Voltaire," 1057). Bolingbroke turned to China for "examples to confirm and illustrate" his deistic arguments by "comparing the effects of natural religion, unmixed and uncorrupted with those of artificial theology and superstition" (4: 264). Swift saw in Temple's lucid summary of the features of the utopian China, a narcissistic reading of travel that fits what Freud termed the "special case" of narcissism, when a delusion is shared by a considerable number of people.

Temple was explicit about his authorities for his ideal view of China:

> The numbers of people and their forces, the treasures and revenues of the Crown, as well as wealth and plenty of the subjects, the magnificence of their public buildings and works, would be incredible, if they were not confirmed by the concurring testimonies of Paulus Venetus, Martinus Kercherus, with several other relations, in Italian, Portuguese, and Dutch, either by missionary Friars, or persons thither upon trade, or embassies upon that occasion: yet the whole government is represented as a thing managed with as much facility, order, and quiet, as a common family. (3: 342–43)

What would otherwise be "incredible" is affirmed for Temple by the "concurring" accounts that stretch from Marco Polo through those of the merchants and missionaries of the Age of Discovery to the accounts of his own time. Temple's attitude toward the travel literature relating to China may itself be understood as echoing a pervasive European sentiment that was neatly summarized by Samuel Purchas, editor of one of the most influential collections of travel writing in seventeenth-century England: "China Authours how diversified soever . . . yet concurre in a centre of Admiranda Sinarum," the wonder of China (12: 57).

As we may describe Nemesis's pool as a fantastic and entrapping interpretation of Echo, so Swift's literary genre—a fantastic travel account—may be understood as an entrapping form of the literature of travel. Echo's return inadvertently feeds Narcissus's delusion; the pool's reflection captures and destroys it. The literature of travel fed a European cultural delusion of which Temple's reading is a representative part; Swift's satiric mirror reflects Modern travel to expose the delusions of Modern discoveries. As Nemesis, Swift turned to the circumstances of the narcissistic encounter: he set his mimetic pool in the literature of travel at the encounter between West and East.

A sense of how Swift worked his travel sources may be gleaned from a closer examination of his borrowing of Temple's comments on the Chinese system of justice. Temple's praise for the carefully turned "hinges" of Chinese justice directly informs his large claim for the Chinese utopia, "framed and policed" with such wisdom that it "in practice" excels Western notions of utopia. Accordingly Gulliver delivers Temple's "hinges of government" maxim with an emphasis on practice: "I could never observe this Maxim to be put in Practice by any Nation, except that of *Lilliput*." But Gulliver, only a page later, must directly contradict himself: "In relating these and the following Laws, I would only be understood to mean the original Institutions, and not the most scandalous Corruptions into which these People are fallen by the degenerate Nature of Man" (*PW*, 11: 60). One is tempted to see the satire working directly and exclusively on Temple: Gulliver, unlike Temple, must spend time living in the country he would otherwise idealize—but the context is larger. Among the travel reports easily available to both Temple and

Swift in Purchas's collection is one by the Jesuit Diego de Pantoia, who made the trip with Matteo Ricci from the mission house in Nanjing to the court of the emperor three hundred leagues away in Beijing. Coming at the end of the Jesuit's fifty-year quest to reach the center of the Middle Kingdom, and as the report of the first Europeans to reach the court at Beijing in the modern era, Pantoia's account should have been a formative document in the history of Europe's impression of the Chinese. But there are problems of Gulliverian proportions in Pantoia's account. It begins conventionally enough with the agreement in a center of Admiranda Sinarum:

> For the greatnesse of this Kingdome, their Lawes and Government conformable to reason, their being so studious as they are, and given to Learning, and to know so much as they know of Morall vertues, and their good capacities gentle, docile, and ingenious, and the great peace and quietnesse which they enjoy, without having any bodie to trouble them with warre, promise much and give great hope, that the vantage which they have over other Nations lately discovered, in the gifts of Nature (being assisted by the grace of God) will helpe them in Gods matters. (*Letters*, 359)

This seemingly clear statement of Pantoia's positive assessment of the Chinese gives way to a point-by-point dismissal of the component parts of an ideal China collage. The architecture, which so many had praised, is nothing to speak of, and the uniformity is such that if you have seen one of China's principal cities, you have seen them all (366). The unwanted sons and daughters of the poor are sold for service and are "the cheapest thing in China" (377). Their soldiers are base and without fortitude (383). It becomes clear, in fact, that Pantoia thinks the government of China, trumpeted as the manifestation of China's "chief art," is as corrupt throughout its extremities as is the court at its center:

> There are no great store of Lawes, but commonly they decide Controversies of their owne heads, and make Lawes in their Jurisdiction after their pleasure, every one diverse. . . . And it is very ordinarie among them to direct all things to their owne profit, whereby of necessitie, they commit many absurdities and wrongs, and take all that they can get: Bribes are usuall, and men use these more then any thing else. (389–90)

The same writer who had spoken of "Lawes conformable to reason," and the relentless Chinese pursuit of "Morall vertues," is here refuting the settled point that the Chinese excelled all nations in the administration of government. What accounts for this startling contradiction?

Pantoia could not come to terms with the disparity between a European ideology that agreed on a center of Admiranda Sinarum and the reality that, whatever China's many virtues, its center had, by the time he arrived there, become corrupt—a core of very human leaders and human institutions.[12] Pantoia's inclusion of both the ideology and the report of his experiences in his travel account make him a nearly perfect model of Gulliver in Lilliput. Gulliver's experiences in the land that "in practice" works the hinges of an ideal government leads him to conclude that it is a land rife with the "most scandalous Corruptions." Pantoia's paean degenerates into blanket condemnation: "Only I will say in generall, that they have many good things belonging unto Government, but not the execution: finally, it is a Government of Gentiles, with a thousand faults" (389). For this specific part of the satire, Pantoia is to Gulliver as Echo is to the mirror. A critical reader like Swift found an experiential corrective to the delusional idealization of China in Pantoia's startling contradictions—Pantoia sets out expecting to find Europe's narcissistic fantasy but reluctantly reports the existence of a real other. Readers of travel like Temple, however, persist in a narcissistic fantasy, ignoring contextualizing contradictions in the construction of an ideal and conveniently remote other.

In Lilliput, one needs the textual comparison with *Of Heroick Virtue* to see that Swift is making references to China, but in Houyhnhnmland, Swift signals the Chinese connection in several overt ways. In the first chapter of the fourth voyage, Gulliver makes a direct reference to the Chinese language: "I plainly observed, that their [the Houyhnhnms'] Language expressed the Passions very well, and the Words might with little Pains be resolved into an Alphabet more easily than the *Chinese*" (*PW*, 11: 226). The relationship of Chinese to the language of the Houyhnhnms is developed when Gulliver follows his direct reference to Chinese by observing "the Grey repeated the same Word twice, as if he meant to teach me the right Accent" (*PW*, 11: 226–27). Later, as he is becoming proficient, Gulliver corrects his "bad Accent" by having members of his master's family pronounce words often (*PW*, 11: 234). Works in Swift's library establish that the pronunciation tones of the Chinese language were referred to as accents in Swift's day, and that this was a feature of the language that attracted considerable attention in Europe.[13] Having directly informed the reader that the Houyhnhnms' language, like Chinese, lacks an alphabet, Gulliver's focus on learning the "right Accent" for pronunciation of Houyhnhnm words invites further comparison of the languages of the horses and the Chinese. In again making reference to the Moderns' search for a universal or Edenic language, parodied in Book 3, Swift is beginning a more general attack on Modern utopian notions.

The extent to which the utopian view of China informed Swift's construction of the rational Houyhnhnms is evident in the debt Book 4 owes to Temple's writing on the Chinese. The fourth voyage begins in fact with Gulliver rushing to utopian conclusions in a manner parallel to Temple's ill-considered conclusions about the Chinese in *Of Heroick Virtue*. In the introduction to his search for heroic virtue in remote regions of the world, Temple offers his "opinion" that one could find among nations "accounted barbarous," some that "have equalled or exceeded all the others, in the wisdom of their constitutions" (3: 322). His opinion is confirmed in his section on the Chinese where he finds a state "contrived by a reach of sense and wisdom, beyond what we meet with in any other government of the world" (3: 340). Likewise, Gulliver forms the opinion upon first seeing the Houyhnhnms that the inhabitants of that land must "needs be the wisest People upon Earth" (*PW*, 11: 225), and upon entering one of their homes he says "this confirmed my first Opinion, that a People who could so far civilize brute Animals, must needs excel in Wisdom all the Nations of the World" (*PW*, 11: 228). Beyond the obvious observation that both Temple and Gulliver believe they have found the wisest inhabitants of earth, Gulliver is like Temple in rashly awarding such laurels to creatures about whom he really knows very little.

The naive optimism of the English statesman and the world traveler may be traced to the power of seductive fantasy of a philosopher's kingdom. Describing his examination by the curious horses, Gulliver observes: "They were under great Perplexity about my Shoes and Stockings, which they felt very often, neighing to each other, and using various Gestures, not unlike those of a Philosopher, when he would attempt to solve some new and difficult Phænomenon" (*PW*, 11: 226). Like his impression that he has found the wisest people on earth, Gulliver's association of the horses with philosophers is confirmed as he learns their language and customs. As Temple, following the Jesuits and various writers on China, located the triumph of Chinese politics in a superior moral philosophy, so Gulliver discovered the source of his equine utopia in the natural rationalism of the philosophic horses.

At the center of the European myth of China was Confucian rationalism.[14] In the travel literature, the myth began with vague notions of wealth and size and took shape around the idea that an enlightened Chinese government provided the organization and stability that allowed for the evident prosperity of the nation. When the Jesuits began to make the Confucian teachings available in Renaissance Europe, Europeans needed little encouragement to view the political and cultural success of the Chinese as a consequence of the rational philosophy of its greatest sage. European commentators, including Temple, generally followed the Jesuit interpretation that made Confucius a sort of conduit for the Chinese to a primitive and pure respect for nature. In summarizing Confucianism, Temple observed: "The chief principle he seems to lay down for a foundation, and builds upon, is, that every man ought to study and endeavour the improving and perfecting of his own natural reason to the greatest height he is capable, so as he may never (or as seldom as can be) err and swerve from the law of nature, in the course and conduct of his life" (3: 333). Gulliver recounts the central precepts of his Houyhnhnm masters in much the same terms: "As these noble *Houyhnhnms* are endowed by Nature with a general Disposition to all Virtues, and have no Conceptions or Ideas of what is evil in a rational Creature, so their grand Maxim is, to cultivate *Reason*, and to be wholly governed by it" (*PW*, 11: 267). Swift was paraphrasing Temple. A chief principle laid down as a foundation is a grand maxim; the verb *to cultivate* here is a metaphor for to "endeavour the improving and perfecting of." Reason is the object in each. Confucius requires, Temple goes on to say, study and philosophy, "which teaches men what is good and what is bad, either in its own nature or for theirs; and consequently what is to be done, and what is to be avoided, by every man in his several station or capacity. That in this perfection of natural reason consists the perfection of body and mind, and the utmost or supreme happiness of mankind" (3: 333). With the very word *Houyhnhnm* meaning "*the Perfection of Nature*," it follows that Gulliver's Houyhnhnm master cannot understand Gulliver's discussion of European law, thinking: "Nature and Reason were sufficient Guides for a reasonable Animal, as we pretended to be, shewing us what we ought to do, and what to avoid" (*PW*, 11: 248).

Temple's mandarins and Gulliver's horses cultivate reason, which teaches individuals what to do and what to avoid. In other words each has natural reason at the center of its moral system. Within each system, moreover, the pursuit of reason and nature is itself sufficient to the requirements of morality.

Centered on reason and nature, the philosophies of the Houyhnhnms and Temple's Chinese have parallel positions on the authority that reason wields. With evident approval, Temple observed that Confucianism "is the learning of the Chinese," such that "All other sorts [of learning] are either disused or ignoble among them; all that, which we call scholastic or polemic is unknown or unpractised, and serves I fear, among us, for little more than to raise doubts and disputes, heats and feuds, animosities and factions in all controversies of religion or government. Even astrology, and physic, and chemistry, are but ignoble studies" (3: 334). In Houyhnhnmland, Gulliver finds the same sentiments and then precisely echoes Temple's opinion of what passes for rational inquiry in Europe. Reporting that the Houyhnhnms have no word to express the meaning of "*Opinion*" since "*Reason* taught us to affirm or deny only where we are certain," Gulliver observes

> that Controversies, Wranglings, Disputes, and Positiveness in false or dubious Propositions, are Evils unknown among the *Houyhnhnms*. In the like Manner, when I used to explain to him our several Systems of *Natural Philosophy*, he would laugh that a Creature pretend-

> ing to *Reason* should value itself upon the Knowledge of other Peoples Conjectures, and in Things where that Knowledge, if it were certain, could be of no Use." (*PW*, 11: 267–68)

For both Temple and Gulliver, the "disputes" and "controversies" engendered by speculative reasoning are evils that their utopian ideals have escaped. Both the Houyhnhnms and Temple's Chinese consider moral philosophy the only proper sort of learning, and each is dismissive of natural philosophy, which is, in China, ignoble and "disused" and, in Houyhnhnmland, simply of "no Use" whatsoever. Here Swift not only adopted Temple's depiction of the Confucian view for Gulliver's Houyhnhnms, he lifted the contrast Temple had drawn between the Chinese and the Europeans as well. With polemic and opinion "unknown" in their respective utopias, Temple and Gulliver lash out at the disputes and controversies that pass under the title of learning in Europe.

The rational disregard for natural philosophy, and speculative reasoning generally, reminded both Temple and Gulliver of Plato and Socrates, whom they ranked beneath the sages of their respective utopias. In *Ancient and Modern Learning*, Temple compared Confucius to Socrates specifically on this issue: "Near the age of Socrates, lived their great and renowned Confutius, who began the same design of reclaiming men from the useless and endless speculations of nature, to those of morality" (3: 456). In *Of Heroick Virtue*, Temple claimed the Confucian Chinese have in practice excelled "the republic of Plato," and refers to "the great and renowned Confucius," as the Chinese "Prince of philosophers" (3: 332). Gulliver is more succinct. Having said that his Houyhnhnm master laughed at the idea of natural philosophy and deemed it "of no Use," Gulliver immediately continues: "Wherein he agreed entirely with the Sentiments of *Socrates*, as *Plato* delivers them; which I mention as the highest Honour I can do that Prince of Philosophers" (*PW*, 11: 268).

While it had become common practice in Europe to refer to Confucius as the Socrates of China, Swift was very specifically following Temple by having Gulliver make the association between his Houyhnhnm master and Socrates on the issue of natural philosophy. By making the Houyhnhnm's agreement with Socrates the highest honor the Western sage could receive, Gulliver assumed the position of Temple in *Of Heroick Virtue* by locating a more potent moral philosophy in a nation remote from the Western tradition.

Temple relates reason to virtue by describing Confucius's writings as "a body or digestion of ethics, that is, of all moral virtues," and making Confucius's "chief principle" the perfection of natural reason. In his summary of Houyhnhnm moral philosophy, Gulliver makes the same association by having the Houyhnhnms' subscription to various virtues follow their "grand Maxim," which is to cultivate reason. But Gulliver's Houyhnhnm master makes the relationship between reason and virtue even more specific in a negative argument, observing that the European "Institutions of *Government* and *Law* were plainly owing to our gross Defects in *Reason*, and by consequence, in *Virtue*; because *Reason* alone is sufficient to govern a *Rational* Creature" (*PW*, 11: 259). In each remote nation, virtue is a consequence of reason. Emphasizing the idea that reason ought to be "sufficient," Swift intended to alert the reader to what is superfluous. Through Gulliver and the Houyhnhnms, Swift has crystallized the argument of Temple and other Modern believers in reason. If human beings are rational animals, and virtue is a consequence of reason, then humans attain virtue through reason.

In following this idea of the sufficiency of reason, it is interesting to notice that even the Houyhnhnms' seemingly singular "disposition to all virtues" derives from Temple's description of Confucian doctrine. Indicating that the Confucians believe that the "perfection of natural reason" leads to the "utmost or supreme happiness of mankind," Temple explains how they go about reaching this perfection: "The means and rules to attain this perfection, are chiefly not to will or desire any thing but what is consonant to his natural reason, nor any thing that is not agreeable to the good and happiness of other men, as well as our own" (3: 333). Reading this, a student of Swift may recall an apothegm from Swift's *Thoughts on Various Subjects*: "The Stoical Scheme of supplying our Wants, by lopping off our Desires; is like cutting off our Feet when we want Shoes" (*PW*, 1: 244). The similarity here is the attempt to do away with human desires and passions. For Temple's Confucians the "means and rules" for doing this are "not to will" things inconsistent with reason. For Swift, this was an example of the worst sort of Modern reasoning.

Even the Stoics recognized the magnitude of trying to suppress the human passions. In Temple's utopia the "means" the inhabitants use to deal with conflicts of passion and reason is simply "not to will" those disagreeable things. When Swift made Gulliver's Houyhnhnms the "*Perfection of Nature*," and endowed them with a "general Disposition to all Virtues," he was playing specifically upon Temple's delusions about the Chinese, as well as upon the Modern optimism more generally. Like Temple's Chinese, Gulliver's Houyhnhnms succeed in living under the "Government of Reason," precisely because "their Wants and Passions are fewer than among us" (*PW*, 11: 242).

~

In looking at later Western representations of the East, Said found a textual "fabric" (*Orientalism*, 24) in which the West cloaks the identity of Eastern Others. The fabric, Said argues, is woven of narcissistic Western images, insuring, as the myth suggests, that there is no real engagement of an Other. These areas of concurrence with the earlier orientalism discussed here may seem, however, at odds at the central point of comparison. Said is, of course, identifying and condemning disparaging Western images of the Orient, used to justify exploitation and oppression, while Swift was calling upon utopian European images of the East. This problem is further complicated by the use here of the term *orientalism*, which is anachronistic and implies a uniformity in Western perceptions of the East, from the Levant to the Far East, that did not exist at a time when nations of the East were still being "discovered" by Western travelers.

But these difficulties inform rather than challenge the narcissistic roots of orientalist discourse. Not every rejection can properly be termed narcissistic. It would be facile, for example, to term the long mutual hostility between Christian Europe and the Ottoman Empire as reflective of the narcissism of one side only. Few things could be clearer from the myth than that narcissism requires an unobtainable or impossible idealization. This is made obvious in the nemesistic pool, but it is clear even from the encounter between Narcissus and Echo. So long as Echo, hidden in the woods, mirrors Narcissus's words, he seeks her. He rejects her only when he sees she is not the other he hopes for—the other he will find in the pool. Locating the prehistory of orientalism in the encounter between Europe and

China provides the clear illustration for impossible idealization fundamental to the claim that orientalism is narcissistic. While Europe's constant contact with the Near East ensured that neither side was to mistake the other for an ideal, China provided a fantastically colored canvas for the European imagination, and distance obscured unpleasant details. While China would, later in the eighteenth and nineteenth centuries, fit rather comfortably into the orientalist framework, the early European encounter with China speaks to the narcissistic construction of the framework itself.

In fact the myth of Narcissus suggests how essential the idealization of China was to what Said terms the "anti-human" discourse of orientalism. This may be illustrated with considerable clarity by recalling Swift's graphic reworking of the Narcissus myth in *The Lady's Dressing Room*. Strephon's ideal, Celia, is found to "shit," exposing "how damnably the men lie" who call Celia sweet and clean. Like Narcissus, Strephon is punished by Nemesis:

> But Vengeance, goddess never sleeping,
> Soon punished Strephon for his peeping.
> His foul imagination links
> Each dame he sees with all her stinks. . . .
> (ll. 119–22)

Strephon's discovery that his Celia is human and not ideal leads him to revile all women. Like Narcissus and Gulliver, the shattering of his ideal leads him to an inhuman place where his libido is overwhelmed by revulsion. In the context of the myth, delusional idealization defines the path to the pool of Nemesis. Swift borrows from the European discourse on the ideal China because it predicts an antihuman discourse. Like Strephon's debilitating "inventory" of the waste products of Celia's body, the Modern responds to its discovery that the Chinese are humans "with a thousand faults" with a discourse, orientalism, that may protect "us" from association with "them." For Swift the utopian image of China was a ready and plentiful source of material demonstrating "how damnably . . . men lie" to themselves. It helped him illustrate how the European experience of travel was taking modern Europe nowhere except deeper into its own increasingly dehumanizing dream of itself.

Chapter Four

POETRY AND SCIENCE

Few discussions of the sense of chaos and the consequent desire for order and certainty in seventeenth-century Europe pass over John Donne's succinct poetic statement of it in his first *Anniversary Poem* (1611):

> And new Philosophy calls all in doubt,
> The Element of fire is quite put out;
> The Sun is lost, and th'earth, and no mans wit
> Can well direct him where to looke for it.
> And freely men confesse that this world's spent,
> When in the Planets, and the Firmament
> They seeke so many new; then see that this
> Is crumbled out againe to his Atomies.
> 'Tis all in peeces, all cohaerence gone;
> All just supply, and all Relation:
> Prince, Subject, Father, Sonne, are things forgot,
> For every man alone thinkes he hath got
> To be a Phoenix, and that then can bee
> None of that kinde, of which he is, but hee.
> (ll. 205–18)

Whether or not one accepts Marjorie Nicolson's argument that this "New Philosophy" broke Donne's youthful skepticism and led to his profound contemplation of divinity, the poem itself argues, more generally, that such divine contemplation is the only sane response to the examination of a dying, disintegrating world.[1] But this passage, in whole or in part, is most often quoted for the clarity of Donne's observations rather than for his conclusions. Drawing starkly contrary conclusions, modern readers are startled that Donne, writing before Descartes, Spinoza, Hobbes, Boyle, Newton, and Locke, suggested that the New Philosophy ends in atomism, that a consequence of falling intellectual hierarchies is the disintegration of monarchal government, that an unreflective individualism is the nearly universal response to the passing of the old authorities. From a modern perspective, Donne can hardly be faulted, given the time he wrote, for failing to see that the disintegrating intellectual, political, and social hierarchies of his "spent" world were also components—material knowledge, representative government, and individual rights—of an emerging new world order.

Such readings assume that a later and hence superior view of the New Philosophy enables one to applaud Donne's prescience in seeing where modern innovations will lead while excusing his failure to understand the remarkable benefits for human society of the falling hierarchies.[2] In such an interpretative framework vastly greater generosity is necessary to find merit in Swift's work. For when Swift wrote about the "world's disease," he, unlike Donne, had the work of scores of New Philosophers to draw upon; he had personal examples, both friend and foe, to observe; and he had the work of the institutions of the New Philosophy, in London and Dublin, to read in their official records.[3] So while modern readings generally credit Donne with being ahead of his time because he identified some profound implications of the new learning, Swift is censured for stubbornly ignoring and denying the evidence that a salutary new order had emerged or was emerging.

If such progressive readings are necessarily overtly hostile to aspects of Swift's work, they are, in their very generosity, as dismissive of Donne's discussion of the world's ills as they are of Swift's. Donne continued the passage above with observations that demonstrate his use of modern phenomena as knowing and poetic:

> This is the worlds condition now, and now
> She that should all parts to reunion bow,
> She that had all Magnetique force alone,
> To draw, and fasten sundred parts in one;
> She whom wise nature had invented then
> When she observ'd that every sort of men
> Did in their voyage in this worlds Sea stray,
> And needed a new compasse for their way;
> She that was best, and first originall
> Of all faire copies, and the generall
> Steward to Fate; she whose rich eyes, and brest
> Guilt the West Indies, and perfum'd the East;
> Whose having breath'd in this world, did bestow
> Spice on those Iles, and bad them still smell so,
> And that rich Indie which doth gold interre,
> Is but as single money, coyn'd from her:
> She to whom this world must it selfe refer,
> As Suburbs, or the Microcosme of her,
> Shee, shee is dead; shee's dead: when thou knowst this,
> Thou knowst how lame a cripple this world is.
>
> (ll. 219–38)

Donne was acutely aware that the age of European exploration was uncovering new worlds and bringing exotic new forms of wealth to Europe. But his appropriation of these discoveries, as with the discoveries of the New Philosophy, was distinctly poetic. It is not that Donne, panicked by the chaos of the collapse of the old order, retreated into a mystical piety, but that he poetically read the modern innovations as the most recent evidence that humans are profoundly ignorant. The Copernican astronomy and the wealth of the East and West Indies are, in Donne's poetic context, only recent indications of how little mortal humans know about themselves and the world, and how vast and unfathomable the creation.

The most significant difference between the early seventeenth century when Donne was writing and the turn of the century when Swift began his literary career may be the province of poetry itself in the European intellectual framework. In Donne's time, the modern discoveries, geographic, astronomic, or philosophic, may still be used to illustrate the mortal condition of fallen humans in a fallen world, and thereby make religion and poetry the only lasting human interests:

> Verse hath a middle nature: heaven keepes Soules,
> The Grave keepes bodies, Verse the Fame enroules.
> (ll. 473–74)

Throughout his writings, Swift had recourse to much of the same material from European culture—New Philosophy, alchemy, travel and discovery, even transubstantiation—that Donne made use of in his *Anniversary* poems and elsewhere. But by the time Swift was searching for fame to enroll in verse, European culture had changed what it valued in ways beyond, perhaps, even Donne's prescient imagination.[4] The riches of the Indies are not properly the stuff of poetry or for contemplation of the deity, but commodities in an emerging European economy. Mechanical philosophers were demonstrating the existence of God and delineating his attributes by way of a Newtonian natural philosophy, and this in lectures delivered at times from the pulpit of Donne's own St. Paul's Cathedral.[5] Rather than calling "all in doubt," this New Philosophy was being preached as a system to end all doubt. And most immediately for Swift, Abraham Cowley, a poet many contemporaries counted among the great English poets,[6] celebrated the modern developments by making poetry one of the diversionary evils that have kept men from discovering "the Americas" just beyond their intellectual horizons. Swift's sustained assault on Modernity is grounded in his early conviction that the Modern is constructed of antihumanist cultural discourses associated with the New Philosophy. The point here is decidedly not that Swift comes to see poetry and science as fundamentally opposed or inimical endeavors. It is rather that he comes to see the ideas about language that grow out of the New Philosophy as inimical to human knowledge, whatever the form of expression.

ECHO AND ODE

Prior to his appearance as a major satirist, Swift had answered Abraham Cowley in an ode that demonstrates that Swift was focused on the modern assault on poetry from the beginning of his literary career. Swift's first published work, an *Ode to the Athenian Society*, is a poem praising the authors of the *Athenian Gazette* as if they were learned men comparable to the members of the Royal Society of London, but working toward different, even contrary, ends.[7] The confused reputation this poem has had with critics[8] stems in large part from a failure to consider seriously the implications of the common assertion that Swift's *Ode to the Athenian Society* is "an obvious reply to" Cowley's ode *To the Royal Society*.[9] Considering how these poems speak to one another reveals Swift echoing Cowley's ode in a way that reflects on the esteemed poet's intellectual poverty. Because Cowley was not merely an important poet but also a representative voice of the New Philosophy and of the Royal Society, Swift's attack is an illuminating first look at Swift's understanding of the Modern.[10] In this attack Swift positioned himself as a defender of poetic sensibilities opposed to the violent narcissism of an age attempting to decontextualize knowledge—to make truth independent of history, tradition, and poetry.

Cowley's poem was written to praise the work of the Royal Society on the occasion of the publication of Thomas Sprat's *History* of the society in 1667. This *History*, which "has occupied an important place in the history of science," was itself a work of praise, intended to vindicate and champion the work of the society's natural philosophers:

> It was the first design of the *History* to explain the nature, organization, work, and aims of the Royal Society to the public, thus showing that the promotion of its affairs was a national, even a patriotic, enterprise that promised both a healing of wounds left by the recent turbulent events [the English Revolution] and great material benefits. The *History* was a piece of public relations, even of propaganda. The material that went into it was carefully supervised and selected, and its omissions and suppressions are as significant as its content. (Aarsleff, 227)

Prefixed to Sprat's *History*, Cowley's poem is an introduction and apology, representing the Royal Society as the offspring of Francis Bacon, a quasi-divine figure analogous to Moses, who had articulated laws for the fundamental reform of the acquisition of knowledge. As the institutional embodiment of the Baconian reforms, the Royal Society had already proven itself and validated Bacon by the heroic work in natural philosophy of the society's early members. Cowley also endeavored to answer the Royal Society's critics, portraying them as foolish, envious, and ignorant.

Swift offered his poem to introduce the forthcoming volume of the work of the Athenian Society, which he represented as a group of "exalted men" (l. 137). He praised their wisdom in looking beyond the "modish" and "narrow" work presently popular to more ancient wisdom revealing "epidemic error and depravity" (l. 139). Like Cowley, Swift defended his society from the obloquy of its detractors, making the censure of the atheist wits of the age a mark of the society's true worth. The nature of Swift's work as a reply to Cowley was particularly pointed in the emphasis he placed on the anonymous publication of the Athenian Society's work. In contrast to Cowley, who was praising a history that trumpeted the accomplishments of the individuals who comprised the Royal Society, Swift was praising the work of those he saw offering knowledge without self-aggrandizing claims for individual members.

If in broad outline these poems by Cowley and Swift have the nature of a call and (contrary) reply, the details show that Swift's response was not so much the expression of a different opinion as a specific attack. Swift was not, that is, simply using Cowley's Pindaric to praise a society he liked better than the Royal Society; he was using Cowley's form, his imagery, and his argument to attack the subject Cowley praises and to suggest a possible alternative.

Cowley's *To the Royal Society* begins with a reading of philosophy as a male figure unaffected by the Fall, but hardly advanced since that time because of the selfish management of knowledge by fallen men.

> Philosophy, the great and only Heir
> Of all that Human Knowledge which has bin
> Unforfeited by man's rebellious Sin,
> Though full of years He do appear,
> (Philosophy, I say, and call it, He,
> For whatsoe'er the Painter's Fancy be,
> It a Male-virtu seems to me)
> Has still been kept in Nonage 'till of late.

Nor manag'd or enjoy'd his vast Estate:
Three or four thousand years, one would have thought,
To ripeness and perfection might have brought
A Science so well bred and nurst. (ll. 1–12)

The failure to arrive at this perfection is traceable to the enemy of Cowley's poem, "Authority," which, "though . . . but Air condens'd" (l. 42), became a "Phantome" (l. 49) only recently put to rout by the heroic philosophical actions of Francis Bacon, "Whom a wise King and Nature chose, / Lord Chancellour" (ll. 38–39).

Cowley traces Bacon's success to an attack on words. Recognizing the ways words are untrustworthy, Bacon moved philosophy from the delusory grip of words to the verity of mechanics:

From Words, which are but Pictures of the Thought,
(Though we our Thoughts from them perversly drew)
To Things, the Mind's right Object, he it brought;
Like foolish Birds to painted Grapes we flew;
He sought and gather'd for our use the Tru;
And when on heaps the chosen Bunches lay,
He prest them wisely the Mechanic way. (ll. 69–75)

Bacon's contribution to the new science begins with a determination to look beyond misleading descriptions to the objects words are supposed to represent. Inherent in the nonlinguistic apprehension of things is the wisdom of mechanics, of seeing how the things of the natural world work independently of human descriptions of them.

Cowley was no doubt at some level struggling to represent the ways Bacon and his followers had changed, as Peter Dear has shown, the traditional distinctions between art and nature.[11] But Cowley's attempt to do so must be judged singularly unreflective. His poem aggressively positions New Philosophers as triumphant successors to poets in a contest for who can most truly represent nature. Cowley's sympathies in this contest permeate his poem, extending to its final lines in which he praised the unadorned style of Sprat's *History*:

'T has all the Beauties Nature can impart,
And all the comely Dress without the paint of Art.
(ll. 183–84)

Cowley was praising the society dedicated, in his own description of it, to removing the human apprehension of nature from the grip of artistic language. And Cowley's poem is even more specifically antipoetic in its argument. Explaining why noble philosophy has not advanced as it should have over the ages, Cowley claimed philosophy has been fed with poetry rather than nature:

> That his [philosophy's] own business he might quite forgit,
> They amus'd him with the sports of wanton wit,
> With the Desserts of Poetry they fed him,
> Instead of solid meats t' encrease his force. (ll. 19–22)

Poetry, for Cowley, is an instrument of diversion that explains why knowledge has advanced little since the Fall and the Baconian attack on words is the explanation for why *scientia* is now able to advance so rapidly. That Cowley used the Pindaric, among the most elaborate and formal of poetic forms, to celebrate the triumph of mechanical descriptions of nature and to condemn the cheat of words, might be taken as a textbook illustration of irony. One need not be Jonathan Swift to recognize it or expose it.

Swift answered Cowley's male philosophy with his own female muse:

> So after the inundation of a war
> When Learning's little household did embark
> With her world's fruitful system in her sacred ark,
> At the first ebb of noise and fears,
> Philosophy's exalted head appears;
> And the dove-muse, will now no longer stay
> But plumes her silver wings and flies away,
> And now a laurel wreath she brings from far,
> To crown the happy conqueror,
> To show the flood begins to cease,
> And brings the dear reward of victory and peace.
> (ll. 11–21)

In contrast to Cowley's conception of poetry as the diversionary enemy of true philosophy, Swift's poem depicts poetry crowning triumphant knowledge. While Cowley celebrated the Royal Society in a form which, by his own argument, was inimical to its work, Swift will use the Pindaric as the muse-sanctioned laurel for the head of a reemerging philosophy represented by the Athenian Society.

Agreeing with Cowley's claim that philosophy has been waylaid since the Fall, Swift implied that the New Philosophy, with its Cartesian foundation of doubt, ought as well to be included in his equation.

> Philosophy, as it before us lies,
> Seems to have borrowed some ungrateful taste
> Of doubts, impertinence, and niceties,
> From every age through which it passed,
> But always with a stronger relish of the last.
> This beauteous queen by heaven designed
> To be the great original
> For man to dress and polish his uncourtly mind,
> In what mock-habits have they put her, since the Fall!
> More oft in fools' and madmen's hands than sages'
> She seems a medley of all ages. (ll. 211–21)

The present philosophy, lying and, perhaps, being laid (as she will be represented much later in Laputa[12]), is of a piece with other gifts that fallen humans misuse. The accomplishment of the Athenian Society has been, not to show the way to her ultimate perfection, but to strip her of some of the "fustian" accoutrements that swell her earthly bulk and obscure her natural connection with the heavens:

> How soon have you restored her charms!
> And rid her of her lumber and her books,
> Dressed her again genteel and neat,
> And rather tight than great,
> How fond we are to court her to our arms!
> How much of heaven is in her naked looks.
> (ll. 228–33)

In Cowley's work and elsewhere, the New Philosophers wanted philosophy represented as a male;[13] Swift pointedly held to tradition, portraying philosophy as a woman who, in contrast to the prostitute materialism of the present, offers herself as a kind of mirror in which a man may "dress and polish his uncourtly mind." Cowley's subject, the Royal Society, leads him to emphasize the masculine subjection of female Nature:

> From you, great Champions, we expect to get
> These spacious Countries but discover'd yet;
> Countries where yet instead of Nature, we
> Her Images and Idols worship'd see
> These large and wealthy Regions to subdu.
> (ll. 109–13)

In contrast to the armed and violent, male philosophy that Cowley portrayed prepared, like Gideon's band, for "glorious Fight" (l. 129), Swift's wisdom is a woman, unadorned and leading men to truth. Swift was praising the Athenian Society in the image of its protectress, later the protector of all the Ancients in the *Battle of the Books*, Pallas Athena.

Confused by Swift's move from the praise of the goddess to his censure of the Athenian Society for praising too highly the virtues of mortal women, critics have censured the poem for employing too many female images. But the poem's reproof of the Athenian Society for exalting mortal women above their worth is completely consistent with its author's satiric temperament. Not comfortable with unrestrained praise of any kind, Swift saw the potential folly in the confusion of his immortal females, muse and philosophy, with mortal women who are as susceptible to the folly of vanity as mortal men. His warning, as perhaps befits his youth, is hardly what we have come to expect from the mature satirist:

> Well—though you've raised her to this high degree,
> Ourselves are raised as well as she,
> And spite all that they or you can do,
> 'Tis pride and happiness enough to me
> Still to be of the same exalted sex with you.
> (ll. 263–67)

The implication is that the Athenians have gone so far in exalting women that Swift must resist the temptation to desire to be a woman himself. Even if this praise has been excessive, Swift saw both men and women elevated by the noble project of the Athenian Society. This uncharacteristic optimism stems from Swift's attempt to counter the Royal Society by praising an alternative: in stark opposition to male, militaristic, materialist images of the New Philosophy, which operate under the seal of an earthly monarchy and a metaphor of empire, Swift offered images of knowledge that are heterosexually dynamic, human beings of both sexes being "raised" when mortal men work under the protection of heavenly female archetypes, wisdom and poetry. Though hardly a modern feminist position, Swift's poem may nevertheless fairly be read as attacking the dehumanizing implications of the New Philosophy's violently aggressive male imagery. Allowing that Swift was not focused on avenues to female empowerment, he was nonetheless identifying, historicizing, and corroborating what is among the most powerful indictments in the arsenal of feminist criticism: inherent in the ideology of the modern project is a violent hostility of the men of science toward women.[14]

Swift's praise for the Athenians is limited by more than his pretended concern over their excessive praise of the female sex. In sharp contrast to the progressive and universal claims Cowley makes for the work of the Royal Society, Swift found a voice in which to say the work of the Athenian Society, after the fate of other human productions, would not last:

> I grieve, this noble work so happily begun,
> So quickly, and so wonderfully carried on,
> Must fall at last to interest, folly, and abuse.
> There is a noontide in our lives
> Which still the sooner it arrives,
> Although we boast our winter sun looks bright,
> And foolishly are glad to see it at its height
> Yet so much sooner comes the long and gloomy night.
> (ll. 275–82)

Swift's muse had taught him that the proper subject of poetry, even a poetry of praise, is mortality. Unlike Cowley, who cast the Royal Society as the elect of a new revelation in which "Bacon, like Moses" led the way to the "promis'd Land" (l. 96), Swift called on the muse to praise those whose anonymity suggests they understand the folly of seeking more than a "short and happy reign"

(l. 303). And while Cowley was in an important sense merely adding an obsolete poetic stamp to the claims the Royal Society was making for itself in Sprat's *History*, Swift reclaimed for the muse the right to name the "chief heroes in the sacred list of fame" (l. 307). Whatever his expectations for the Athenian Society, Swift's first purpose in his poem was to expose that contradiction in Cowley's poem, which made poetry an irrelevance by subordinating it to the New Philosophy.

Swift took the issue of irrelevant knowledge from Cowley and made it a major conceit of his poem. To do this Swift played with Cowley's language, demonstrating his own ability to draw poetic meaning from words Cowley employed in the pedestrian service of the new natural philosophy. Near the end of his ode, Cowley said the detractors of the Royal Society call the most important things impertinences, in the sense of irrelevancies:

> The things which these proud men despise, and call
> Impertinent, and vain, and small
> Those smallest things of Nature let me know
> Rather than all their greatest Actions do.
> (ll. 152–55)

Swift picked up Cowley's use of the word *impertinent* and used it six times in his *Ode*, four times in his third stanza to refer to himself and his poetry. Referring to his "young and (almost) virgin-muse" (l. 62), Swift observes:

> No wonder then she quits the narrow path of sense
> For a dear ramble through impertinence,
> Impertinence, the scurvy of mankind,
> And all we fools, who are the greater part of it,
> Though we be of two different factions still,
> Both the good-natured and the ill,
> Yet wheresoe'er you look you'll always find
> We join like flies, and wasps, in buzzing about wit.
> (ll. 68–75)

The ill-natured faction makes "Railing a rule of wit, and obloquy a trade" (l. 84), but Swift's good nature:

Begets a kinder folly and impertinence
  Of admiration and of praise.
(ll. 79–80)

Playing with the word *impertinence*, Swift contrasted his own benign irrelevance as a poor poet with the impudence of the great poet Cowley, and his great subject, the Royal Society. The significance of the play on the word's two meanings, irrelevance and impudence, becomes clear when one notices that Swift used it in Cowley's pattern. Referring to the philosophy that "before us lies," Swift used the word, as Cowley does, in a list of three pejoratives: "Of doubts, impertinence, and niceties" (l. 213). Swift was, in effect, specifically identifying himself as one of Cowley's "proud men" who despise the new philosophy and impudently charge it with irrelevancy. Having made his own poetic muse impertinent as well, Swift contrasted his own youthful literary irrelevance with the consequential impudence born of the New Philosophy's claims for its irrelevant discoveries.

The movement back and forth between impertinence as irrelevance and impertinence as impudence is dizzying, but the implication is profound when understood in the context of Swift's lifelong satiric assault on the Modern. Swift set himself, as irrelevant poet and impudent critic of the New Philosophy, in opposition to the Royal Society's impudent claims for universal knowledge. Impertinence is, in Swift's handling, a word that expresses the components of modern hubris: prideful impudence built on transient matter. Impertinence also expresses the appropriate response to hubris: an impudence, derived from a traditional poetic respect for human limitations, toward grand claims for human accomplishments. However impertinent Swift's youthful muse may have been in praising what is so far above her, her ultimately pertinent theme of the mortality of human things stood in stark contrast to the impertinence of Cowley and the New Philosophers, who not only claimed to have discovered the way to the promised land, but who have, in an ode, announced they have obviated the pernicious influence of poetry itself.

Swift had, in his first printed work, begun to see his opposition to Cowley, the Royal Society, the Modern generally, in terms of an impudent response to a burgeoning cultural narcissism. This becomes clear in Swift's poetic response to Cowley's references to painting and painters. Rejecting words, which "are but Pictures of the Thought," Cowley also rejected the visual arts:

> Who to the life an exact Piece would make,
> Must not from other's Work a Copy take;
> No, not from Rubens or Vandike;
> Much less content himself to make it like
> Th' Idaeas and the Images which ly
> In his own Fancy, or his Memory.
> No, he before his Sight must place
> The Natural and Living Face;
> The real Object must command
> Each Judgment of his Eye, and Motion of his Hand.
> (ll. 79–88)

This sentiment is again expressed in Cowley's final lines in which Sprat's *History* is described as having "all the Beauties Nature can impart," but "without the paint of Art" (ll. 183–84). As the new philosophers have produced superior representations of nature by forgoing rules of art in favor of the naked perception of the "real Object," so Sprat, a new historian, has triumphed by forgoing eloquence.

These modern devaluations of the aesthetic in art, poetry, philosophy, and history propel Swift to a consideration of the poetic implications of the metaphor of art itself. Imagining himself a painter, Swift asks what subject of his age is worthy of representation:

> Were I to form a regular thought of fame,
> Which is perhaps as hard t'imagine right
> As to paint Echo to the sight:
> I would not draw the idea from an empty name;
> Because, alas when we all die
> Careless and ignorant posterity,
> Although they praise the learning and the wit,
> And though the title seems to show
> The name and man, by whom the book was writ,
> Yet how shall they be brought to know
> Whether that very name was he, or you, or I?
> (ll. 158–68)

His image of the painter trying to represent Echo is one of folly and frustration, which has at its unreachable center the poetic figure of the disembodied voice.[15] His conviction is that time disembodies all voices, though the learned may continue to speak as echoes from the past. Swift's struggle to find his own echoing voice led him to confront the problem of writing in an age when poetry, even in the voice of its most esteemed poet, was ceding its claims to be the medium between humans and nature:

> Less should I daub it o'er with transitory praise,
> And water-colours of these days,
> These days! where even the extravagance of poetry
> Is at a loss for figures to express
> Men's folly, whimsies, and inconstancy,
> And by a faint description makes them less.
> Then tell us what is fame? where shall we search for it?
> Look where exalted virtue and religion sit
> Enthroned with heavenly wit,
> Look where you see
> The greatest scorn of learned vanity. (ll. 169–79)

Hindsight perhaps allows us to spy in these early lines the revelation that was to come to Swift. His appraisal of the age in which he lived allowed no fit subject for a poetry of praise: it demanded one who could expose folly, a destroyer rather than one who could sing praise. His use of the image of the painter cast him already in that satirist's role. While Cowley had invidiously introduced Rubens and Vandyke to illustrate the superior representation of nature by the New Philosophers, Swift made the voice that cannot confidently be attached to any name, mock transitory, "water-colour" praise. The modern age is for Swift a time in which fame is sought not in "virtue" or "religion" or in "heavenly wit," but in illusory mechanical representations of the ineffable.

Swift's earliest answer to this modern dilemma was this first printed poem. He offered his impertinent voice in praise of the Athenian Society as an alternative to Cowley's sanguine substitution of the New Philosophy for the "Desserts of Poetry" (l. 21). But Swift's recognition that even poetry in "these days" is "at a loss" to express the modern impertinence, suggested a path other than the poetry of praise. The clue to Swift's alternative path is in the metaphor of travel. Cowley had made the vista opened by the New Philosophy analogous to the discovery of America.[16] In *To the Royal Society*, he called the members of the society "great champions" who would discover "spacious countries" for learning. Swift used the metaphor to contrary effect:

> We often search contentedly the whole world round,
> To make some great discovery,
> And scorn it when 'tis found. (ll. 142–44)

The expatiating inquisitiveness, which Swift always associated with the best of ancient learning, is mocked by the narrow impertinence of the modern vision.[17] Those not "studied in the world's disease" (l. 138) travel to discover, not answers to their own inadequacies, but confirmation of their own grandiose images of themselves. Swift's attempt to find an echoing voice in a poetry of praise led him to a consideration of the vanity of his age. We may come to understand this early poem as posing a question Swift spent the remainder of his literary career answering. What is the echoing voice for an age that prepares itself for travel by stripping itself of its traditional concepts of virtue, religion, art, and poetry, and congratulates itself, even as it sets out, on its triumphant arrival?

THE ECHO OF BABEL

Cowley was a remarkably propitious target for Swift. There were easier marks among the New Philosophers—spittle-weighing projectors and the like—who might have helped the young satirist to an earlier recognition of his wit. But Cowley was a giant among men of letters, much admired by Swift's mentor, Temple, for precisely the kind of heroic verse Swift imitated in his odes, and Cowley was an active participant in the design and development of the Royal Society. The rich irony of Cowley, the great poet ceding the representation of nature to the New Philosophers, helped Swift form the idea that the *via moderna* of the New Philosophy was not a triumph of reason over the superstitions and intellectual hegemonies of late medieval Europe, but a reaction to the philosophic (including "new" natural philosophies), artistic, and literary humanism of the Renaissance.

Swift's study of Cowley's situation led Swift to view humanistic knowledge, crowned in his poem by poetry, as threatened by the seductive, reductive certainties of the emerging mathematically based philosophies. The path from Swift's critique of Cowley's ode to Swift's early satires is illuminated by an historical sense that the arrogant certainty of the modern claims are rooted in a profoundly delusional narcissism.

If the Modern does not really begin with Descartes, the fiction that it does is useful for those who champion as well as those who attack Modernity.[18] By making Descartes a leader of the Moderns and the first fatality in the *Battle of the Books*, Swift affirmed Descartes's importance as a primary mover of the Modern. It is interesting in this context to see Descartes's distinctions between poetic knowledge and his own project. In the *Discourse on Method*, Descartes juxtaposed poetry and mathematics as he reviewed the fields of study he would reject:

> I esteemed Eloquence most highly and I was enamored of Poesy, but I thought that both were gifts of the mind rather than fruits of study. Those who have the strongest power of reasoning, and who most skillfully arrange their thoughts in order to render them clear and intelligible, have the best power of persuasion even if they can but speak the language of Lower Brittany and have never learned rhetoric. And those who have the most delightful original ideas and who know how to express them with the maximum of style and suavity, would not fail to be the best poets even if the art of Poetry were unknown to them.
>
> Most of all was I delighted with Mathematics because of the certainty of its demonstrations and the evidence of its reasoning; but I did not yet understand its true use, and, believing that it was of service only in mechanical arts, I was astonished that, seeing how firm and solid the basis, no loftier edifice had been reared thereupon. (1: 85)

Descartes's indirection may lead modern readers to see him distinguishing the rhetorical and artistic ends of oratory and poetry from the physical or material ends of mathematics. But this is a misreading. Poetry and eloquence generally are necessarily the fruits of individual minds, whereas mathematics is, at least potentially, the basis of a process of objective construction. It is, interestingly, the common ends of these disciplines that define Descartes's view of mathematics and poetry. The "true use" of mathematics that Descartes's method advances is the ultimately persuasive argument—the form of communication that is not rhetorically eloquent, but merely and universally (more common than the language of Lower Brittany) certain. The "delightful original ideas" that define Descartes's concept of poetry give way to what he most "delighted" in, the study of mathematics, and his own "original idea" is that mathematics provides the model for the "long chains of reasoning" that make "nothing so remote that we cannot reach to it, nor so recondite that we cannot discover it" (1: 92). Descartes may be read as sharing Plato's suspicion that poetry is too idiosyncratic—the fruit of individual inspiration—to be welcome where reason governs, but the distinction between Plato and Descartes on this point is crucial. Whereas Plato bans poetry from the Republic because it is a powerful counterforce to reason that, in Plato's conception, is seeking to strengthen or extend its tenuous grasp on human behavior, Descartes may merely dismiss poetry as a pleasant irrelevancy, a formerly powerful but unstable authority now replaced by an emerging rational system that delivers—certainly and progressively—truth.

As Rodolphe Gasché has explained in a study of the modern philosophical notions of reflexivity, Descartes's fundamental contribution to the Modern is best understood in terms of the human study of our own reflection:

> The philosophy of reflection is generally considered to have begun with Descartes's *prima philosophia*. There are good reasons for this assumption, for in Descartes the scholastic idea of *reditus* undergoes an epoch-making transformation, whereby reflection, instead of being merely the medium of metaphysics, becomes its very foundation. With Cartesian thought, the self-certainty of the thinking subject—a certainty apodictically found in the *cogito me cogitare*—becomes the unshakable ground of philosophy itself. No longer does the essence of the human being reside primarily in grounds ontologically and theologically independent of him. . . . With the ego as *cogitans* be-

> coming its own *cogitatum*, a major paradigm of reflection, and of ensuing philosophy, is set forth. (17)

From Swift's perspective this "major paradigm of reflection" is not distinguishable from the concept of narcissism: Descartes's long chains of reasoning are infallible avenues to truth because they are self-reinforcing—projection and reflection. Descartes's unification of all knowledge is supportable, not because it is a unification of all knowledge, but because it is *Descartes's* unification. The Cartesian claim that "no knowledge that can be rendered doubtful should be called science" (1: 87) means, of course, that science is that knowledge Descartes or his followers judge certain. In defining a separate scientific discourse, Descartes is excluding most branches of learning, including poetry, from their ancient claims to *scientia*.

One would like to follow Marjorie Nicolson's explanation that the new philosophy of the seventeenth century made it so that "[t]he language of poetry and science was no longer one when the world was no longer one."[19] But the suggestion of separately developing discourses obscures the self-informing reflectiveness inherent in the New Philosophy's appropriation of *scientia* to itself. Most interesting in Gasché's account of philosophic reflexivity is the idea that the Cartesian paradigm is predictive of the philosophy that follows: "From here on, the history of the development of the philosophy of reflection becomes almost predictable. Take, for instance, the case of Locke, for whom reflection is also the fundamental method of philosophizing, inasmuch as it is the sole means of discovering logical categories" (17). Gasché acknowledges the odd position of a philosopher in the modern world by observing that Locke's reflection is "*empirical* reflection . . . belonging by right to psychology and not to philosophy" (17). By Descartes's definition of science, philosophy joins poetry in relinquishing its claims on whole areas of knowledge. Whatever Locke's contributions to modern psychology, his greatest contribution to the "predictable" path of the modern discourse generally is his fundamentally Cartesian discussion of language.[20] In his *Epistle to the Reader* prefaced to *An Essay Concerning Human Understanding*, Locke distinguishes his task from those of the "Master-Builders" of his age—Boyle, Sydenham, Huygens, and the "incomparable Mr. Newton"—by claiming his *Essay* is intended only to remove some of "the Rubbish, that lies in the way of Knowledge," in the form of "uncouth, affected, or unintelligible terms" (10). Locke saw his work on language as contributing to the process of the pursuit of "the true Knowledge of Things" in the context of the project of the Royal Society.[21] As Aarsleff has pointed out, Locke's discussion of language begins with and culminates in a scientific doctrine that is inherently antipoetic. Tracing many of Locke's ideas on language to Robert Boyle, Aarsleff observes:

> Boyle and his eminent friends did not depreciate poetry because they were illiterate and uncultured boors, for obviously if man can hope to gain real knowledge, poetry is of no consequence. The angels do not entertain *themselves* with poetry, though in the human perspective their entertainment is poetry and beautiful music; but for them it is enough to intuit directly. The order they contemplate demands no embellishments. (62)

From this linguistic assumption of the Modern, as developed in Book 3 of Locke's *Essay*, Aarsleff sees the linguistic development of the Modern over the last three centuries:

> From the slow beginnings of artificial signs—or words and speech—man's control of the world steadily grew as reflection was offered new material to work on. The fruitfulness of language and reflection worked for the reciprocal benefit of each to produce the "origin and progress of language." This process opened the way for the history of thought, as Locke had intimated. . . . For a long time the signs of language retained elements of gestural expression in a mixture of song and poetry that was to play a large role in Romantic esthetic. But the union was gradually resolved as language was refined to meet the practical demands of knowledge and control over things. Music moved into its own sphere, and the poet was left to make the best of a language that was largely foreign to his purposes. (30)

One remarkably "predictable" development of the Modern as a consequence of establishing human thought as self-reflecting activity is an extraordinary increase in "the practical demands" of the Baconian enterprise—the extension of power over things. Another is (or should be) the death of poetry. Although it seems unlikely that even the youthful Swift feared for the long-term health of poetry, he was clearly concerned that many of his most influential contemporaries favored an untroubled pond of self-affirming physico-mathematical knowledge over the contextualizing pool of the humanist tradition.

Swift dispatches Descartes with true poetic economy. In the *Battle of the Books* the author of the debased modern epic—that is, the Epic of the Modern—begins by calling upon "a hundred tongues, and mouths, and hands, and pens, which would all be too little to perform so immense a work" (*OAS*, 14). Such is the nature of the modern project of accretive knowledge that no number of appendages or orifices or machines could possibly broadcast the Modern's claims for itself adequately. After the Moderns ineffectively initiate the battle and after certain gaps in the manuscript, Aristotle meets Descartes on the field:

> Then Aristotle, observing Bacon advance with a furious mien, drew his bow to the head and let fly his arrow, which missed the valiant Modern and went hizzing over his head. But Des Cartes it hit; the steel point quickly found a defect in his head-piece; it pierced the leather and the pasteboard and went in at his right eye. The torture of the pain whirled the valiant bowman round till death, like a star of superior influence, drew him into his own vortex. (*OAS*, 14)

Bacon is missed, not as many interpretations suggest, because Swift valued Bacon above Descartes: the equanimity of terming them both "valiant" moderns could hardly be clearer. Rather Aristotle's thought passes by appearance, "the furious mien," to reach the intellectual source of the New Philosophy. The mechanistic exterior of Descartes's thought—his books represented by the leather and pasteboard of his "head-piece"—is betrayed by the sensitive flesh that lies beneath or behind it.

These relatively transparent allegorical aspects of Swift's attack are subordinate to the prescient satiric thrust at Descartes's vortices. Modern readers generally suppose that the weakness in Descartes's head-piece corresponds to his physics, which, virtually every modern discussion notes, was superseded by Newtonian physics. Such a reading fails to recognize that Descartes saw his philosophical method and his physics as interdependent, with his physics demonstrating the efficacy of his approach.[22] Swift here works with the sublime linguistic irony of this interrelationship. For in piercing the mechanistic exterior, the arrow spins the sensitive, mortal being, Descartes, into a proof of his essentially narcissistic system. As one who has resolved to proceed from his own head "in the form of lines" (17) taken from geometry, Descartes ends up being destroyed by his own circular metaphor, the whirlwind that has at its center a self-created vacuum. In Swift's fiction, as well, perhaps, as in an informed reading of the dismissal of Descartes's physics, the Cartesian system is one that, when historicized by Aristotle's arrow,[23] devolves into the vacuous center of its author's ultimately self-referential projections.

Also in the *Battle of the Books*, Swift represents Cowley confronting his paradoxical existence as at once a poet and a man of the new science. Meeting Pindar on the field of battle, the Modern is overwhelmed by the ancient poet he has imitated. Facing certain death, Cowley begs for his life, offering his horse, his arms, and the ransom his "friends will give":

> "Dog!" said Pindar, "let your ransom stay with your friends; but your carcass shall be left for the fowls of the air and the beasts of the field." With that he raised his sword, and with a mighty stroke cleft the wretched Modern in twain, the sword pursuing the blow; and one half lay panting on the ground, to be trod in pieces by the horses' feet; the other half was borne by the frighted steed through the field. This Venus took, washed it seven times in ambrosia, then struck it thrice with a sprig of amaranth; upon which the leather grew round and soft, and the leaves turned into feathers, and being gilded before, continued gilded still; so it became a dove, and she harnessed it to her chariot. (*OAS*, 17)

The fate Cowley meets is to be cleft into his ancient and modern parts. A poet known for his wit, and especially his love poetry (hence the protection of Venus), Cowley discovered Pindar at a time when he had become deeply involved in the political and intellectual movements of his day. With odes written to Thomas Hobbes, Dr. Charles Scarborough, and the Royal Society, Cowley has offered the ransom of modern "friends" to his ancient teacher.

Swift's allegory separates Cowley, the great poet, from Cowley, the friend of the New Philosophy. The poet who has used Pindar to liken Hobbes's reason to Achilles' shield is made carrion; the author of the "The Mistress" and other poems is immortalized as a poet who, Swift is sure, will one day be counted an ancient in the ever unfinished battle of the books.

Larger poetic implications of the modern whirlwind are explored in *A Tale of a Tub*, where Swift's Hack is in many respects a Cartesian, not the least in his intention to present his readers with "the most finished and refined system of all sciences and arts" (*OAS*, 121). A decidedly modern reading of Xenophon's dictum that Homer covered all topics in his poems leads the Hack to identify the Epic poet as his most formidable competitor:

> I must needs own it was by the assistance of this *arcanum* that I, though otherwise *impar*, have adventured upon so daring an attempt, never achieved or undertaken before but by a certain author called Homer, in whom, though otherwise a person not without some abilities and, *for an ancient*, of a tolerable genius, I have discovered many gross errors, which are not to be forgiven his very ashes, if by chance any of them are left. For whereas we are assured he designed his work for a complete body of all knowledge, human, divine, political, and mechanic, it is manifest he hath wholly neglected some, and been very imperfect in the rest. (*OAS*, 122)

The *arcanum* that raises the Hack to his universal task is an alchemical recipe that distills an infinite information delivery system of "abstracts, summaries, compendiums" and the like from "all modern bodies of arts and sciences whatsoever" (*OAS*, 121). Homer is, therefore, appropriately taxed with a deficient account of the *opus magnum*, and a superficial understanding of the texts of the seventeenth-century alchemists, Michael Sendivogius, Jacob Boehme, and Thomas Vaughan. As the Hack's criticisms of Homer descend from the arcane to the more mundanely ridiculous—Homer is censured for "ignorance in the *common law of this realm*, and in the doctrine as well as discipline of the Church of England" (*OAS*, 122)—the modern reader recognizes the humorous absurdity of the Hack's argument.

But Swift's attack is methodological: an epitomized *reductio ad adsurdum* of the modern project itself. Alchemy is a seedbed of the

Modern, both in its experimental approach to the acquisition of knowledge,[24] and, more importantly for Swift, in its grandiose expectations to reduce reality to a controllable system. Modern science takes not only its basic empirical methodology from alchemists; it also takes their most fundamental end. The distinction between the two modern enterprises, then, is one of adaptation in which the mad project of individual alchemists is expropriated by a mercantile mentality of progressive accumulation. Bacon's trade "for God's first creature, which was *Light*," was, for Swift, a path to the intellectual tyranny that values the present moment over all that have come before. Swift's specific satiric target in the Hack's discussion of Homer is William Wotton, whose *Reflections on Ancient and Modern Learning* is a proto-Hegelian argument that the Moderns have necessarily surpassed the ancients in virtually every field of knowledge. Swift reduces Wotton's reflections to their logical, solipsistic conclusions by exposing the absurdity of judging Homer by Wotton's immediate concerns. But Swift attacks Wotton's *Reflections* as one preposterous illustration of the tyranny of modern narcissism itself. Flush with his success in dispatching Homer from the intellectual stage, Swift's Hack reduces his technique to a cardinal principle of modern discourse: "But I here think fit to lay hold on that great honourable privilege, of being the *last writer*. I claim an absolute authority in right, as the *freshest modern*, which gives me despotic power over all authors before me" (*OAS*, 123).

In the formation of the Modern, Swift sees the intellectual violence inherent in the idea that knowledge may be accumulated progressively. The modern dismissal of Homer as irrelevant to our present concerns is indicative of an antihumanist ideology. The "honourable privilege" of this ideology is the concept of chronology in the scientific sense of measuring the passage of time without "the cheat of words." The logically predictable end of the Hack's work and modern project generally is prefigured in the Hack's first and most expansive modern claim on posterity: "What I am going to say is true this minute I am writing." For, as death, "a star of superior influence," fixes Descartes in the void of his own language, so the Hack ends up "living fast to see the time when a *book* that misses its tide shall be neglected as the *moon* by the day," and "trying an experiment very frequent among modern authors, which is *to write upon nothing*" (*OAS*, 162, 163).

The Hack's desperation to keep writing his momentary experimental existence *and* universal system against the rush of time is Swift's representation of the paradoxical textuality of the modern project itself: inherent in the belief in ultimately progressive construction is the crisis that makes the critical assertion of ego a textual sea wall built of sand. Swift's reply to Cowley recognizes the emblematic irony of the linguistic and intellectual suicide inherent in the attempt of a great poet to extol poetically an age that was attempting to define itself in opposition to artistic representations of reality. Cowley was, after all, singing the praise of a society whose motto, *Nullius in verba*, speaks verbally, and hence ironically, to the very ambiguity of language the society's members hoped to deny.[25]

Swift's *Ode* set the stage for his major satiric assaults on modern narcissism. In the Ovidian myth, Tiresias tells Liriope, the mother of Narcissus, that her child will live so long as he never knows himself. Unlike Tiresias, who sees the impossibility of explaining the terrible irony of the narcissistic position, Swift in the *Ode* is trying to forewarn, to suggest there are alternatives to the tragedies inherent in the working out of the modern "paradigm of reflection."

But the *Ode* is in many respects both a first and last attempt to reach a prophetic strain, to point out a better path to those who are lost. The hopelessness of writing poetry in the "These days!" of Swift's *Ode* echoes across the decades to the "those days" of the introduction to Pope's *Dunciad*, where the poet responds in "*the only way that was left*." Inspired by Swift, Pope indites his indictment of the Modern as the perfectly ordered song—an unimpeachable witness against the cacophony of chaos itself. But Swift abandoned the form that is, in this first poem—

> at a loss for figures to express
> Men's folly. (ll. 172–73)

The muse of poetic "extravagance" has given way to a nemesistic muse who is never at a loss for figures of folly. As Nemesis, Swift is bound neither to warn Narcissus nor to protect Echo. He is an avenger. His discourse is with Narcissus. He works to intercept Narcissus, to understand him, to reflect him. When, in the *Battle of the Books*, Swift's narrator calls on the muse for inspiration, it is an afterthought, grotesque, and in prose, and this is emblematic both of what the Moderns are doing to humanist discourse and of Swift's conviction that he will serve poetry and all it represents, not as a great poet himself, but as the enemy of poetry's enemies. His great work will be to paint Echo, to mirror the Modern with textual images of its "unbodied hope."

Chapter Five

TRANSUBSTANTIATION, TRANSMUTATION, AND CRITICAL THEORY

> The method of interpreting Scripture does not widely differ from the method of interpreting nature—in fact, it is almost the same.
>
> Spinoza, *Theologico-Political Treatise*

By arguing that Swift may serve as one of the "best critics" of our contemporary critical discourse, Edward Said suggests tentatively that Swift was "methodologically unarmed" (*World*, 28). There is something almost heroic, perhaps even religious, in imagining the restless and agitated, but unarmed, voice from the early eighteenth century speaking effectively against the theoretical arsenal of modern discourse itself. And Swift's satiric attack in *A Tale of a Tub* on "conquest and systems" suggests the possibility that he would revel in the characterization that pits his unsystematized verbal energy against the oppressive critical machinery of the descendants of Richard Bentley and William Wotton, the ill-fated lovers of the *Battle of the Books* and "brother *modernists*" of *A Tale*. Said might agree, however, that Swift would revel in this characterization of his critical art, especially to the extent he regarded it untrue.

It is typical of the problem of finding Swift's position with respect to his satiric mirror that the same work that provides the most substantial material for reading Swift as a kind of intellectual anarchist, *A Tale of a Tub*, begins its final paragraph with a statement on method: "In my disposure of employments of the brain, I have thought fit to make *invention* the *master*, and to give *method* and *reason* the office of its *lackeys*" (*OAS*, 164). Since the speaker here, Swift's Hack, has informed the reader that he is continuing to write though he has nothing more to say, this statement on method might be read as a reiteration of a point he has made a number of times. In this reading the Hack is merely reasserting his place among the esteemed group of "innovators in the empire of reason" whose intellectuals are overturned—the modern madmen the Hack aspires to be counted among. But Swift has added something here. The Hack acknowledges that his mad modern discourse works on a pattern that employs method and reason as servants, perhaps messengers, of an inventive master. If even the Hack recognizes a power arrangement in his mode of intellectual discourse, a reader must be wary of any conclusion that would leave Swift methodologically defenseless. And indeed this final opportunity to laugh at the Hack's quintessentially modern attitude has all the trappings of the nemesistic pool. While the modern reader laughs at the Hack's ridiculous subordination of method and reason to a fanciful invention, the reader is also being invited to consider, at his or her peril, what the noncomical relationship of invention and rational method is. Even a Cartesian claim that one follows a path (*hodos*) of reason to come upon (*invenire*) or discover new knowledge makes reason and method servants of invention, while nevertheless omitting the *meta* of method: methods are ways after. More than a linguistic game, the Hack's happy statement of method reflects the usually unacknowledged epistemological paradox of modern empiricist thought. Late twentieth-century readers know the paradox well because of the initially shocking work of Thomas Kuhn: even in the hard sciences, new directions are dependent on unaccountable imaginative leaps. Along with historians of science, Swiftians now trace the issue back to conflicts between Renaissance thinkers and the New Philosophers. Over the course of this and the following chapter, it should become clear that Swift's lampoons of various early modern intellectual discourses are methodological: the various methodological claims of his Hack serve as comic masks that mislead and entrap, and in so doing, undermine modern claims for the certain and cumulative acquisition of knowledge.

Put another way, if Swift has a methodology of his own, it must somehow be detectable (like the existence and properties of antimatter through its contact with matter) in the substantial commentary by Swift's characters on their own methodologies as well as those of other Moderns. Modern critics have generally not distinguished carefully enough between Swift's satires on the methods of the cultural and intellectual phenomena he expected his readers to consider discredited—the scholastic debasement of the Roman Catholic Church and the mystical materialism of the alchemists—and the main focus of his satire, the methods of the new science. Following Swift's "*phenomenon* of *vapours*" through Bentley and Wotton to the work of the Royal Society's most considerable members, Robert Boyle and Isaac Newton, reveals that Swift's attack on modern methodologies depends on links he sees between discredited doctrines of transubstantiation and transmutation, on the one hand, and modern, supposedly rational, methodologies on the other. As Nemesis, Swift constructs a satiric mirror in which the reflection of the Modern emerges from the associations with the intellectual, religious, and social phenomena Moderns claim to reject.

Discerning the modern face in the satiric mirror requires seeing how *A Tale* traces transubstantiation, transmutation, and the New Philosophy's "Theory of Air" to a common critical theory through which spiritual and material realities are textualized and (mis)interpreted. The least familiar of the linked phenomena, and the most important to understanding the *Tale*'s satire on Modernity, is the debate on air or ether or subtle vapors that pitted Descartes against Hobbes and was supposedly resolved by Robert Boyle, a founder of the Royal Society and its most important member prior to Newton. The chapter following this one demonstrates that Newton's *Principia*—arguably the single most formidable work of the modern era—is, when read in its seventeenth-century context, permeated by a theory of ether, and that this theory of air informs Swift's "*phenomenon* of *vapours*" in the *Tale*'s "Digression on Madness." The present chapter delineates the context necessary for reading the attack on the new science by showing how transubstantiation and transmutation are, for Swift, the work of modern critics who knavishly pave ready linguistic paths between matter and spirit, making way for the truly credulous: scientists/critics who believe reason or method may be used to take human beings in one (positive) direction.

~

Said offers a cryptic clue toward distinguishing between Swift's method and what Swift considers the modern method. When Said claims "critics are not merely the alchemical translators of texts into the circumstantial reality or worldliness" (*World*, 35), one is left to translate, without help from Said, his use of the term "alchemical." Readers may be inclined to substitute a word like "magical." But the reader of *A Tale of a Tub* will see that Swift leads Said to distinguish between his (Said's) own critical methods and modern alchemical criticism. In fact, returning to *A Tale* to investigate the relationship between alchemy and criticism, one discovers an initially unaccountable charge against the Modern: Swift seems to define the Modern as a sustained period of alchemical translation.

Swift's depiction of the Modern begins in an historical place that, from a modern perspective, is as strange as any one might imagine.

> When the works of Scotus first came out, they were carried to a certain library and had lodgings appointed them; but this author was no sooner settled than he went to visit his master Aristotle; and there both concerted together to seize Plato by main force and turn him out from his ancient station among the divines, where he had peaceably dwelt near eight hundred years. The attempt succeeded, and the two usurpers have reigned ever since in his stead. (*OAS*, 5)

This place is, for Swift, both the beginning of the Modern and the beginning of modern criticism. Typically this passage contains a joke. It is from John Duns Scotus, the thirteenth-century scholastic philosopher and theologian, that the word *dunce* derives. So here Swift, who will encourage Pope to write the *Dunciad*, is suggesting the modern period begins with the original dunce. The joke is misleading only if one fails to recognize the ways it resonates, not unlike, perhaps, the humorless linguistic linking of Narcissus with narcosis. Scotus was, of course, known as the subtle doctor for drawing philosophic distinctions so fine his critics doubted their existence, and his philosophy was and is most often discussed by way of the challenges he raised against the theology of Thomas Aquinas. For Swift these things made Scotus a true modern and a true critic, for he is one whose reputation depends upon controversies he created through a deconstructive critique of Thomas's attempt at synthesis. Historians of philosophy, such as Frederick Copleston, have, from a very different perspective and without reference to Swift, essentially confirmed Swift's reading, tracing the "*via moderna*" of fourteenth-century Western philosophy to a critical spirit present in the works of Duns Scotus (3: 11).

Those who study the history of philosophy may be roiled at the significance being attached to admittedly crude characterizations of the schoolmen. It is worth, however, pushing Swift's joke a step further. Scotus is said by Swift to have teamed up with Aristotle to remove Plato from his "station among the divines." For Swift, Scotus's infamous contribution to Western thought and the rise of modernism is his distinction between metaphysics and theology. In the context of critiquing the Thomistic synthesis, Scotus's argument that "God is not the subject of metaphysics," is generally considered to have driven the wedge between philosophy and theology that was worked by later, increasingly modern, thinkers. Swift's jokes tend to have these odd resonances. The original dunce is the original modern because he is a Christian theologian who, presumably unwittingly, contributes to the modern split that defines the material and spiritual worlds as discontinuous discourses. Swift is, in effect, drawing a line from the original dunce to Ockham to Descartes, Spinoza, and Hobbes, to the Freethinkers and Deists, and he would likely continue the line through the *philosophes* to Nietzsche's conclusion that God is dead.[1] In this context the Subtle Doctor's confrontation with Aquinas, the Angelic Doctor, is a vastly degenerate type of the war in heaven in which Satan is, in the language of *A Tale of a Tub*, a "true modern critic," one who has made his reputation as "*a discoverer and collector*" (45) of the faults of the writer who strove for the harmonious synthesis of Christian theology and Greek rationalism.

This Fall that demarcates the onset of the Modern in Swift is a specifically critical one. The legacy of the Subtle Doctor's mind-splitting distinctions is a horrible confusion, which is modern, not as determined by chronology, but by rational method. Swift's speaker in *The Mechanical Operation of Spirit* distinguishes between "the Indians and us" by focusing on their ability to demarcate categories of experience. While the Indians' so-called superstition never allows "the liturgy of the *white* God to cross or interfere with that of the *black*," Europeans "Who pretending by the lines and measures of our reason to extend the dominion of one invisible power [God or the good] and contract that of the other [the Devil], have discovered a gross ignorance in the natures of good and evil, and most horribly confounded the frontiers of both" (*OAS*, 172). The Indians, whatever the faults of their religious doctrines, are different from modern Europeans because they do not suppose their reason will enable them "to extend the dominion" of the good in a way that diminishes the province of evil. This context explains why Aquinas himself makes Swift's list of Moderns: his attempt at synthesis is a grand act of rational hubris. Scotus is singled out as the initial modern villain because he begins the corrosive critical discourse that ends, in Swift's reading, with a "fellowship of Christ with Belial" (*OAS*, 172)—the debilitating inability to make any meaningful, critical judgment. Swift's charge might be glossed by recalling Milton's claim that "Good and evil . . . grow up together almost inseparably" and are so "intermixed" it is hard to imagine distinguishing the one from the other.[2] Swift would read this ethical statement in the context of the Puritan project to use reason to "extend the dominion" of the good to the realization of a Christian commonwealth—a new Eden—in Great Britain.[3] While we do not know if Swift specifically connected Scotus and Milton, other than as "brother *modernists*," he would hardly be surprised that scholars have linked Milton's portrait of Satan in *Paradise Lost* with the theology of the *Doctor Subtilis*.[4]

The Modern for Swift is historically, culturally, and geographically definable. Rather than a culminating step in human history, the Modern is a phenomenon limited (in his time) to a particular part of the globe and further limited within the West to those who seek to extend human dominion via "the lines and measures" of human reason. The irony of the modern project is that the critical method that seems to make the infinite extension of dominion possible (the legacy of Aquinas) is the same method that reduces positive construction to a horrible confusion (the legacy of Scotus).[5]

Swift's strange suggestion that the Modern is the extension or the realization of the scholastic project turns on the idea that modern critical methods share the characteristic of replacing human beliefs in "things invisible" with the methods themselves. While the Hack delights in the way the search for systems ends up making reason and method the lackeys of an invented master, Swift historicizes the modern project by illustrating how the method that reduces Christian claims for "things invisible" to temporalities, is the same method that builds and dooms the supposedly rational or secular systems of the Moderns. In other words, instead of seeing the modern ideas that coalesced under the term *enlightenment* as a reaction to the authority of Christianity or the authority of Aristotle, Swift sees the Modern as a comic-tragic working out of the scholastic attempt at synthesis, which leads inevitably to the destruction, first of modern Christianity, then of modern reason. Swift writes this satiric history in what seems from the modern perspective a most unaccountable way: by reading modern intellectual systems, and particularly modern critical theory, as an extension of the Roman Church's fraudulent doctrine of transubstantiation.

The narrative of *A Tale* links modern intellectual systems and transubstantiation by tracing the Roman Church's pervasive corruption to the temporally successful development and application of critical theory. The Hack's tale of Christian history takes the form of an allegory with coats (Christian doctrine) being passed from a father (Christ) to his three sons, Peter, Martin, and Jack, referring of course to Simon Peter, Martin Luther, and John (Mad Jack) Calvin. The harmony among the three brothers for the first seven years—that is, seven centuries—after the death of the father is shattered when they arrive in a town where they meet three women who correspond to covetousness, ambition, and pride. From this time on the brothers are in a frenzy to be accepted in the town, but they are shunned because of their simple dress—the coats—and they begin consulting their father's will, that is, the Scriptures, for a way out of their predicament. It is at this point they discover the great facility of critical theory.

Finding that the fashion of the town demands wearing great shoulder-knots on their coats, one brother suggests they qualify the prohibition against adornment by looking for references to shoulder-knots in their father's will: "'Tis true,' said he, 'there is nothing here in this Will [the Scriptures], *totidem verbis*, making mention of *shoulder-knots*, but I dare conjecture we may find them *inclusivè*, or *totidem syllabis*'" (*OAS*, 100). Failing to find a direct reference to shoulder-knots, the brother has proposed searching for the constituent words, or failing that, for the syllables that make up those words. This elementary semiotic approach uses Latin terms to obfuscate the base intentions of its author under the cover of a learned methodology. But a particular syllable cannot be found, and increasingly arcane authorities must be called on to mask ever more implausible methodologies. Reduced to looking for the occurrence of individual letters, *S*, *H*, *O*, *U*, etc., in the Scriptures, the brothers fail to find the letter *K*. But their confidence in the development of interpretive theory has grown such that they are able to explain away the letter *K* as a modern corruption of *C* by way of reference to some ancient manuscripts.

The brothers' success with shoulder-knots encourages them to value learning quite literally, as they begin to see a connection between interpretive theory and material gain. This becomes evident when gold lace becomes the fashion of the town. Shoulder-knots were a superficial ornament, but this lace "*aliqou modo essentiae adhaerere*" (*OAS*, 101), suggesting that the brothers understand they are now attacking the essential meaning of the coats themselves. For this, the brothers decide, their ad hoc semiotics will not do, and so they turn to the great pagan philosopher, rehabilitating "that wonderful piece *de Interpretatione* which has the faculty of teaching its reader to find out a meaning in everything but itself, like commentators on the Revelations who proceed prophets without understanding a syllable of the text" (*OAS*, 101). This passage contains a layered satire that speaks to Swift's view of the Church's hypocritical use of the "pagan" philosophers as well as what he sees as the

Moderns' apocalyptic preoccupation. Directly relevant here is a layer relatively close to the surface. What the brothers have found in this work by Aristotle is quintessential literary theory: it is an abstract construction that has no essential meaning, but gains authority in its application. Like the Book of Revelation, such works are wholly dependent on the abilities and the intentions of those who apply them.

Both the abilities and the intention of the brothers have been well established by this point in the narrative, and they use their critical skills to advance themselves in the world until they have gained a home, that is, the see of Rome, for themselves. But this success is tempered by a most curious result of the application of critical theory in Swift: it leads to madness. The most accomplished critic among the brothers, Peter, uses his skill to dominate his brothers. At a meal one day, Peter cuts slices of bread and presents them to the others as mutton. When they object he responds with this argument:

> "Look ye, gentlemen," cries Peter in a rage, "to convince you what a couple of blind, positive, ignorant, wilful puppies you are, I will use but this plain argument: By G—, it is true, good, natural mutton as any in Leadenhall market, and G— confound you both eternally if you offer to believe otherwise." Such a thundering proof as this left no further room for objection. (*OAS*, 117–18)

The "great deal of reason" the brothers suddenly discover in Peter's doctrine of transubstantiation is, of course, the decision to humor a dangerous madman. The satirist has positioned himself as one who considers Peter's appeal to authority a damnable fraud, and those who accept the material impossibility that bread is mutton, he casts as fools under the sway of a knave.

It is instructive that Swift's ridicule of the Roman Church's doctrine of transubstantiation appealed to the Reformed Christians who formed the bulk of his contemporary audience as well as it appeals to modern secular readers. With transubstantiation, as with his portrayal of Peter generally, Swift is seen dealing, in his inimitable way, with the fact of the Roman Church's pervasive corruption. However odd and wonderful Swift's presentation of his satiric indictment of Peter appears, it is, to the modern reader, a reasonable position. As Moderns, we need not look to Swift's personal faith or any appeal to Christian authority to understand why he paints Peter as he does.

Recognizing, however, that this account of this particularly significant moment in the history of Christianity is the Hack's account, adds a troubling dimension to this seemingly obvious satiric strain. If the ridicule of Peter and his doctrine belongs to the satirist, how are we to distinguish the satirist's position on transubstantiation from the Hack's? The answer lies in a direction that grows increasingly troublesome for a modern reader as he or she advances toward the nemesistic mirror. In order to distinguish the Hack's view of Peter from the satirist's view, one must look ahead to where the Hack discovers that the madness he sees in Peter's doctrine is the same as that he finds—and strongly commends and recommends—in the actions or doctrines of Calvin, Descartes, Alexander the Great, himself, and other innovators. And this observation begs the Hackean question, What is embodied in this doctrine of transubstantiation? The body of the Hack's version of the doctrine is the confusion of the literal with the metaphorical, of the lamb with the Messiah. That the Messiah becomes mutton, which is itself only bread, reflects, on the satiric level, the failure of Peter's call to authority to transform, much less transcend, the material world.

For the Hack, however, Peter's doctrine of transubstantiation can be said to fail only to the extent it fails to bring over the two brothers. The intent and method of Peter's doctrine are, for the Hack, the essential ingredients of Modernity itself. In fact, the idea for transubstantiation does not originate in the Church but is appropriated by Peter from an alderman/alchemist. The alderman's speech on beef that "comprehends in it the quintessence" of various meats, pudding, and custard, is "cook[ed] up" by Peter into the doctrine of transubstantiation that finds in bread "the quintessence of" not only the lamb, "but a wholesome fermented liquor" diffused throughout the bread. From Peter's alchemical manipulations the Hack takes us directly to his own doctrine, which is representative of modern intellectual discourse. What Moderns are looking for, the Hack recognizes, is "an universal system," preferably one that can be contained in "a small portable volume." Our means to that end are the same as Peter's, for we may cook as well as Peter, distilling, according to the Hack's recipe, from "all modern bodies of arts and sciences whatsoever," together with a "quintessence of poppy" and three pints of forgetfulness, "an infinite number of abstracts, summaries, compendiums"—the information systems that are the mutton of our fraudulent transubstantiation (*OAS*, 121). "We of this age," boasts the Hack, "have discovered a shorter and more prudent method to become *scholars* and *wits*, without the fatigue of reading or thinking" (*OAS*, 131). Effortless education, painless labor, material salvation—these are constituents of the Hack's definition of modern happiness, the "perpetual possession of being well deceived" (*OAS*, 144).

Swift's linking of transubstantiation and transmutation has nuances that depend on the historical context of the development and use of these terms. On the one side, transubstantiation is an Aristotelian term used to explain the liturgical event that originated in Christ's statement at the Last Supper that the bread is his body and wine his blood. While commentators from the patristic theologians forward used a variety of such terms to try to speak about the mystery of that liturgical moment, it was appropriately enough the Council of Trent that officially gave the event a name rooted in natural philosophy.[6] Swift's satiric suggestion that this labeling is best understood in terms of Peter's debasement of the lamb to mutton illustrates his idea that the Aristotelian explanation of a transcendent moment of religious experience is a kind of unparalleled intellectual and religious travesty. Before the mystery was defined materially—that is, in terms of a physical switching of substances—the scriptural event was available to the faithful in any number of modes of understanding. Once it was reduced to a specific sequence of material occurrences, it became the material of worldly arguments and religious schisms. Historically this is reflected in the fact that none of the major Christian sects of the Reformation disputed the "real presence" of Christ in the Eucharist: the Reformed Christians objected to the Tridentine doctrine that insisted that bread and wine were physically replaced by the body and blood. From Swift's perspective the argument is a rational absurdity because it is premised on the reduction of a transcendent religious event to a mechanical operation. Here it is important to emphasize that Swift is not offering a personal belief against a scientific or material explanation of a religious doctrine. He is not witnessing to the transcendent truth of the "real presence." He is, rather, suggesting that a religiously divisive debate over the physical events of the Eucharist has all the rational merit of an argument about, for example, the physical modes of communication between Homer and his muse. It is for Swift a terrifying reduction of the human intellect, perfectly represented in Peter's doctrine of transubstantiation, to make all modes of human experience submit to a materialist discourse.

Peter's transubstantiation heralded the debasement of Christianity to just another flawed system, which, "after the fate of other systems," according to the speaker of the *Argument Against Abolishing Christianity*, "is generally antiquated and exploded" (*PW*, 2: 27). Swift suggests that alchemical transmutation, which gives Peter the idea for his doctrine, moves quickly to fill the void left by the exploded "system of the Gospel." Swift understood that serious alchemists were not trying to change lead into gold as an end in itself, but for the key—the philosopher's stone or the elixir—that would allow transformation at every level of the human experience, including transformation of the human spirit.[7] While Peter was debasing the Church's claim that it could save souls by turning Christian doctrine into a knavish material system, the alchemists were hard at work trying to turn material knowledge into a kind of transcendent spiritual salve. So, while transubstantiation is the final critical travesty in Peter's mad descent into a materialist critical theory, transmutation is the critical principle that allows the alchemist to claim that his secret knowledge of the working of nature leads to the ultimate transformation of the human spirit.[8] In each case transcendent knowledge—supernatural, spiritual, poetic—is mediated by, that is, becomes dependent upon, materialist critical principles of transformation. The fluid movement of claims for material transformation between the transmutation of alchemical learning and the transubstantiations of modern Christianity is fully delineated when Jack, who has come to be easily confused with Peter, declares the parchment on which the Scriptures are written "'to be meat, drink, and cloth, to be the philosopher's stone and the universal medicine'" (*OAS*, 154).

The argument that Swift uses transubstantiation and transmutation to lay the groundwork for an assault on the New Philosophy is, at this point, a deduction that wants demonstration. One important component of the deduction is the observation that, without some other substantial satiric target, Swift's ridicule of victims that his readers would generally agree were culpable would, as Edward Rosenheim has argued, make his work a species of comedy other than satire.[9] Beyond the lampoons of Roman Catholics, Calvinists, or Alchemists, there must be satiric targets Swift's readers will not so readily recognize as either foolish or depraved.[10] The second component of the present deduction is that the additional satiric targets will be linked to the more obvious targets by the transubstantiating or transmuting methodologies. Its seems, that is, that the elaborate methodological interrelationships of the apparent targets in *A Tale* would serve Swift's attack on his primary targets. The most apparent target, beyond the mad, modern Christians and the alchemists, is the modern critic who is linked to the others in just this way, by a shared methodology. On the one hand Peter's development of transubstantiation is an interpretative critical enterprise that gives rise to Jack and his alchemy; on the other hand, the Hack himself is a critic who offers a universal system of all learning by way of an alchemical recipe of a "great philosopher of *O. Brazile*" (*OAS*, 121). So Swift's attack on the critical writers of the "commonwealth of learning" is linked by way of a modern methodology of transformation to the Christians Swift's readers would have generally recognized as debased and to the learning they would consider occult.

This methodological trail leads up to a demonstration that Swift's satire aims ultimately at the new science. While many of Swift's readers shared his derogatory view of the Grub Street writers themselves, few would readily see the justice of attacking Wotton and Bentley under the rubric of Grub Street, nor of the associations the Hack draws between the hacks of Grub Street and the members of the Royal Society. This is not to say his readers would miss the slanderous implications of such associations. Rather, the more modern the reader, the more likely he or she is to think the associations are merely slanderous.

The modern point of view has led critics to treat the satire on Bentley and Wotton as a satire on criticism separate from the attack on science. And this failure to follow the methodological associations led critics to overlook the target at *A Tale*'s center. Put another way, the modern confidence that Swift, for all his wit and just moralizing, did not really understand our modern scientific methodologies has led critics, until recently, to turn a blind eye to Swift's attack on figures among his contemporaries whose contributions to Modernity have almost never been questioned, such as Robert Boyle and Isaac Newton. This omission is all the more surprising since for Swift and his contemporaries, Wotton, Bentley, Boyle, and Newton were very clearly associated. Following the modern methodologies in *A Tale* reveals that Swift was attacking the new science as yet another fraudulent doctrine of material transformation.

Chapter Six

A CRITICAL THEORY OF AIR

A third supposition may be, that the soul has a power to inspire any muscle with this spirit, by impelling it thither through the nerves. But this too has its difficulties, for it requires a forcible intending the spring of the aether in the muscles, by pressure exerted from the parts of the brain: and it is hard to conceive, how so great force can be exercised amidst so tender matter as the brain is. And besides, why does not this aethereal spirit, being subtil enough, and urged with so great force, go away through the dura mater and skins of the muscle; or at least so much of the other aether go out to make way for this, which is crouded in? To take away these difficulties is a digression; but seeing the subject is a deserving one, I shall not stick to tell you how I think it may be done.

—Isaac Newton, "An Hypothesis . . . on Light"

As belief in the "bright dawn" (Davis, 207) of the Modern age has dimmed, Swift's "benighted" view of science has moved steadily toward critical light. Ann Cline Kelly, Kenneth Craven, and Frederik Smith are among those who have made major contributions to a new understanding of Swift's representations of Science.[1] And Douglas Lane Patey has uncovered unrecognized cultural assumptions that skewed earlier critical attempts to deal with this issue. At the center of Patey's argument that Swift has been misread is a claim that is, independently but not coincidentally, central to Stephen Toulmin's argument in *Cosmopolis* that the Modern has been misread. While Toulmin describes the development of the new philosophy in the context of a "*counter*-Renaissance"—a reaction against Renaissance humanism—Patey claims that "Twentieth-century students too seldom realize that the familiar posture of the new scientists in rejecting previous authorities was less often an attempt to clear away past errors in order to make room for a new probabilistic experimental science than to clear away the probabilism of Renaissance humanists in order to make room for a new philosophic and scientific certainty" (817).

In other words, we have based our readings of Swift's satire on science on a flawed "'received view'" of Modernity (Toulmin, 16). Once one allows for the possibility that the New Philosophy was less directly a rejection of Aristotle and scholasticism, as it claimed, and more directly a rejection of Renaissance humanism, Swift's sustained attack on the new science assumes an immediacy that positions Swift as one who represented a crisis inherent to modernity itself even as the Modern was taking shape.

It is one important thing to say Swift's attack on science may have a contextual validity; it is another thing to argue that Swift's thinking on the new science is relevant in any direct way to the discourse on the end of modernism. The link here works in this way. The author, who often is called the greatest satirist to write in English, took aim at the New Philosophic work that culminated in Isaac Newton's *Principia.* No one questions the relevance of Newton's work to our contemporary discussions of Modernity; the contention here is that Swift's work is similarly relevant, particularly to our postmodern—in the sense of from beyond the Modern—discourse on what Modernity is or was.

On the face of it the argument that Swift in any direct way challenged Newton must be judged improbable. The references to Newton in the *Travels* have generally been read to support the assertion that Swift understood little about Modern science. With no direct references to Newton in the body of *A Tale of a Tub*, many critics have considered Newton's *Philosophiae naturalis principia mathematica*, first published in 1687, to be too recent to have been digested for the 1704 *Tale.* And there is a long-standing (though unaccountable) belief that the *Principia* was, in the years before Samuel

Clark's Boyle lectures in 1704–5, too difficult to read for all but a small group of mathematicians. What possibility then, that a "man of letters" would have taken on so formidable a work?

There is at least one more reason why Newton's *Principia* cannot be a target of Swift's *Tale*. Swift himself suggested there was nothing more preposterous. And this is where the story begins to turn. In the "Apology" that prefaced the 1710 edition of *A Tale*, Swift rails against those who had used the word *banter* to dismiss his satire. Describing *banter* as a term that had originated among criminals and descended to use by pedants, Swift claims that it "is applied as properly to the production of wit as if I should apply it to Sir Isaac Newton's mathematics" (*OAS*, 70). Coming, as this does, in a work that uncovers a number of Swift's satiric targets, the misdirection of Swift's reference to Newton's *Principia* should hardly deflect us at all.[2] At its first level Swift's comment suggests a parallel that makes *A Tale* no more easily dismissed, at least as banter, than the first great work of the Royal Society's president. Had Swift called upon Aristotle's *Physics* instead, we might accept the parallel as a straightforward rhetorical point. But in an "Apology" to a work that links the "societies of Gresham" with Grub Street, Swift's direct reference to Newton is far from subtle. Swift has issued a challenge to the reader, asking that *A Tale*, which combines "the noblest and most useful gift of human nature" with humor, be considered as seriously as the defining work of the most esteemed natural scientist of the age. The parallel Swift draws sets his notoriously difficult (but greatly enjoyed) production of wit against the ponderously forbidding (but greatly admired) work of his scientific adversary. Swift suggests that, while he would not use the word *banter* to attack Newton's mathematics, he would not hesitate to use what his critics perceive as banter—wit and humor—against the work Moderns would think least susceptible to those talents.

Newton's text is, in fact, a key document in the cultural milieu that *A Tale* ridicules. While Clarke's Boyle lectures of 1704–5 were indeed an important step in bringing Newton's work to a large audience, Bentley's 1692 Boyle lectures positioned the *Principia*, with Newton's assistance, as an incontrovertible answer to atheism. With Bentley a primary and named target in both the *Battle of the Books* and *A Tale*, the strange thing indeed would be if Swift were uninterested in the work that inspired what was then Bentley's most prominent and ambitious work—his Newtonian Boyle lectures. These were delivered and published in the years during which Swift suggests he composed *A Tale*.[3] Moreover, when *A Tale* appeared in 1704, it received its most damning and most prominent denunciation in—where else?—Samuel Clarke's Newtonian Boyle lectures.[4] The idea that Swift, writing in 1710, is referring to Newton's *Principia* in a deferential, straightforward way is entirely improbable.

I attempt to illuminate Swift's attack on the new science and Newton in two parts. The first involves locating Sir William Temple, William Wotton, and Richard Bentley, with respect to the New Philosophy and Newton. Wotton and Bentley are consistently represented in Swift's work as lackeys (they had Newton's support) of a new "Newtonian" religion. In the second section I argue that Swift, reading Newton in seventeenth-century context, identified an attempt to repress a "theory of air" in the *Principia* and that this provides a model for the Hack's phenomenon of vapors in *A Tale of a Tub*. Swift saw in Newton's great work what he considered a rational lacuna. I argue that this rational gap has important correspondences to relevantly recent critical consideration of Newton's alchemical work and of the social dimensions of the new scientists' construction of "truth."

A NEW SCIENTIFIC BATTLE OF THE BOOKS

Swift's satiric thrusts at Wotton and Bentley have often been construed as wholly local or personal attacks stemming from their dispute with Sir William Temple.[5] Because even the issues of the local controversy have been poorly understood, the important links the pair provide between modern critics and modern scientists have been overlooked. Swift's interest in Wotton and Bentley arises from his relationship with Temple, but Swift's attack on the "brother modernists" is focused, not on the details of their arguments with Temple, but on their modernist agenda. Following the lines of his attack on Wotton and Bentley through to the political and religious claims they were making for the New Philosophy leads directly to the targets in the eye of Swift's satire, Robert Boyle, Isaac Newton, and the scientific foundations of the modern project.

In 1690, Sir William Temple, Swift's mentor and one of the most prominent persons in England, published an essay entitled *Of Ancient and Modern Learning.*[6] A gentleman essayist, Temple rebukes writers who are making grandiose claims for the superiority of the achievements of the Moderns in the arts and sciences over those of the Ancients. In 1692, in what was then an unrelated event, Richard Bentley delivered the first Boyle lecture. Bentley's Boyle lectures are important in intellectual history because Bentley, following the mandate of the great chemist, Robert Boyle, who endowed the lectures, intended to show how natural philosophy could be used to effectively counter the atheism it was often credited with engendering. Bentley had something remarkable and new to bring to the discussion on the relationship of God and natural philosophy. The "very excellent and divine Theorist Mr. *Isaac Newton*" had not long since discovered the principles of gravitation that showed the Creator's hand ever at work in every body's relationship to every other body.[7] Definitively silencing atheists by way of a Newtonian theology was no mad scheme out of Bentley's imagination, but had the considerable support of the great scientist himself, as is evidenced by Newton's correspondence with Bentley.

In 1694, William Wotton, a minor Anglican cleric and close colleague of Bentley's, published his *Reflections on Ancient and Modern Learning.* So settled are critical misperceptions of this episode that an authoritative recent edition would have it that Wotton's *Reflections* were "by no means abusive of Temple" (*OAS*, 606). In fact Wotton's work accuses Temple of promoting atheism and belonging "to those whose Interest it is" to reduce "the *Christian Religion* . . . [to] an Empty Form of Words" (preface, 6). Wotton traces the inspiration for his attack to Bentley's lectures "against Atheism." For Wotton and Bentley, Temple's rebuke of the Moderns had to be answered in the interest of religion itself.[8]

In his Boyle lectures, Bentley provided the lines of attack that Wotton aimed directly at Temple. Scorning Libertines who believed "men first sprung up, like Mushrooms," Bentley argued that "if infinite Ages of Mankind had already preceded, there could nothing have been left to be invented or improved by the successful industry and curiosity of our own" (1: 13; 3: 22). The recent discoveries by "Luminaries of this Island" show how untenable a belief in an eternal world is. Focusing Bentley's argument on Temple, Wotton suggests Temple is "a Libertine" who would have us believe "Men, like Mushrooms, sprung out of the Earth" (*Reflections*; preface, 8). Wotton later owns that he wrote because Temple had "treated with Contempt" the "Inventions and Discoveries of the present Age, especially by *Men of Gresham*" (*A Defense*, 474). The character of the group that Wotton's *Reflections* would make Temple a member of, as well as the group's agenda, is described in Bentley's first lecture:

> If Atheism should be supposed to become universal in this Nation (which seems to be design'd and endeavour'd, though we know the gates of Hell shall not be able to prevail) farewell all Ties of Friendship and Principles of Honour; all Love for our Countrey and Loyalty to our Prince; nay, farewell all Government and Society it self, all Professions and Arts, and Conveniences of Life, all that is laudable or valuable in the World. (3: 39)

The Ancient/Modern controversy that inspired the *Battle of the Books* and *A Tale of a Tub* is the one that made modern learning not only superior to ancient learning, but a proof and requirement of faith, civil society, and personal decency. Far from "unabusive" to Temple, Wotton and Bentley cast the influential gentleman essayist as a chief propagator of an insidious, immoral, specifically anti-Christian system of atheism.

With important limitations and different circumstances, Swift might have found considerable merit in Wotton's reading of Temple as irreligious. Temple's deistic assumptions are accessible to any serious reader of his work.[9] But what interested Swift far more, as will become evident, was the progressive, scientific doctrine that was being marshaled by Wotton and Bentley to combat the elder statesman's genteel and very nearly innocuous admonishment of the Moderns. In his preface, Wotton says he will answer Temple's irreligious admiration for ancient learning "by shewing how the World has gone on, from Age to Age, improving" (preface, 5–6). While Bentley directly propagates the theological implications of the new,

Newtonian science, Wotton is an historian of the movement, showing how human history has been moving inevitably to this moment when the New Philosophy—when modern science—would bring us to ultimate knowledge, not excluding certain proof of the deity and of his constant and necessary involvement in the material world.

Swift's attacks on Bentley and Wotton are the most transparent of *A Tale*'s satiric strains; he sees the two, as the Hack sees reason and method, as the lackeys of the modern scientists' invention. Wotton, in Swift's satire, is nearly always ridiculed for his belief in continuous progress. Thus Swift has the Hack call on "Mr. W[o]tt[o]n, Bachelor of Divinity" as an authority when ridiculing Homer for his ignorance of alchemy and the laws of the Church of England (*OAS*, 122). And when the Hack says he has learned from "a very skilful *computer*" that "there is not at this present a sufficient quantity of new matter left" to fill a volume (*OAS*, 131), Swift is reducing to an absurdity Wotton's enthusiastic claim in the *Reflections* that such strides have been made in natural and mathematical knowledge that "the next Age will not find much Work of this kind to do" (386). Wotton is, accordingly, credited in the Dedication to Posterity with having "written a good sizeable volume against a *friend of your governor*" (*OAS*, 78). With Time as the governor of Posterity, Temple is cast as Time's friend who warns against modern hubris, and Wotton as Time's enemy, who has written to show that the ravages of time are defeated by the progressive accumulation of knowledge.

Bentley, on the other hand, is associated in Swift's satires with a principle of gravitation. In the *Battle of the Books*, Swift describes Bentley's unsuccessful attempt to knock Aesop and Phalaris from their place among the ancients in the royal library: "But endeavouring to climb up [Bentley] was cruelly obstructed by his own unhappy weight and tendency towards his centre, a quality to which those of the Modern party are extreme subject" (*OAS*, 5–6). In his fourth Boyle lecture, Bentley had, without reflecting on his own body, claimed that Newton's principle, with its centripetal force, was generally accepted: "'Tis now a matter agreed and allowed by all competent Judges, that every Particle of Matter is endowed with a Principle of Gravity, whereby it would descend to the Centre, if it were not repelled upwards by heavier bodies" (23). Swift was thinking specifically of Bentley's Boyle lectures when drawing his Newtonian portrait of Bentley. Ridiculing atheists who pretend to explain the composition of the human body, Bentley compares their arguments about the relationship of bone to flesh to the preposterous suggestion that "the Lead of an Edifice should naturally and spontaneously mount up to the Roof, while lighter materials employ themselves beneath it" (4: 13). Swift applies Bentley's clumsy rhetorical illustrations to a description of Bentley armed for battle: "His armour was patched up of a thousand incoherent pieces, and the sound of it as he marched was loud and dry, like that made by the fall of a sheet of lead which an Etesian wind blows suddenly down from the roof of some steeple" (*OAS*, 17–18). While mocking Bentley's rhetoric, Swift is here beginning to expose what he believes is the dangerous foolishness of Bentley's enterprise. Just as one might point out that lighter substances do support sheets of lead found on roofs, one might attack Bentley's thesis that God exists by attacking his Newtonian science. Swift moves the lead from any roof to that of a steeple because Bentley is, in a sermon, making the existence of God dependent on the truth of a particular natural philosophy.

Wotton and Bentley are ridiculed as lackeys of the new science, but the messengers in Swift's satires lead up to the modern inventors themselves. Referring to the "Catholick Principle of Gravitation" (4: 6) throughout his Boyle lectures, Bentley introduces Newton's *Principia* (1687) and announces he will "proceed and build upon it as a Truth solidly established" (7: 9). There may be little original in Bentley's conception of men "as Spectators in this noble Theatre of the World" (1: 11), unless it is that humans are spectators rather than actors. But the parody is established by noticing that Bentley views his Newtonian theater of the world as a refinement of that of Epicurus: "Now this is the constant Property of *Gravitation*; That the weight of all Bodies around the Earth is ever proportional to the Quantity of their Matter. . . . This is the ancient Doctrine of the *Epicurean* Physiology, then and since very probably indeed, but yet precariously asserted: But it is lately demonstrated and put beyond controversy by that very excellent and divine Theorist Mr. *Isaac Newton*" (7: 8). Having acknowledged the common basis in "an inherent principle of Gravitation," Bentley distinguished between the "miserable absurd stuff" of the "*Epicurean* Theory" and that of Newton by noting that "supine unthinking Atheists for a thousand years" have thought bodies tended toward "a *Vacuum* or Nothing" and had no explanation why bodies sometimes deviate "from the Perpendicular" (7: 20).

Swift makes Bentley's distinction a matter of mere name-calling. Setting out his theory of "oratorial receptacles or machines," Swift's Hack argues from Epicurus that not only is air "a heavy body," but words "are also bodies of much weight and gravity" (*OAS*, 88). Following the Epicurean theory, the Hack arranges auditors on a perpendicular line "from the zenith to the centre of the earth" to catch the heavy words that fall in a straight line (*OAS*, 89). But the Hack confesses that "there is something yet more refined in the contrivance and structure of modern theatres." Here the bodies of heavy words fall to the bottom, the large portion of wit runs "much upon a line and ever in a circle," the "whining passions . . . are gently wafted up by their own extreme levity to the middle region, and there fix and are frozen," while bombast and buffoonery "by nature lofty and light, soar highest of all and would be lost in the roof," if not for the twelve-penny gallery (*OAS*, 89). In the *Tale* as well as in Bentley's lecture, the Newtonian system is a refinement of the Epicurean because it explains not only the movement on a line from the zenith to the center of the earth, but how all the various bodies find their appropriate places in the universal theater. Just as the architect of Swift's theater provided a gallery at the roof so that nothing is lost, Bentley is at pains to explain that "the smallest Corpuscle of Vapour" though "exhaled to the top of the Atmosphere" will not be lost: "many Experiments" having proven that there is a top, "the whole Terraqueous Globe" has not "lost the least particle of Moisture, since the foundation of the World" (4: 23–24). Swift suggests that, notwithstanding the abusive rhetoric against Epicurus and his followers, the Newtonian theater is a "contrivance and structure" for utilizing words "of much weight and gravity" within or on top of a system the religious of the period generally considered the most nefarious source of atheism.

Whereas Swift's theater of gravity might be understood to represent the structures being built, with Newton's sanction, on the "Truth solidly established" of Newton's *Principia*, Bentley's reference to a "Corpuscle of Vapour" points in the direction of an increasingly detailed representation of the modern system.[10] In his fourth Boyle lecture, Bentley argues that the "Mechanical or Corpuscular Philosophy," which is "the oldest, as well as the best in the world" has been restored by "excellent Wits of the present" age, particularly Robert Boyle: "It principally owes its re-establishment and lustre, to that Honourable Person of ever Blessed Memory, who hath not only shewn its usefulness in Physiology above the vulgar Doctrines of Real Qualities and Substantial Forms; but likewise its great serviceableness to Religion itself" (4: 4–5). Bentley's claim is expansive. It is not only the case that Boyle, by rehabilitating and advancing the theories of the atomists, has surpassed the natural philosophy of the schoolmen; he has bettered them in theological matters by making a notoriously atheistic approach to nature serviceable to religion. In his *Reflections* on Temple's essay, William Wotton confirms this formulation, linking the "*Corpuscular* Philosophers" with "New Philosophers." For the Greek half of the equation, Wotton goes back to Epicurus's source: "*Democritus* supposes that the Northern Snows being melted by the Summer Heats, are drawn up in Vapours into the Air; which Vapours circulating towards the South, are, by the Coldness of the *Etesian* Winds, condensed into Rain, by which the *Nile* is raised. . . . *Democritus's* Opinion of this *Phaenomenon* seems not amiss, though his Hypothesis of the Cause of it is wrong in all probability" (126). But the true understanding of the "*Corpuscularian* Philosophers" was limited to "just what might be collected from the Observation" (243) of the most obvious qualities of such phenomena. In the pipes and vials of the "New Philosophers," however, more precise and even unseen characteristics, such as Boyle's "Springs" of air, can be recognized and experimentally verified. Particularly because of Boyle's work, the "History of Air" is a body of knowledge on a natural phenomenon "whose Theory" is nearer to "being compleated" (244) than any other.

Wotton is confident, moreover, that the charge that the theory might, considering its source, promote atheism has been met in a most dramatic way:

> By this *Air-Pump*, as it is usually called, he [Boyle] discovered abundance of Properties in the Air, before never suspected to be in it. . . . How far they may be relied upon, appears from this; That though *Hobbes* and *Linus* have taken a great deal of Pains to destroy Mr. *Boyle's* Theory, yet they have had few or no Abettors: Whereas the Doctrine *of the Weight and Spring of the Air*, first made thoroughly intelligible by Mr. *Boyle*, has universally gained Assent from Philosophers of all Nations who have, for these last XXX Years busied themselves about Natural Enquiries. (183)

That Hobbes (not to mention the Jesuit, Francis Hall Linus) would attack Boyle's theory of air underscores the social and political dimensions of Boyle's scientific agenda. Noting that Hobbes had been involved in a protracted dispute with Descartes over whether the subtle fluid that fills apparently empty spaces was corporeal or not, scholars have recently read Boyle's experimental work on air as an approach to intellectual order that was competitive with that of Hobbes on social and political levels.[11] While Hobbes's materialist natural philosophy was explicitly linked to his political conception of the Leviathan, Boyle's Baconian approach was one designed to draw men who would otherwise waste their time in idle philosophic disputes into an ultimately cooperative enterprise in pursuit of the perceivable facts of the order of nature. If Boyle's method stood in sharp distinction from that of Hobbes's, their ends were similarly distinct. While Hobbes hoped, like Lucretius, to lead men from the superstitious forces that governed their lives to a rational order, Boyle was certain the pursuit of the secrets of nature was one with an understanding and appreciation of the Creator. When Hobbes attacked Boyle, he did so as one asserting that matter existed everywhere against one who believed in the existence of a vacuum or a void. While the plenist/vacuist characterization of the Hobbes/Boyle debate is problematic, it would point up, to one interested in ironies, just how completely the world had been turned: the atheist seemed to be arguing against the Lucretian void; the religionist defending it.

Though Wotton and modern history generally have considered Boyle to have prevailed in his dispute with Hobbes, the triumph from the Swiftian perspective belonged, if not to Hobbes, then to

Epicurus himself, and the evidence for this is clear from Bentley's lectures. Quoting Boyle, Lucretius, and Newton, in his seventh sermon, Bentley asserts: "Now since Gravity is found proportional to the Quantity of Matter, there is a manifest Necessity of admitting a *Vacuum*, another principal Doctrine of the *Atomical* Philosophy."[12] It is perhaps unnecessary to appeal to a seventeenth- or eighteenth-century perspective to notice that when the argument for the existence of God comes down to whether or not one perceives (in Bentley's phrase) the "Finger of God" in the way bodies may act on one another across a void,[13] one has moved so far into the Epicurean camp that the God of the Christian revelation seems even more rationally remote than Epicurus's atomistic gods. And so it is no accident when Swift has his Hack digress in the paragraph immediately preceding the Hack's "explanation" of his own system of vapors to acknowledge the madness of William Wotton—one incomparably fit "for the propagation of a new religion" (*OAS*, 142). Wotton, with his "brother *modernists*," were in historical fact advancing a "new religion" that saw Newtonian theory as the incontrovertible triumph of measured Anglican thought.[14]

The Hobbes/Boyle debate on air should lead us to consider that the tub of *A Tale of a Tub* is an empty barrel intended to divert the wits who "pick holes in the weak sides of Religion and Government" (*OAS*, 79). More specifically, the Hack tells us that his *Tale* is a tub thrown into the water of contemporary discourse to divert the whale, which is Hobbes's *Leviathan*, from smashing the ship of state, which includes the church, until an academy can be established that will "employ those unquiet spirits," the wits of the kingdom (*OAS*, 79–80). With a great deal of that *Tale* taken up by various doctrines of air, from that of the learned Aeolists, to Jack's inspiration, to the Hack's own system of vapors, we would have to be surprised if Swift were not making some reference to the debate that put Hobbes against Descartes and Boyle against Hobbes and that seemed to be finally resolved in the joint forces of the Royal Society's most prominent representatives. With this debate featured as evidence of the happy and religious triumph of the New Philosophy in those works by Wotton and Bentley that inform the *Battle of the Books*, it was most certainly an object of Swift's critical scrutiny.

NEWTONIAN VAPORS

Robert Boyle was in attendance on December 9, 1675, when these observations from Newton's "Hypothesis," were read:

> It is to be supposed therein, that there is an aethereal medium much of the same constitution with air, but far rarer, subtler, and more strongly elastic. . . . But it is not to be supposed, that this medium is one uniform matter, but compounded, partly of the main phlegmatic body of aether, partly of other various aethereal spirits, much after the manner, that air is compounded of the phlegmatic body of air intermixed with various vapors and exhalations: for the electric and magnetic effluvia, and gravitating principle, seem to argue such variety. (*Papers and Letters*, 179–80)[15]

In *A Tale* the vapors and exhalations are in a "perpetual circulation." In Newton the "vapors and exhalations" are likewise continually circulating:

> Nature making a circulation by the slow ascent of as much matter out of the bowels of the earth in an aereal form, which, for a time, constitutes the atmosphere; but being continually buoyed up by the new air; exhalations and vapors rising underneath, at length (some part of the vapours, which return in rain, excepted) vanishes again into the aethereal spaces, and there perhaps in time relents, and is attenuated into its first principle: for nature is a perpetual worker. (*Papers and Letters*, 181)

As Wotton recognized, the gross observation from which the more refined points are drawn may be traced all the way back to Democritus. But like other later atomists, Newton would take the observations a good deal further. Out of his perpetually circulating exhalations and vapors, which rise up from the earth as mists and smoke, and can return in rain, Newton thinks he perceives the grand design of the Creator:

> Perhaps the whole frame of nature may be nothing but various contextures of some certain aethereal spirits, or vapours, condensed as it were by precipitation, much after the manner, that vapours are condensed into water, or exhalations into grosser substances, though not

> so easily condensible; and after condensation wrought into various forms; at first by the immediate hand of the Creator; and ever since by the power of nature; which, by virtue of the command, increase and multiply, became a complete imitator of the copies set her by the protoplast. Thus perhaps may all things be originated from aether. (*Papers and Letters*, 180)

If, from Swift's perspective, "all occultism may be traced to an ultimate quest for the original of all things; a quest of which an ultimate aim was the achievement of universal systems" (Starkman, 45), then claims like this may be a clue to how Swift came to portray modern science as one of several branches of the madness that comprises Modernity. Here, in the words of perhaps the greatest scientist of all time, one may discern the modern methodology by which a common observation—vapors rise up from the earth and rain falls from the clouds—becomes by way of metaphor and analogy the evidence of the material mastery of a supernatural design.

Once language builds a material bridge between the natural and the supernatural, a number of possibilities arise.[16] To see this, one traces the way Newton moves from the cosmic level of circulating vapors and exhalations—these are fundamental to the development of his theory of gravity and so to the organization and movement of the planets—to the microcosm, that is, to living bodies. In what he calls "a digression," Newton undertakes to answer the problem of what causes "animal motions." Explaining this by way of his system of "aethereal spirits" presents a number of difficulties, including the problem of how "so great force [as are these spirits] can be exercised amidst so tender matter as the brain is." The answer, Newton supposes, is that

> There is such a spirit; that is, that the animal spirits are neither like the liquor, vapour, or gas of spirit of wine; but of an aethereal nature, subtil enough to pervade the animal juices, as freely as the electric, or perhaps magnetic, effluvia do glass. And to know, how the coats of the brain, nerves, and muscles, may become a convenient vessel to hold so subtil a spirit, you may consider, how liquors and spirits are disposed to pervade or not pervade things on other accounts than their subtilty. (*Papers and Letters*, 183)

And to understand how this ethereal spirit can cause movement in gross muscles, one need turn only to what we have learned from the alchemists:

> Aqua fortis, which will not pervade gold, will do it by addition of a little sal armoniac, or spirit of salt: lead will not mix in melting with copper, but if a little tin or antimony be added, they mix readily, and part again of their own accord, if the antimony be wasted by throwing saltpeter or otherwise: . . . And, in like manner, the aethereal animal spirit in a man may be a mediator between the common aether and the muscular juices, to make them mix more freely. . . .
>
> Thus may therefore the soul, by determining this aethereal animal spirit or wind into this or that nerve, perhaps with as much ease as air is moved in open spaces, cause all the motions we see in animals. (*Papers and Letters*, 184)

Newton concludes his digression on how the system of ethereal wind that moves the planets may also explain "all motions" in animal bodies by noticing that what he has said of the movement of muscles "may be applied to the motion of the heart," excepting only that the heart is continually generative ("by the fermentation of the juices with which its flesh is replenished") of the wind that moves the body. Newton's entire discussion of the ether that moves animal bodies is informed by certain experiments of "Mr. Boyle," which led Newton to suppose that "the spring of aether" is "many degrees stronger than that of air" (*Papers and Letters*, 182). Newton develops his theory of air within the tradition of the most prominent member of the Royal Society.

It is easy from our late twentieth-century perspective to misapprehend the significance of this "hypothesis" to Newton's work. Newton's hypothetical speculations do not sit alongside his concrete mathematical work in optics or in the laws of motion and gravity; these speculations, at least at this time, underlie his conception of how nature works.[17] Newton acknowledges as much in a letter to Robert Boyle. Outlining a system of ascending and falling "particles of vapors, exhalations, and air," nearly identical to that put forward in his "Hypothesis," Newton concludes the letter to Boyle with a connection he claims to have made while setting out this system:

> I shall set down one conjecture more, which came into my mind now as I was writing this letter. It is about the cause of gravity. For this end I will suppose ether to consist of parts differing from one another in sublety . . . yet the grosser ether in the air affects the upper regions of the earth, and the finer ether in the earth the lower regions of the air, in such a manner, that from the top of the air to the surface of the earth, and again from the surface of the earth to the center thereof, the ether is insensibly finer and finer. (*Papers and Letters*, 253)

It is clear from these works that his reading of the debate on air informs his understanding of his theory of light as well as his theory of gravity. A late seventeenth-century reader turning to the *Principia* with what Wotton called the "History of Air" in mind might be forgiven for seeing Newton's own theory of air, not so much hidden in the great work, as forcibly restrained, like steam from a pot with a very heavy lid.[18]

In his preface to the first edition (1687), Newton placed himself among "the moderns" who reject "substantial forms and occult qualities," and who propose to "subject the phenomena of nature to the laws of mathematics" (1: xvii). From these mathematical propositions set out in the first two books, he develops a third, the "System of the World," in which he derives "from the celestial phenomena the forces of gravity. . . ." He also tells us he had wished to accomplish more, and that he suspects his work will be useful toward those goals:

> I wish we could derive the rest of the phenomena of Nature by the same kind of reasoning from mechanical principles, for I am induced by many reasons to suspect that they may all depend upon certain forces by which the particles of bodies, by some causes hitherto unknown, are either mutually impelled towards one another, and cohere in regular figures, or are repelled and recede from one another. The forces being unknown, philosophers have hitherto attempted the search of Nature in vain; but I hope the principles here laid down will afford some light either to this or some truer method of philosophy.[19]

This, then, is a work that offers a system of the world, referring to the macrocosm, but its author suggests that it offers as well the method for perceiving all "the rest of the phenomena of Nature." One familiar with Newton's "Hypothesis," or the debate on air more generally, would reasonably expect that the "forces" and "particles" Newton refers to here are elements of a system of aethereal vapors.[20] What the author of *A Tale of a Tub* would likely notice from Newton's preface is that this work claims to contain a new method from which the system of the world and the workings of all nature might be derived. Swift might also have noticed that the *Principia* would work very well under the motto, *diu multumque desideratum* (much desired for a long time), which he would later affix to *A Tale*. For it is, Newton informs us, only through the "solicitations" of Edmund Halley, who "continually pressed" him to communicate his work to the Royal Society, and then only because of that society's "kind encouragement and entreaties," that he even considered publishing his *Principia*. But because he had not yet finished work on the lunar motions, he "deferred publication" (18). Like *A Tale*, then, the *Principia* was a work whose author claimed it was something entirely new, that it was systematic and universal, that, as it offered a true philosophical method, it was for the benefit of mankind, and, not the least, that it was a work *diu multumque desideratum*. The point here is not that these features are unique to *A Tale* and the *Principia*. The point is that at the time *A Tale* was being composed, the most prominent and formidable work to employ these conventions was the *Principia*, and Wotton and Bentley, among others, were arguing (literally and figuratively from the pulpit) that it was the great work that delivered on its universal promise.

The first indication a suspicious reader might find of the presence of the ethereal vapors in the *Principia* is in Newton's explanation of his first definition on the first page of the work. Though it is significant to our discussion that Newton's first illustration of body or mass is by way of air, it is the medium he claims he will *not* talk about that is most interesting here:

> Thus air of a double density, in a double space, is quadruple in quantity; in a triple space, sextuple in quantity. The same thing is to be understood of snow, and fine dust or powders, that are condensed by compression or liquefaction, and of all bodies that are by any causes whatever differently condensed. I have no regard in this place to a medium, if any such there is, that freely pervades the interstices be-

> tween the parts of bodies. It is this quantity that I mean hereafter everywhere under the name of body or mass. (1: 1)

A reader coming to Newton from Boyle's work, or that of Descartes or Hobbes, among others, would likely identify the "medium" Newton is saying he will not discuss as the "subtil matter" that had dominated the seventeenth-century debate on air. This statement in which Newton claims the medium will have no place in this discourse has itself a syntactically insinuating quality not, perhaps, unlike the ethereal substance. The paragraph would read better (here and in the Latin original[21]) without the interposed statement, yet its presence is barely noticeable to the reader looking forward to Newton's promised mathematical demonstrations. While mathematical arguments dominate the work that follows, various "exhalations and vapours," increasingly fine and subtle, make their way into the interstices of Newton's demonstrations. It is not that the ethereal medium lacked a place in Newton's *Principia*; it lacked the explanation the "perfect mechanic" would give it.

Newton indirectly acknowledges such an explanation is wanting:

> I here use the word *attraction* in general for any endeavor whatever, made by bodies to approach to each other, whether that endeavor arise from the action of the bodies themselves, as tending to each other or agitating each other by spirits emitted; or whether it arises from the action of the ether or of the air, or of any medium whatever, whether corporeal or incorporeal, in any manner impelling bodies placed therein towards each other. (1: 192)

Noticing that Newton is working to avoid embracing a particular explanation of the how and why of the attractive forces, one may nevertheless recognize that the only options he offers the reader are those that fall within the seventeenth-century debate on air. The only real choice Newton offers is that one may explain the "how" of attraction by either corporeal or incorporeal spirits. Thus avoiding the dispute between Hobbes and Descartes, Newton nevertheless suggests some such spirit of air must be called upon to explain the action.[22] Seeing the attractive force through the lens of its Epicurean original, Swift will not allow his Hack to dodge the questions of how or why it operates.

Setting out his system, Swift's Hack draws an analogy between the vapors that rise in the body and cause madness in a human being and the various mists that rise from the earth and cause storms in the atmosphere:

> For the *upper region* of man is furnished like the *middle region* of the air; the materials are formed from causes of the widest difference, yet produce at last the same substance and effect. Mists arise from the earth, steams from dunghills, exhalations from the sea, and smoke from fire; yet all clouds are the same in composition as well as consequences, and the fumes issuing from a jakes will furnish as comely and useful a vapour as incense from an altar. Thus far, I suppose, will easily be granted me; and then it will follow that, as the face of nature never produces rain but when it is overcast and disturbed, so human understanding, seated in the brain, must be troubled and overspread by vapours ascending from the lower faculties to water the invention, and render it fruitful. (*OAS*, 139)

Here Swift's Hack moves from the microcosm to the macrocosm, portraying nature as a perpetual circulator of steams and vapors and exhalations. Only the odd selection of illustrations distinguishes this description from the work of Europe's greatest scientists.

Tracing the violent actions of Henry IV of France to a vapor finally released by the "state-surgeon" who stabbed him to death, the Hack asserts that he can explain the actions he observes in terms of attractive forces and movement of vapors:

> Now, is the reader exceeding curious to learn from whence this *vapour* took its rise, which had so long set the nations at a gaze? What secret wheel, what hidden spring, could put in motion so wonderful an engine? It was afterwards discovered that the movement of this whole machine had been directed by an absent *female* whose eyes had raised a protuberancy, and before emission, she was removed into an enemy's country. What should an unhappy prince do in such ticklish circumstances as these? He tried in vain the poet's never-failing receipt of *corpora quaeque*, for
>
> > Idque petit corpus mens unde est saucia amore:
> > Unde feritur, eo tendit, gestique coire. Lucr.
>
> Having to no purpose used all peaceable endeavours, the collected part of the semen, raised and inflamed, became adust, converted to

> choler, turned head upon the spinal duct, and ascended to the brain. (*OAS*, 140)

A reader sympathetic to the new science will be appalled by the comparison. Newton's attractive force of planetary bodies has been reduced to a burlesque of sexual concupiscence. In recognizing this reduction of the greatest principle of the "divine theorist," we should notice that Swift is historicizing the New Philosophy's rehabilitation of the ancient atomists. What distinguishes the New Philosophy from its atomist originals is a reluctance to confront the implications of its discussions of "the movement of this whole machine." Swift sees the modern future in its Lucretian past. The Hack strives to be what Newton calls "the most perfect mechanic" by asking and answering the questions Newton himself shrinks from: What is the "secret wheel," the "hidden spring" that will allow the "perfect mechanic" to realize Newton's "wish" at the outset of the *Principia*, that the principles therein may explain "the rest of the phenomena of Nature"? Swift's mechanic is one who takes the New Philosophy to its most ancient "hidden spring," a spring of air that, as in Lucretius, may as assuredly explain the rise and fall of the planets and the tides as it does the swelling and ebbing of human sexual organs.

Newton's avowed intention to avoid discussing the medium "which freely pervades the interstices between the parts of bodies" is an increasingly futile battle. In his second book he performs an experiment with a pendulum to test for the existence of "some subtle fluid, which freely pervades the pores of all bodies," and constitutes the hypothetical "ethereal medium extremely rare and subtile" (1: 325). Though he initially quantifies the existence of this substance based on the experiment, he offers an alternative explanation for the results, which leads him to conclude that resistance of this ether is "either nil or wholly insensible." That his apparent inability to measure the subtle substance in no way dissuaded him from assigning significance to it has been explained in terms of his growing interest in alchemy.[23] But even without access to Newton's interests in alchemy, a reader may notice from the *Principia* itself that the ethereal medium is never far from Newton's thought. Consider

Newton's explanation of the movement, aspect, and influence of comets:

> And it is not unlikely but that the vapor [of the comet's tail], thus continually rarefied and dilated, may be at last dissipated and scattered through the whole heavens, and by little and little be attracted towards the planets by its gravity, and mixed with their atmosphere; for as the seas are absolutely necessary to the constitution of our earth, that from them, the sun, by its heat, may exhale a sufficient quantity of vapors, which, being gathered together into clouds may drop down in rain, for watering of the earth, and for the production and nourishment of vegetables; or, being condensed with cold on the tops of mountains (as some philosophers with reason judge), may run down in springs and rivers; so for the conservation of the seas, and fluids of the planets, comets seem to be required, that, from their exhalations and vapors condensed, the wastes of the planetary fluids spent upon vegetation and putrefaction; and converted into dry earth, may be continually supplied and made up; for all vegetables entirely derive their growths from fluids, and afterwards, in great measure, are turned into dry earth by putrefaction; and a sort of slime is always found to settle at the bottom of putrefied fluids; and hence it is that the bulk of the solid earth is continually increased; and the fluids, if they are not supplied from without, must be in a continual decrease, and quite fail at last. I suspect, moreover, that it is chiefly from the comets that spirit comes, which is indeed the smallest but the most subtle and useful part of our air, and so much required to sustain the life of all things with us. (2: 529–30)

Here the terrestrial observations of Democritus on the rise and fall of the water and vapors of rain are understood as the pattern of the cosmos. And the most subtle of nature's "exhalations and vapors" are those that scatter from comets bringing the ethereal matter of the stars into our field of nature, sustaining and replenishing all life as we know it. Here Newton the mechanic reveals his suspicions—"perhaps . . . all things . . . originated from aether" (*Papers and Letters*, 180)—that the hidden spring of the great machine is found in a vapor, closely analogous to those rising from the earth to the clouds, but more subtle, and intrinsic to all action in the microcosm as well as the macrocosm.[24]

As Nemesis, Swift represents the New Philosophy's rehabilitation of the systems of the Corpuscular Philosophers in a way that challenges its claim on rational thought. If, as Newton suggests, a system of vapors will explain "all motions we see in animals," or all "the rest of the phenomena of Nature," let it explain the motions we have witnessed in a few notable animals:

> Of such great emolument is a tincture of this vapour which the world calls *madness*, that without its help the world would not only be deprived of those two great blessings, *conquests* and *systems*, but even all mankind would unhappily be reduced to the same belief in things invisible. Now, the former *postulatum* being held, that it is of no import from what originals this *vapour* proceeds but either in what *angles* it strikes and spreads over the understanding or upon what *species* of brain it ascends, it will be a very delicate point to cut the feather, and divide the several reasons to a nice and curious reader, how this numerical difference in the brain can produce effects of so vast a difference from the same *vapour*, as to be the sole point of individuation between Alexander the Great, Jack of Leyden, and Monsieur Des Cartes. The present argument is the most abstracted that ever I engaged in; it strains my faculties to their highest stretch; and I desire the reader to attend with the utmost perpensity, for I now proceed to unravel this knotty point.
>
> There is in mankind a certain ⋆ ⋆ ⋆ ⋆
> ⋆
> ⋆ ⋆ ⋆ ⋆ ⋆ ⋆ ⋆ ⋆
> ⋆
>
> Hic multa ⋆ ⋆ ⋆ ⋆ ⋆ ⋆
>
> desiderantur. ⋆ ⋆ ⋆ ⋆ ⋆ ⋆
> ⋆
> ⋆ ⋆ ⋆ ⋆ And this I take to be a clear solution of the matter. (*OAS*, 142–43)

What is so ardently desired (*desiderantur*), that is, what is so obviously missing, in the Hack's system of vapors is some explanation of how his or Newton's theory of mechanical or chemical movement of vapors tells us anything about the phenomenal diversity of human experience. The Hack's "clear solution of the matter" is a mechanical explanation that can hold together only by creating a void, not in nature, but in rational discourse. The only way to explicate an ultimate mechanical system is by way of the occult—the Hack's "things invisible"—or by omitting the occult basis of the material system. In the first case are systems like those of Peter (Roman Catholicism) or Jack (Calvinism) or of the alchemists, which are clearly built on occult foundations, and in the second, systems like those of the Hack and of Newton and, perhaps, of Epicurus, which leave out, or attempt to leave out, the occult foundations of their mechanical philosophies.

Although Swift must certainly have been aiming at the entire seventeenth-century debate on air—a primary project of the New Philosophy—there is no better demonstration of the gap he represents in his satire than that that bedevils the text of the greatest scientific work of the period. Newton's avowal in the opening passage of the *Principia* that he has "no regard in this place" for the ethereal medium is belied by his troubled regard for ether, and what it represents, throughout the text. In the *General Scholium*, added to the 1713 edition of the *Principia*, the struggle between the claims of the New Philosophy to deal only in fact confirmed by experiment comes face to face with its necessarily occult origins and ends. Now addressing the question Swift's Hack had posed, Newton seems to make diversity a matter of faith: "All that diversity of natural things which we find suited to different times and places could arise from nothing but the ideas and will of a Being necessarily existing" (2: 546). Newton appears to be making the point that no chemical or mechanical system will account for the great variety found in nature. And though arguing God is the proper subject of natural philosophy, Newton would seem to be directing his readers further in the direction of faith for their perceptions of the deity: "In bodies, we see only their figures and colors, we hear only the sounds, we touch only their outward surfaces, we smell only the smells, and taste the savors; but their inward substances are not to be known either by our senses, or by any reflex act of our minds: much less, then, have we any idea of the substance of God" (3: 546). Newton is suggesting sentiments not unlike those expressed in Swift's "Digression on Madness" that even scientists who dissect bodies, claiming to find secret inner workings, deal only with the surfaces of things. Following in this line, Newton acknowledges he does not understand the cause of gravitation and excludes hypotheses about such causes from the domain of experimental philosophy. Then, however, Newton shows himself to be a mechanic as confused as Swift's Hack:

> And now we might add something concerning a certain most subtle spirit which pervades and lies hid in all gross bodies; by the force and action of which spirit the particles of bodies attract one another at near distances, and cohere, if contiguous; and electric bodies operate to greater distances, as well repelling as attracting the neighboring corpuscles; and light is emitted, reflected, refracted, inflected, and heats bodies; and all sensation is excited, and the members of animal bodies move at the command of the will, namely, by the vibrations of this spirit, mutually propagated along the solid filaments of the nerves, from the outward organs of sense to the brain, and from the brain into the muscle. But these are things that cannot be explained in few words, nor are we furnished with that sufficiency of experiments which is required to an accurate determination and demonstration of the laws by which this electric and elastic spirit operates. (2: 547)

Having made our inability to know the "inward substances" of gross bodies the evidence that we have no idea of the "substance of God," Newton has here begun to tell us about the "most subtle spirit," which "lies hid" in all bodies. It is, in other words, not that God is unknowable by mechanical means; it is rather the case that we have not yet a sufficiency of experimentation to apprehend the hidden particle that constitutes the work of the prime mover. The apprehension of God, in the New Philosophy, is dependent on the discovery of that next, still more subtle particle that, when we find it experimentally, will complete the system and explain the "rest of the phenomena of Nature," including the movements of the brain and muscle of the human microcosm. The subtle spirit, like the next subatomic particle, cannot "be explained in a few words": its existence occupies the gap in the text of the *Principia*, which, Swift suggests, corresponds to a void—*Hic multa desiderantur*—inevitable in the explication of every "universal" system.

Swift's rational void is a representation of his perception of what separates alchemists from the new scientists: scientists omit or deny the mystical foundations of their essentially alchemical work. Swift's critique of Newton has received twentieth-century corroboration that should lead to a reconsideration of the value of Swift's critique of the Modern generally. Since John Maynard Keynes purchased and wrote on Newton's alchemical manuscripts, we have known that Newton was at least as serious about his alchemical work as he was about those disciplines that are now generally called science.[25] This discovery is necessarily something more than an adjustment of naive beliefs in the existence of a clean line of separation between Baconian science and alchemy because, as the Modern's greatest scientist, Newton had become emblematic of the demonstrable triumph of rationality over the mystical blindness of the premodern past. That his remarkable scientific achievements were driven by his alchemical interest, as well as his interpretation of *Revelation*,[26] suggests that reason and method were, in Swift's terms, the lackeys of an incomparable mystical invention.

Since it is safe to assume Swift had no access to the manuscripts that directly reveal Newton's millenary alchemy, how is it that Swift would recognize the nonrational sources of the great scientist's work? Rather than any prophetic or otherwise mystical explanation, the answer would seem to be that Swift read skeptically and in context. One need not, that is, have access to unpublished manuscripts to recognize Robert Boyle's interest in alchemy and debt to alchemists. Knowing the importance of what Wotton calls "The History of Air" to the New Philosophy generally, and particularly to Boyle and the Royal Society, Swift would not have accepted the modern distinction between Boyle's chemistry and Newton's physics.[27] Instead, Swift noticed that both scientists' systems dealt with ethereal matter, one that Boyle is willing, without committing himself of course, to discuss in terms of Paracelsus's *quintessence*. We may recognize something of Swift's contextual reading of the New Philosophy, in Gail Chistianson's biographical reading of the 1675 "Hypothesis":

> Newton conceived of nature as "a perpetuall circulatory worker, generating fluids out of solids, and solids out of fluids, fixed things out of volatile, & volatile out of fixed." He further conjectured that

> a subtle and elastic ether or spirit was the causative agent of such diverse phenomena as gravity and magnetism. We can discern the mind of a master alchemist behind these thoughts. For Newton the universe had become nothing other than the mighty crucible of God in which the first matter of creation is being constantly transformed. (Christianson, 234)

Swift makes a larger charge. The New Philosophers are influential examples of a dangerous modern type, each an innovator "in the empire of reason" who would "reduce the notions of all mankind exactly to the same length, and breadth, and height of his own" (*OAS*, 141). In section 2 of *A Tale* the Hack describes a religious sect that worships God as a tailor: "They held the universe to be a large *suit of clothes*, which *invests* everything: that the earth is invested by the air; the air is invested by the stars; and the stars are invested by the *primum mobile*" (*OAS*, 97). Swift sees the New Philosophers as authors of a comparable religion in which the universe is composed of corpuscles or particles or subtle vapors and God is the "perfect mechanic" or the original chemist.

Swift's representation of emergent modern science situates it in the political and social contexts in which the scientific methodologies are made and function. Nowhere is this more immediately evident than in Swift's hint, mentioned earlier, that his satire aims at Newton:

> As wit is the noblest and most useful gift of human nature, so humour is the most agreeable; and where these two enter far into the composition of any work they will render it always acceptable to the world. Now, the great part of those who have no share or taste of either, but by their pride, pedantry, and ill manners, lay themselves bare to the lashes of both, think the blow is weak because they are insensible; and where wit hath any mixture of raillery, 'tis but calling it banter and the work is done. This polite word of theirs was first borrowed from the bullies in White-Friars, then fell among the footmen, and at last retired to the pedants, by whom it is applied as properly to the production of wit as if I should apply it to Sir Isaac Newton's mathematics. (*OAS*, 70)

Wotton had used the word *banter* repeatedly in attacking *A Tale*, and both Wotton and Bentley had used Newton's work as a quasi-divine weapon in their intellectual battles for modern superiority. Arguably nothing would be more offensive to the "brother modernists" than to see the greatest work of their "divine theorist" put on a par with the work Wotton had called "one of the Prophanest Banters upon the Religion of Jesus Christ . . . that ever yet appeared" (*A Defense*, 534).

But Swift aims to offend more than Wotton and Bentley. In fact his point in drawing our attention to Newton is to warn against thinking he wrote so formidable a work merely to mock those he considers mere pedants. White-Friars, where Swift says the word *banter* was coined, was a criminal area of London known as Alsatia, and Alsatia was "known as a headquarters for the manufacture of counterfeit coins."[28] As all Swift's readers knew, Newton was the Warden and eventually the Master of the Mint, who was famous for aggressively prosecuting coiners. A major part of Newton's strategy in this effort involved hiring agents—often criminals themselves—to trap counterfeiters.[29] With this reference, Swift is mocking the "divine theorist" back to the squalid social and political context in which, Swift was confident, each of us spends not a little of our lives. Just as Newton's lofty reputation at the Mint depended upon interaction with a violent human world, so, Swift suggests, his "incomparable" intellectual achievement owes much to pedants like Wotton and Bentley, the intellectual equivalent of the bullies of White-Friars.

If Swift's "hint" in the "Apology" takes a low road of *ad hominem* (counter)attacks, the attack that the hint points to in *A Tale* is socially and politically profound. Consider that it is in the context of a parody of New Philosophy's systems of "aethereal spirits or vapors" that the Hack discovers the source of "all those mighty revolutions that have happened in *empire*, in *philosophy*, and in *religion*." And consider this discovery in comparison with Thomas Kuhn's *The Structure of Scientific Revolutions*. Like Swift, Kuhn attacks the new science's claim that it offers a steady path to objective truth. Like Swift, Kuhn confutes as irrational the modern belief that science consists of a steadily progressive accumulation of knowledge. Aristotle's statement in Swift's *Travels* might, in fact, now be categorized as a Kuhnian view of science:

> [Aristotle] found, that *Gassendi*, who had made the Doctrine of *Epicurus* as palatable as he could, and the *Vortices* of *Descartes*, were equally exploded. He predicted the same Fate for *Attraction*, whereof the present Learned are such zealous Asserters. He said, that new Systems of Nature were but new Fashions, which would vary in every Age; and even those who pretend to demonstrate them from Mathematical Principles, would flourish but a short Period of Time, and be out of Vogue when that was determined. (*PW*, 11: 197–98)

Unlike Swift, Kuhn sees the explosions of scientific systems as evolutionary, proposing, as a new paradigm of scientific advancement, "the selection by conflict within the scientific community of the fittest way to practice future science" (172). Swift, on the other hand, sees in the intellectual violence of scientific revolutions the same potential for human violence that is associated with political and religious revolutions. Following the parody of Newton, Swift's Hack makes his most chilling and most often quoted observation: "Last week I saw a woman *flayed*, and you will hardly believe how much it altered her person for the worse" (*OAS*, 145). The monstrousness of the Hack's dementia is all the more evident when we notice he is offering the results of this and other "late experiments" to save us the charges of "all such expensive anatomy for the time to come" (*OAS*, 145). The practical and commercial concerns of the Hack's material system allow him, with supreme detachment, to reduce a human being to so much torn flesh on the table. As important to Swift's critique of the Modern as exposing the irrational origins of supposedly rational modern thought is a prefiguring of the end of the modern "conquests and systems" (*OAS*, 143) in the Hack's inhuman materialism. If Kuhn has begun a recognition of the first part of Swift's critique with a historical examination of scientific revolutions, perhaps I. I. Rabi may be said to have begun a discussion of Swift's conclusions. Rabi initially refused to join the project to build the atomic bomb, saying he did not want to make "'the culmination of three centuries of physics' a weapon of mass destruction" (Rhodes, 452). But the three centuries from Newton to Hiroshima end with Rabi's comment, "We thought of human beings as matter."[30] From the Swiftian perspective there is nothing mystical or irrational in this formulation. Inherent in the reduction of *scientia* to modern science is the reduction of the human being to so many vapors in a monstrously rational machine.

Newton opens his correspondence with Bentley by observing: "When I wrote my Treatise about our System, I had an eye upon such Principles as might work with considering Men for the Belief of a Deity; and nothing can rejoice me more than to find it useful for that purpose" (*Papers and Letters*, 280). Elsewhere in the correspondence he indicates he is specifically aware that the Boyle lectures were delivered as sermons.[31] With Newton's blessing, Bentley was preaching a Newtonian theology. In *A Tale*, Swift makes the pulpit one of three "oratorial" machines by which words, "bodies of much weight and gravity," may be hurled down and leave "deep *impressions*" on auditors: "By the *pulpit* are adumbrated the writings of our *modern saints* in Great Britain, as they have spiritualized and refined them from the dross and grossness of *sense* and *human reason*" (*OAS*, 89). Connecting words and gravity, writings and spiritualized sense and reason is Swift's way of indicating that he recognizes the mysterious "new religion" (*OAS*, 142) of the Newtonian Anglicans to be, like Peter's debased version of Christianity, an essentially critical enterprise: "Now this physico-logical scheme of oratorial receptacles or machines contains a great mystery, being a type, a sign, an emblem, a shadow, a symbol, bearing analogy to the spacious commonwealth of writers, and to those methods by which they must exalt themselves to a certain eminency above the inferior world" (*OAS*, 89). As Peter rehabilitated Aristotle's *de Interpretatione* to raise himself to certain eminency, so it is "those methods" of writers in Great Britain that allow them to turn "the dross and grossness" of sense and reason into mystical systems they think appropriate to deliver from pulpits.

~

The methodology of the Modern for Swift is Cartesian, a collection of long chains of reason, though in Swift these chains do not link empirically obtained data to truth, but bind occult originals in madness. When the Hack tells us he has made method and reason the lackeys of invention, he has recognized the pattern of modern discourse he first identified in the scholastic reduction of the scriptural communion to transubstantiation.[32] While the critical methodology, borrowed from Aristotle, has the effect of debasing the revealed original, it is a kind of philosopher's stone for natural philosophy, showing how virtually any material observation—that clothes often distinguish individuals or that vapors rise from the earth—may form the basis for a system that explains the soul of the human being as surely and certainly as it explains the cosmos. Swift's statement, in the "Apology" prefaced to the 1710 edition, that his satire aimed at corruptions in religion and learning can be accepted with this critical caveat. The full force of the satire comes not in Swift's ridicule of the corruptions his readers would generally accept—those of the Roman Church and the mad claims of the alchemists—but in showing that the world that claimed to reject those corruptions—the Reformed Churches and the New Philosophy—were, or were becoming, extensions of those corruptions. Swift does not merely suggest invidious similarities by mixing diverse elements in his tub. He follows a methodological line along which he seeks to define the Modern. To be modern in the context of *A Tale of a Tub* means to believe a doctrine in which salvation, transcendence, or ultimate knowledge is inherent in material transformation, or to propound such a doctrine for personal gain. The scholastic project that reduces the bread that is Christ to mutton does so critically, by commenting on the transcendent text in a way that insists its truths must be material. Once the gospel has been reduced to a system that may be exploded, it is not hard to see how the "scholastic midwifery" might work in the opposite direction, transmuting material observations—like those of Newton—into mystical truths. The critical theory of *A Tale* is a terribly constructive paradigm, for it allows Moderns to take the commonplace—simple bread, clothes, sexual desire, even flatulence—and transmute them through the medium of language into degenerate, always false, systems of ultimate truth. And the nemesistic mirror reflects an image of a modern world capable of no intellectual activity other than such delusional, self-destructive transmutation.

If Swift deserves Edward Said's encomium, "our best critic,"[33] it is in part because he is able to speak from "far outside" the intellectual assumptions of Modernity. It is not right, that is, to conclude that Swift anticipates Kuhn or Rabi or Toulmin, or for that matter, that he in any precise way shares postmodern intellectual concerns. Swift was a skeptic who lived in an intellectual moment when formidable thinkers, Descartes and Newton chief among them, thought it was necessary and possible to "save humanity from skepticism."[34] Penning his own "divine treatise" that was "Written for the Universal Improvement of Mankind," Swift reflects modern science as an extension of his satire on modern religions. He represents the general project of the New Philosophers as a paralogistic scheme in which the social and political authority of the Christian Revelation, severely attenuated since the Reformation, could be shored up or replaced by the work of "Divine theorist[s]" in natural philosophy. In distinction from later modernist formulations that see them opposed, modern religion and science are turned together in Swift's *Tale* as social and political manifestations of a common messianic discourse.

Chapter Seven

CRITICAL NEMESIS

As an interpretative construct, the Nemesis myth points in a direction away from that of most traditional Swift criticism, because the literary dynamic that becomes primary is not that between satirist and subject but between the reader and the text as reflecting pool. In a review of the history of Swift criticism through the early 1960s, Milton Voigt observed that "No critic of the *Tale* appears willing to view it apart from Swift's intention, a reflection of the assumption that the meaning of a satire is indistinguishable from the author's intention" (59). Voigt was writing in a critical environment when the problem of authorial intention was being generally discussed, and many (though far from all) subsequent studies of Swift were written with an awareness of this discussion. But it is the continuity Voigt recognizes that is remarkable, rather than any incipient change.[1] Is it possible that from 1704 until 1964, the work of critics has continually reflected a common assumption the critics brought to *A Tale*? If this is the case with respect to the widely shared assumption about authorial intention, does it follow that the widely divergent assumptions of critics on other issues account for the wide divergence in critical appraisals of the work? In the context of the myth, the question becomes: has Swift constructed a textual mirror that throws back the narcissistic assumptions of those who claim to illuminate the text? And if this should prove to be the case, how likely is it that any study since the 1960s escapes this satiric trap?

These questions bring to mind powerful textual evidence for understanding Swift's *Tale* as a snare particularly alluring to narcissistic critics. Swift's Hack happily suggests as much for his text:

> But the reader truly *learned*, chiefly for whose benefit I wake when others sleep, and sleep when others wake, will here find sufficient matter to employ his speculation for the rest of his life. It were much to be wished, and I do here humbly propose for an experiment, that every prince in Christendom will take seven of the *deepest scholars* in his dominions, and shut them up close for *seven* years in *seven* chambers, with a command to write *seven* ample commentaries on this comprehensive discourse. I shall venture to affirm that whatever difference may be found in their several conjectures, they will be all, without the least distortion, manifestly deducible from the text. (*OAS*, 150–51)

This passage has always made critics uncomfortable, though it is easily enough evaded by way of the very assumption that Voigt attributes to all critiques of the *Tale*. That is, one can agree that the Hack's text is a fustian work, sufficiently mystical and incoherent that hundreds, perhaps thousands, of interpretations might work each as well as another, in contrast to Swift's determinate satiric text. In fact the Hack's wild contradictions and unabashed claims for the obscurity of his text are reasonably read as signals that Swift reviles both characteristics of modern hack writing. Swift's text must be, the reasoning goes, a kind of meta-text that uses the Hack's pointless modern esotericism within its own carefully directed rhetorical structure. The critic's work—the search for this determinate meaning in the satires—puts the most sophisticated reader in much the same position as the most naive: every reader wants to know where Swift stands.

The encounter between Nemesis and Narcissus holds forth little hope for such an approach. Whatever Narcissus may pick up about Nemesis in the process, his lesson is all about himself. We can, without too much trouble, see that something very like this happens in those readings that locate Swift in hopeless misanthropy and madness. The best of such readings to consider in this respect may be the first because it laid the charge of misanthropy against Swift long before the *Travels*, suggesting that such readings of Swift are not necessarily the result of simple, easily dismissible confusions of author and character (Swift and Gulliver). This first attack on Swift's respect for humanity came, appropriately enough, from the Anglican divine who was the most considerable of the Newtonians, Samuel Clarke.[2] It was first delivered in 1705, the year following the publication of *A Tale*, from the pulpit of St. Paul's in the Boyle lecture series. Though the author of *A Tale* had not yet been identified, Clarke was certain enough of the author's character to discuss him in a section of the lecture entitled "Profane and Debauched Deists, Not Capable of Being Argued With."

> They indeavour to ridicule and banter all *Humane* as well as *Divine* Accomplishments; all Virtue and Government of a Man's self, all Learning and Knowledge, all Wisdom and Honour, and every thing for which a *Man* can justly be commended or esteemed more excellent than a *Beast*. They pretend commonly in their Discourse and Writings to expose the Abuses and Corruptions of Religion; but (as it is too manifest in some of their modern Books, as well as in their Talk,) they aim really against all Virtue in general, and all good Manners, and against whatsoever is truly valuable and commendable in Men. Of which a late Author has given us a very impious and profane * Instance. [*A Tale of a Tub.] They pretend to ridicule certain Vices and Follies of ignorant or superstitious Men; but the many very profane and very lewd Images, with which they industriously affect to dress up their Discourse, show plainly that they really do not so much intend to expose and deride any Vice or Folly, as on the Contrary to foment and please the debauched and vitious Inclinations of Others as void of shame as Themselves. (29–30)

Reading Swift's satire has led Clarke to articulate a formula for misanthropy by which the penchant of writers like the author of *A Tale* to ridicule indiscriminately leads inevitably to the discovery that they are unable to see the value of human beings above animals. In drawing the author of *A Tale* as an enemy of "all Virtue," Clarke anticipated and rejected as a pretense Swift's claim, in the

1710 "Apology," that his work attacks only corruptions in religion and learning. So although it is unlikely Clarke recognized the extent of the use of parody in *A Tale*, he made a defense based on misreadings of parody—the centerpiece of Swift's "Apology"—irrelevant to his charges against *A Tale*: one who would approach the subjects of religion and learning as the author of *A Tale* did, Clarke asserts, shows the depravity of his true aims, whatever he might claim to the contrary.

Clarke had a critical advantage over most subsequent critics of *A Tale* because his own work was more apparently a target of the satire than that of most commentators. He begins his Boyle lectures, entitled *A Demonstration of the Being and Attributes of God* and *A Discourse Concerning the Unchangeable Obligations of Natural Religion and the Truth and Certainty of the Christian Revelation*, by asserting that it is "most certain that no Argumentation . . . can possibly be made use of on the side of errour, but may also be used with much greater Advantage, on behalf of Truth" (*Demonstration*, 260). Making extensive use of Newton's *Principia*, Clarke further claims to argue by as "Mathematical" a method as possible. In this context, it is inconceivable that Clarke would fail to see himself linked with Bentley and Wotton as one of *A Tale*'s "brother *modernists*," accused of contriving and propagating a "new religion" (*OAS*, 142). Bentley, the first Boyle Lecturer, had been the first to use Newton's work to demonstrate the existence of God, and he is ridiculed in *A Tale* specifically for doing this from the Anglican pulpit.[3] Clarke may, however, have felt the sting of the satire more directly than those who are named in *A Tale* because he began preaching his Newtonian theology in his first series of lectures in 1704, the same year *A Tale* appeared.

Responding as one who has recognized his face in the satire, Clarke begins to repeat himself, trying to nail down the case for the satirist's misanthropy. Such writers, he says,

> Discover clearly, that they have no Sense at all of the Dignity of Humane Nature, nor of the Superiority and Excellency of their Reason above even the meanest of the Brutes. They will sometimes in Words seem to magnify the Wisdom and other natural Attributes of God; but in reality, by ridiculing whatever bears any resemblance to it in Men, they show undeniably that they do not indeed believe

> there is any real difference in Things, or any true Excellency in one thing more than in another. By turning every thing alike, and without exception, into ridicule and banter; they declare plainly, that they don't believe any thing to be wise, any thing decent, any thing comely or praise-worthy at all. (*Demonstration*, 30)

Clarke's repetition of his formula for misanthropy signals the way his reading of Swift's satire is less a critique of another's work than a reflection of his own assumptions. In charging Swift with turning all things equally in his tub of ridicule, Clarke has himself narrowed the difference between the attributes of "Humane Nature" and the attributes of God. Particularly in this second exposition of the path to misanthropy, one can be offensive to the divine by mocking the claims human beings make for their own accomplishments. In his example—what debauched authors "sometimes" seem to do—Clarke reveals the fundamental narcissism of his happy human/divine construct, unwittingly acknowledging his nemesis. With Clarke's work a "Demonstration of the Being and Attributes of God," where has he found misanthropy? In the character of authors who "sometimes in Words seem to magnify . . . natural Attributes of God." One becomes a depraved and debauched despiser of "Humane Nature," it seems, when one pretends to do what Clarke does in earnest—when one parodies works like Clarke's own. Clarke makes the author of *A Tale* a misanthrope, not for ridiculing all "resemblance" between God and humans, but very specifically for ridiculing Clarke's understanding of his own close resemblance to the deity. In this, among the earliest of recorded confrontations with Swift's text, the critic claims to reveal the fundamental position of *A Tale*'s author but instead unwittingly uses the Swiftian text to reflect the narcissism of his own theological project.

The elucidation of one individual's narcissistic response to *A Tale* will hardly seem significant unless it somehow informs a more general response to Swift's satire. Freud delineates a path from individual to cultural narcissism that is identical in many respects to the path described in Swift's "Digression on Madness."[4] In *Civilization and Its Discontents*, Freud discusses various ways individuals try to avoid "frustration from the external world," including one approach that makes reality itself an enemy:

> One can try to re-create the world, to build up in its stead another world in which its most unbearable features are eliminated and replaced by others that are in conformity with one's own wishes. But whoever, in desperate defiance, sets out upon this path to happiness will as a rule attain nothing. Reality is too strong for him. He becomes a madman, who for the most part finds no one to help him in carrying through his delusion. . . . A special importance attaches to the case in which attempts to procure a certainty of happiness and a protection against suffering through a delusional remoulding of reality is made by a considerable number of people in common. The religions of mankind must be classed among the mass-delusions of this kind. No one, needless to say, who shares a delusion ever recognizes it as such. (32)

Swift's Hack and Freud agree on the essential characteristics of the development and consequences of extreme narcissism. In each it begins with an individual's attempt to find a "path to happiness," and in each this path leads to a happiness that is delusional. The Hack, of course, defines happiness as "a perpetual possession of being well deceived" (*OAS*, 145). In both Freud and Swift the delusional path leads to madness. Freud has made madness the usual result of extreme narcissistic ambition. Swift uses a musical metaphor to express the same idea:

> There is a peculiar *string* in the harmony of human understanding which, in several individuals, is exactly of the same tuning. This, if you can dexterously screw up to its right key and then strike gently upon it, whenever you have the good fortune to light among those of the same pitch they will, by a secret necessary sympathy, strike exactly at the same time. And in this one circumstance lies all the skill or luck of the matter; for if you chance to jar the string among those who are either above or below your own height, instead of subscribing to your doctrine they will tie you fast, call you mad, and feed you with bread and water. (*OAS*, 142)

In both Freud and Swift, the individual narcissist who finds no followers is a common mad person. Explicit in Swift's text and implicit in Freud's is a corollary by which the narcissist who finds a group with which to share his or her delusional desires is equally as mad as the conventional lunatic, but will be hailed as a great visionary. Freud illustrates collective madness by referring to "the religions of mankind," while Swift makes the "propagating of new religions" one of a triumvirate, with military conquests and new schemes in philosophy, of the human revolutions that can be traced to the collectivization of initially individual narcissism.

In this context, Clarke's narcissistic reading of *A Tale* is satirically revealing, not only on an individual but on the cultural level as well. When Clarke sees himself ridiculed among the "brother modernists" in *A Tale*, he responds by placing that discourse outside the system that links human beings with nature and God. Swift's text prompts in Clarke a deconstructive tautology: writers like the author of *A Tale* "are first to be convinc'd of the true Principles of *Reason*, before they can be disputed with" (*Demonstration*, 31). But how are they "to be convinced" if they cannot "be disputed with"? If they "are not capable of being argued with," how are they to be led to accept Clarke's "true Principles"? With Clarke a modernist personally, philosophically, and theologically committed to a conception that portrays humans as rational creatures on a rational path, Swift's text becomes, in Clarke's reading, a jarring inconsistency, the human production that is nowhere on the path, nowhere within an otherwise all-encompassing order. Swift is made one with "no Sense at all of the Dignity of Humane Nature" in this very early critique, precisely because his text is "not capable of being argued with." He is a misanthrope because, instead of contributing to the achievements by which Moderns bridge the gaps between the human and divine orders, his text is, in Clarke's reading, an instrument of confusion, chaos, disorder.

At the other extreme of the criticism that sees Swift as a depraved misanthrope is the now nearly pervasive view that Swift's Anglicanism guides his deepest satiric designs. The readings that contribute to this critical conclusion turn on the issue of order, as Ronald Paulson forthrightly states in opening one of the earliest, most extensive, and substantial attempts to uncover a coherent structure and plan in *A Tale*:

> My justification for analyzing the *Tale of a Tub* lies in the evident need for a close reading, which Swift himself made a gesture toward sanctioning when he wrote his "Author's Apology" to meet the ac-

> cusations of irreligion that were promptly leveled at his book. Over and over through the years since its publication, and largely because of its form, the *Tale of a Tub* has been accused of being (1) an outright attack on religion, (2) an expression of disorder which is nihilistic, or (3) an elaborate joke which disregards over-all unity for the hilarity of momentary incongruities. (*Theme and Structure*, 1–2)

Notice that Paulson, writing in 1960, sees himself joining the critical debate on *A Tale* begun in attacks like Clarke's and initially responded to by Swift, but left unanswered in the intervening 250 years. Paulson positions his work as a defense of Swift, following a "sanctioning" gesture he perceives in Swift's "Apology."

To defend Swift's text from the persistent charge of irreligion, Paulson must show that the work's "eccentric" form is in fact ordered in some perceptible way. The order Paulson finds, "a logically arranged encyclopedia of Gnostic sufficiency," is less important, here, than noticing how the frame he chooses for his task shapes his discovery of Swift's religious position. In other words, having set himself up as the critic who will finally answer charges that *A Tale* is irreligious or otherwise depraved, and having taken his lead from Swift's own defense of his work, Paulson locates Swift in *A Tale* in the "The Christian View of Man," the title of Paulson's concluding chapter. Reassuring us that his conclusion about Swift's view of human nature in *A Tale* "is perhaps not so pessimistic as it may at first sound," Paulson points to the moderate character of Martin:

> The picture we are given [of the moderns] is of a man with a head that aspires ever upward but with a body so heavy that as soon as he gets off the ground he tumbles down again. It is therefore clearly better to walk on the earth, because in this posture and place the weight of one's lower parts acts as ballast and balance, even assists gravity, rather than acting as a handicap. It should be noted that when weight is used in the proper way, like the knife, it can be good, as when "the *Weight* of *Martin's* Argument" and his "Gravity" sustain him against Jack's blandishments and make Jack "fly out, and spurn against his Brother's Moderation . . . " In short, the human body, whatever its limitations, is God-given and good. (*Theme and Structure*, 231)

Though, for Paulson, Swift is indeed a harsh critic of the unbalanced activities and aspirations of human beings generally, and of the Moderns specifically, he also affirms the good that balanced human activity can lead to. The Anglican Martin is representative of the sustaining nature of balanced weight against the assaults of a decidedly unbalanced world. With Martin as the only figure in *A Tale* with an obvious correspondence to the biographical Swift—both may be construed as defenders of Anglican Christianity—Paulson's "Christian View of Man" became a fixture in Swift criticism through the closing decades of the twentieth century.

Paulson's view, then, is as nearly diametrically opposed to Clarke's as possible. Instead of an atheist, Swift is an orthodox Christian. Instead of a work that creates only chaos by ridiculing indiscriminately, *A Tale* is a work marked by "a strikingly periodic order," (*Theme and Structure*, 233) a masterpiece of parodic control. Instead of denigrating all that is virtuous in human beings, Swift's work affirms a specifically moral view of human nature sustainable through all the foolish excesses humans are given to. In radical contrast to Clarke and all those judged "guilty of the gravest misconceptions" for finding "irreligion or nihilism" in *A Tale*, Paulson makes a mighty contribution to locating Swift on the side of the angels, where Swift in the "Apology" claimed to belong. Is it possible that even such a happy reading of Swift is prey to a nemesistic trap? Is it possible such critiques are more similar to than different from Clarke's because they are more nearly reflections of the critics' assumptions than of the satirist's position?

One need only see how Paulson spends the considerable critical capital he gains from reading *A Tale* to answer these questions affirmatively: "The first point I have tried to prove in this study is that the *Tale of a Tub* is not simply a *jeu d'esprit*, but rather falls easily within the area of literature which is concerned with moral problems—what Leavis calls the 'great tradition'" (*Theme and Structure*, 233). Precisely like Martin, Swift, as seen by Paulson, is one who "doubtless would have delivered an admirable lecture of morality" (*OAS*, 67), had the eccentricities of his age not demanded something else. Paulson's discovery of the moral order lying under the eccentric surface means Swift should be admitted to a club from which he had been specifically excluded by the critic who was its founder. Instead of using his reading of Swift to mock the pretensions of F. R. Leavis's invidious comparison of Swift and Blake, Paulson uses the order he has deduced from the work to argue that Swift be admitted to a club, wholly invented by a critic who explicitly excluded not only Swift but Sterne and, most vehemently, James Joyce. Leavis's rejection of Joyce's *Ulysses* is illustrative of the impetus behind Paulson's efforts with Swift. Leavis says:

> I know that Mr. T. S. Eliot has found in Joyce's work something that recommends Joyce to him as positively religious in tendency (see *After Strange Gods*). But it seems plain to me that there is no organic principle determining, informing, and controlling into a vital whole, the elaborate analogical structure, the extraordinary variety of technical devices, the attempts at an exhaustive rendering of consciousness for which *Ulysses* is remarkable. (39)

Without a "determining, informing, and controlling" structure, Joyce's work cannot be "positively religious." In fact, Leavis goes on to call *Ulysses* "a pointer to disintegration," a reading he sees verified in Joyce's influence on writers like Djuna Barnes, Henry Miller, and Lawrence Durrell, who "'do dirt' on life."[5] More than two centuries after Clarke had made the disorder of *A Tale* the evidence of an irreligion degrading to "Humane Nature," Leavis uses the disorder of the masterwork of another Irish writer to charge its author with an irreligion defined in terms of its failure to affirm—What are the opposites of the accusations made?—the possibilities for order and cleanliness in human experience. In this context Paulson's rehabilitation of Swift is heroic and prodigiously ironic. Instead of using his reading of Swift to ridicule the narcissistic pretensions of critics who set themselves up as priestly arbiters of moral, religious, and literary order, Paulson accepts the terms defined by critics from Clarke to Leavis and undertakes the Herculean task of cleaning up and ordering *A Tale of a Tub*. He succeeds by making its eccentric surface a mask for the phlegmatic, sedate, critically acceptable Martin, who represents its author. He succeeds, that is, by finding in *A Tale* his own critical assumptions about what "falls easily within the area of literature which is concerned with moral problems."

Writing 250 years after Clarke, Paulson comes to an opposite, happy conclusion, not because critical assumptions have changed, but because Paulson can not imagine what Clarke could not deny, that Swift's satire is aimed at Paulson as reader. Clarke, like Thackeray and even Leavis, rails irrationally against the discourse that mocks self-satisfied rationality, the railing itself corresponding to Narcissus's impotent rage at the discovery of his limitations. Paulson's critique corresponds to an earlier point in the myth, the happy identification. Like Martin trying to deliver an admirable lecture on morality against Jack's mad antics, Swift has tried to offer a work of moral literature against the Gnostic enthusiasm—and Paulson has offered an ordering critique of Swift against the raging condemnations of less perceptive critics. The one positive image Paulson finds in the satiric mirror is a happy referent for his own measured critical activity.

In an environment of ever-accelerating critical obsolescence, Paulson's critique, now more than thirty years old, may be judged as quaintly archaic as Clarke's warning against "down-right *Atheism*." But the remarkable, unperceived continuity in the terms of the critical debate from Clarke to Leavis should make us wary of the presumption that all has changed in the decades since Paulson discovered the moderate Christian order of *A Tale*. Even among critiques published in the 1990s, including those that in one way or another define themselves against the last thirty some years of Swift criticism, the "Christian View of Man" has remained a kind of critical safe haven.

Two particularly interesting examples of the resilience of the "Christian View" are Melvin New's provocative discussion of Swift and Thomas Mann in *Telling New Lies* and Richard Nash's attempt, in "Entrapment and Ironic Mode in *A Tale of a Tub*," to bring Reader Response Theory to *A Tale*. New says he is "arguing against" Philip Harth's approach in *Swift and Anglican Rationalism*, which "remains after thirty years the most cogent, convincing, and useful reading . . . of *A Tale of a Tub*" (208). His opposition to Harth is epitomized by the claim that "the critic who privileges Christianity as a way of explaining human pride, self-deception, limitation, and the like, has already failed to negotiate the irony of *Tale of a Tub*" (170). But recognizing this critical trap does not allow New to avoid it. Only a few pages later, he assumes that "Swift has located himself—that is, Martin, or Anglicanism, or rational Christianity, or simple reason"—in Martin's moderate Christianity. That Swift's position may be equated with Martin's is, precisely as New suggested, a failure to negotiate irony. It is at such points—when critics fail to negotiate irony—that we find the tools for dismissing Swift. New accordingly considers Swift compromised by his moderate Christianity, the power of Swift's critique diminished by the weakness of Martin's untenable position. Instead of actually opposing the "Christian View," New merely distinguishes his use of it, saying it makes him think less of Swift's satiric accomplishments, rather than more. The assumption itself persists.

Richard Nash similarly hopes to distinguish his reading from "the various interpretations of *Tale of a Tub* offered over the past thirty years." But Nash does not equate Swift with Martin. Finding various critical warnings against this trap, he establishes a powerful case for reading Martin as one of the targets of *A Tale*'s satire, rather than the lone representative of Swift's positive positions. It is possible to further Nash's argument about Martin by showing Martin to be very much a part of *A Tale*'s attack on Newtonian Anglicans. But despite beginning the demolition of the Swift/Martin foundation of the "Christian view," Nash nevertheless clings to the Christian reading itself. And despite purporting to use Reader Response Theory to recover *A Tale* from decades of deadening professional readings, Nash keeps the "Christian view" reading afloat on a sea of extra-textual evidence, such as Swift's sermon on the Trinity. The meaning Nash would have each reader involved in creating is not, it seems, independent of the professional readings that have dominated Swift criticism.

I have singled out Nash and New from among recent studies because these extraordinarily fine readings follow different paths to a common insight about Swift, and then each shrinks from the insight by recourse to the very critical tradition he purports to be rejecting. If we put New's assertion that "the critic who privileges Christianity . . . has already failed to negotiate the irony of *Tale of a Tub*," together with Nash's demolition of the reading that equates

Martin with Swift, we are led to consider the possibility that there is no positive referent in *A Tale*.

To consider this possibility seriously, we may briefly consider whether Nash is correct in severing Swift's position from that of Martin. Martin's reputation among critics for salubrious moderation arises from the scene in section 6 of *A Tale* in which he encourages Jack, at the time of the split with Peter, "not to damage his coat by any means" (*OAS*, 128). Nash points to contemporary uses of the word *moderation*, including some by Swift, to argue that Swift is attacking the kind of moderation Martin exhibits, a reading with powerful textual support. It is not simply that Martin's attempt to deliver "an admirable lecture of morality" is ineffective with Jack, whose rage toward Peter is not controllable. Martin's approach to Jack actually helps destabilize Jack, loosening the vapor that ascends to Jack's brain:

> Martin had still proceeded as gravely as he began, and doubtless would have delivered an admirable lecture of morality . . . but Jack was already gone a flight-shot beyond his patience. And as in scholastic disputes nothing serves to rouse the spleen of him that *opposes*, so much as a kind of pedantic affected calmness in the *respondent*; disputants being for the most part like unequal scales, where the *gravity* of one side advances the *lightness* of the other, and causes it to fly up and kick the beam; so it happened here that the *weight* of Martin's argument exalted Jack's *levity*, and made him fly out and spurn against his brother's moderation. (*OAS*, 128–29)

Nash's argument that we should be wary of accepting Martin's moderation as something the satirist is endorsing may be made more emphatic by noticing that Martin is linked with *A Tale*'s chief pedant, Richard Bentley. As Bentley offered words of "weight and gravity" from the Anglican pulpit by using Newtonian natural philosophy against atheism, Martin himself offers his "weight" and his "gravity" against Jack's burgeoning madness. Here the point is not that the English Church had based its belief on natural philosophy from the time of the Reformation, but that at least since the Reformation Martin was always affecting a "phlegmatic and sedate" countenance, his very moderation serving to inflame the forces, Roman Catholic and Calvinist, that were making a burlesque of Christianity. That Anglicanism would, in Bentley and Clarke's Newtonian lectures, stake the ever more precarious condition of its coat/doctrine on a principle of gravitation so moderate and reasonable that it is finally indisputable, is the occasion for a rarity—an intellectually resonant pun. The *weight* of Martin's reasoned moderation becomes, in the modern Anglican pulpit, Newton's *gravity*, a scientific principle that is, according to Bentley, of "such good sense and true Syntax and harmonious Measure," and "eternal usefulness" that it "cannot possibly be conceived" (8: 42) without reference to the phlegmatic and sedate God who is its author. When Swift allows Martin to leave the stage of *A Tale* by showing Peter and Jack "a fair pair of heels," the image is no longer one of sustaining moderation, but of a church on the run.[6] Whereas Peter has traded his sacred doctrine for transubstantiation, and Jack becomes a raving religious alchemist, Martin's famed resistance to those modern methodologies is represented in *A Tale* as giving way to Wotton and Bentley and Clarke's "new religion," of spiritual materialism: "By the *pulpit* are adumbrated the writings of our *modern saints* in Great Britain, as they have spiritualized and refined them from the dross and grossness of *sense* and *human reason*" (*OAS*, 89). In this context Swift's claim in the "Apology" that *A Tale* "celebrates the Church of England" should direct our attention to the rest of his sentence: "as the most perfect of all others in discipline and doctrine."[7] Given the portrait of "all others" in the work, Swift's claim amounts to little more than a distinction between residents of successive circles of Hell. The Anglican pulpit, as it appears in *A Tale*, is one more oratorical machine, delivering words of "much weight and gravity" to credulous fools and eager knaves.

Without Martin as the textual reflection of Swift, the text has no figure representing Swift, and critics like Nash are forced beyond the text for evidence of Swift's position. Because all the substantial evidence for Swift's Christian view dates from periods after the publication of *A Tale*, critics who make such arguments are in the uncomfortable position of suggesting that *A Tale* would remain a supremely problematic work had Swift died the week it went to press. Irvin Ehrenpreis, perhaps the most influential proponent of the Christian view, may have indirectly acknowledged this problem when he went to extraordinary lengths to try to back-date the composition of Swift's *Sentiments of a Church of England Man* to the period of the publication of *A Tale*.[8] If we feel the need to look to subsequent writing by Swift for insights into Swift's position in *A Tale*, why not consider what he said, not about his religion but about his writing and himself? Writing to Pope in September 1725, Swift claims: "The chief end I propose in all my labours is to vex the world rather than divert it, and if I could compass that design without hurting my own person or fortune I would be the most indefatigable writer you have ever seen, without reading" (*Corr.*, 3: 225).

Whether this celebrated letter is read as an intimate communication between friends or as posturing for posterity, Swift's statement about his relationship with his writing is consistent with both his definition of satire and the epitaph he wrote for himself. The mirror of satire he proposes makes fools of those diverted by his satires and provokes impotent fury in those who recognize themselves; his final words position him as one who champions human liberty—not by satisfying the expectation of his readers, but as an avenger (*vindicator*) shaking or jolting (*vexare*) his readers into unbearable experiences of self-recognition, or narcissistic denial. It is this "chief end"—an intention to mortify—that enrages his enemies, Wotton, Bentley, and Clarke, not to mention Thackeray, Leavis, and other proponents of interpretations that see Swift as mad or misanthropic or both. It is this apparent end—the critical vexatiousness of Swift's satires—that leads friendly twentieth-century critics to seek hidden order in the works, or at least Christian explanations for critical chaos.

If we will seriously consider that Swift writes to exact vengeance, we are forced to recognize that the work of critics is necessarily a first line of the satiric attack. Not only are we specifically portrayed as venomous asses in *A Tale*, but our work, beginning with a rehabilitation of Aristotle's *de Interpretatione*, provides the foundation for modern materialist methodologies. Swift's seemingly eccentric location of the origins of the Modern in a debased critical function is independently supported. His first modern, Duns Scotus, is seen in the history of philosophy as one whose "critical spirit" informed subsequent, increasingly materialist, philosophic approaches.[9] More provocative, though perhaps necessarily less conclusive, the critic credited with beginning the postmodern attack on positivist criticism, Jacques Derrida, makes *de Interpretatione* the first work he attacks in *Of Grammatology*. That Swift and Derrida independently place this seldom discussed Aristotelian work near the beginnings of their attacks on the Modern might seem less significant if their arguments did not have other remarkable similarities. Derrida makes Aristotle's work a text of only apparently stable meaning that has influenced logocentric criticism generally. While Derrida's critique imagines critics building unwittingly on the shifting sand of the Aristotelian claims, Swift locates the Modern in what is, at least initially, a depraved recognition of the usefulness of so unstable a text.

Both Swift and Derrida argue that the "truths" arrived at through the application of an Aristotelian critical theory are untenable. Each suggests that modern critical projects are centered on concepts that make the rational universal systems derived from them something closer to what is meant by religion than what is meant by science or philosophy or criticism. Only Swift traces the foolishness of such grand claims to a particular historical moment, and critical knavery.

There is a happy, and therefore extremely suspect, possibility that Swift would see the fulfillment of his linking of *de Interpretatione* with the *Revelation* in what, for progressive Modernists, is the critical apocalypse of deconstruction. Once beyond the naive expectation that language is or can be certain or literal or linear, our culture might move beyond the Modern, beyond the cleanliness and order of modern systems that vitiate humanistic discourse and the "human liberty" Swift claimed to champion. It is probable, however, that Swift would judge deconstruction a system ultimately as naive as the systems it purports to overturn—a system that privileges concepts of paralysis, invariably, and ironically, constructing satisfying critical destinations from a linguistic inability to move. The apocalyptic implications of Swift's satires are much more likely to be understood in the relationship Swift is always insisting upon between criticism and the world. Peter rediscovers *de Interpretatione*, not out of a detached scholarly interest, but because he recognizes it can be useful to him in the material world. His modern criticism is not an attempt to think critically about anything, but rather to order the world in a way that is increasingly satisfying to his narcissistic desires. Freud, for one, would agree with Swift that there are apocalyptic implications inherent in such a critical project:

> But even where it [sadism] emerges without any sexual purpose, in the blindest fury of destructiveness, we cannot fail to recognize that the satisfaction of the instinct is accompanied by an extraordinarily high degree of narcissistic enjoyment, owing to its presenting the ego with a fulfillment of the latter's old wish for omnipotence. The instinct of destruction, moderated and tamed, and, as it were, inhibited in its aim, must, when it is directed towards objects, provide the ego with the satisfaction of its vital needs and with control over nature. (*Civilization*, 81)

Writing between the First and Second World Wars, Freud goes on to recognize that we have gained control over nature such that we would "have no difficulty" in destroying ourselves (*Civilization*, 112). In this context, *criticism* is both something more and something less than what we usually mean by the term. It is more in the sense that it underlies the Baconian project of knowledge and power, which has its roots, according to Swift, in self-serving critical interpretations of the Scriptures by the Roman Church and of nature by alchemists. As such, modern social and intellectual systems are, in the Swiftian context, ultimately narcissistic critical projects, ways of structuring the world to satisfy narcissistic expectations. Criticism is something less because it is not about discerning, but about ordering and controlling.

In this context, Swift might covet for his own work Leavis's description of Joyce's *Ulysses* as "a pointer to disintegration." The work that will not conform to the critic's self-satisfying system is the work to admire, the work with a fair claim on posterity. In casting himself in the role of Nemesis, Swift has made it a mistake to assume that any representation of the writer's positive position appears in his work: the work is meant to tear down, to deconstruct, to break the presumptions of its "beholders." Nemesis is not present in the mirror she presents to Narcissus, but only behind its creation. Narcissus is not destroyed by discovering Nemesis in the mirror, but in discovering his own reflection. And Nemesis's position is not affirmative of any particular god or religious system, but only of the divine generally because she is destructive of ways humans have of confusing the human and the divine. From a critical perspective, Clarke's critique, among the earliest readings of *A Tale of a Tub*, may have come nearest to a kind of critical truth when it identified *A Tale*'s author as one not "capable of being argued with."

~

"Homer more than any other," Aristotle says in the *Poetics*, "has taught the others the art of framing lies in the right way" (2336–37). He had no better student than Jonathan Swift, who employs not only paralogisms of the sort Aristotle is considering, but also Homer's great liar, Sinon, in undermining critical reductions of his *Travels*.

One of Swift's most interesting liars is Don Pedro de Mendez who, though he appears ever so briefly in the Swiftian glass, exercises an enormous influence on modern readings of the *Travels into Several Remote Nations*. A thorough review of the criticism concerning Mendez would not be useful here, but a brief discussion of some relatively recent comments will be helpful in locating the present argument. A revealing exchange occurs in the pages of *American Notes and Queries* in the mid-1980s. An admittedly speculative note suggested the possibility that Swift might be playing on the name Mendez to suggest both mendaciousness and mendicancy in conjunction with the name Pedro and its symbolic connection to the Church of Rome.[10] Two prominent Swiftians joined forces to pen an angry response to the unreasonable and "contentious" suggestion that Don Pedro is himself a satiric figure. Marshaling authorities in impressive, one might say remarkable, number, the rebuttal begins by asserting that all the critics agree Don Pedro is "the incarnation of a *vir bonus*" (Real and Vienken, 136). The angry response to the speculative suggestion is understandable. With the satiric ground shifting so constantly beneath the critical path of Swift studies, mere speculations about this rare, seemingly fixed, patch of solid earth appeared positively irresponsible.[11]

The most interesting thing to arise from the speculative questioning of Mendez's role in the *Travels* was a ringing defense by Maurice Géracht in *Swift Studies* of the reading that sees Mendez as the Good Samaritan. More certainly persuasive than Géracht's main argument—that Mendez would be recognized by Swift's contemporaries as a Marrano Jew—is a nuanced reading of the Samaritan story itself. Emphasizing the importance of the fact that the Samaritan of the scriptural parable is an outsider, Géracht suggests the satiric nature of a story that exposes vice by locating moral action in an outcast. Because he recognizes this dimension of the original story, Géracht is able to use Mendez the Samaritan in a reading that is not, or at least not traditionally, "soft" school. Rather than a redemptive figure, Mendez is, in Géracht's reading, a figure with a scriptural referent in whom the relentless satire of the *Travels* is extended rather than ended or redeemed. A formidable reading of Mendez as the good man, Géracht's reading, like other Good Samaritan interpretations, is constructed from a highly selective reading of the few pages in which Mendez appears.

Nothing could be more obvious than that Mendez is indeed the *vir bonus*. But he is something else as well. He is Gulliver's first "gentle reader."

A first step in stepping beyond the Good Samaritan interpretation is to notice that Don Pedro's actions go beyond what it seems likely even the Samaritan himself would do. The Samaritan would most certainly fish a desperate man from the sea. He would likely provide him passage. If he were extremely conscious of Christian imagery he might offer to lend Gulliver "the best Suit of clothes he had" (*PW*, 11: 228). Don Pedro goes much further. He allows himself to be measured for Gulliver's clothes, though he has a ship full of men who might be instructed to do this. He takes Gulliver into his home until he can persuade him to return to England. Most unaccountably, he suffers Gulliver's insults for no apparent reason since there is no reason he must see Gulliver. Would the Samaritan pester the obnoxiously condescending Gulliver, as Don Pedro does, with "earnest Request[s]" (*PW*, 11: 287) to join him at his table? We can choose to disbelieve Gulliver on this point, but then we would have no basis for discussing any of Mendez's actions, since we have only Gulliver's report. The question then is, why would this apparently seasoned captain, having already done more for a completely destitute, lunatic sailor of a foreign and competing nation than is easily believable, regularly invite him to his table only to suffer his insults? The answer may be that, like any gentle reader, Mendez is interested in Gulliver's story.

Gulliver's interpretation of his episode with Mendez is, in contrast to his report of the events, most certainly suspicious. The importance of the encounter with Mendez for Gulliver is not in the news that he was saved by the actions of Mendez, which he takes to be an unlucky twist of fate, but in the witness Mendez provides for Gulliver's veracity. When Gulliver first gives Mendez a "Relation of [his] Voyage," the captain looks upon it "as if it were a Dream or a Vision," deeply offending Gulliver who "had quite forgot the Faculty of Lying." Invited by Gulliver to raise whatever objection he has, Mendez eventually comes around: "The Captain, a wise Man, after many Endeavours to catch me tripping in some Part of my Story, at last began to have a better Opinion of my veracity" (*PW*, 11: 287).

Unlike some witnesses to the veracity of earlier voyages who have such physical evidence as miniature animals, Mendez, like every subsequent reader, has only Gulliver's "Relation" on which to base his judgment. Gulliver's success in making his case to Mendez prepares us for Gulliver's next and final chapter that begins by addressing the "gentle reader" directly and proceeds with a defense of the literal truth of the account. Though Gulliver recognizes that readers may, with Mendez, initially think he is mad or dissembling, he expects us to be dissuaded from this impression by his detailed account of his experiences. For Gulliver, Mendez is not a Samaritan, but rather the type of the gentle reader.

In the final chapter the satirist intrudes upon the case Gulliver is earnestly making directly to the reader by having Gulliver quote Sinon, the most celebrated liar of antiquity, in support of his veracity. This is of course a clue. It points to the reason Swift made the captain who is witness to Gulliver's veracity a Portuguese sailor named Mendez. One Portuguese sailor was well known to Swift's English audience. His name was Mendez and he was, like Sinon, known as a paradigmatic liar. Though Ferdinand Mendez Pinto was, it seems certain, among the greatest of European travelers of the period, he crafted an account of his travels in which he freely mixed fiction with his recollections of his remarkable experiences. Dorothy Osborne, writing to the young William Temple, seems to have well understood the nature of the work:

> Have you read the Story of China written by a Portuguese, Fernando Mendez Pinto I think his name is? if you have not, take it with you, tis as diverting a book of the kinde as ever I read, and is as handsomly written. you must allow him the Priviledge of a Travellour & hee dos not abuse it, his lyes are as pleasant harmlesse on's as lyes can bee, and in noe great number, considering the scope hee has for them; there is one in Dublin now that ne're saw much further, has tolde mee twice as many (I dare swear) of Ireland. (Letter 59, 148)

Joseph Addison writing as Isaac Bickerstaff in the *Tatler* for November 22, 1710, was less inclined to allow Pinto the status of a traveler at all, linking his account with that of Sir John Mandeville, a wholly fictional work, and saying he read these travels as he read the travels of Ulysses and Spenser's Red-Cross Knight. In William Congreve's *Love for Love*, Foresight says to Sir Sampson, "*Ferdinand Mendez Pinto* was but a Type of thee, thou Lyar of the first Magnitude" (2, i: 235–37). When Gulliver says his own experience of travel has shown how "the Credulity of Mankind [is] so impudently abused," and given him a "great Disgust" for the "Books of Travel" he once enjoyed (*PW*, 11: 291), he is distinguishing his own work from works like the type of travel account represented by the account of Mendez Pinto. Just as Gulliver defends his veracity by identifying with the truthfulness of Sinon, so he makes the first judge of his adventure with the Houyhnhnms, a Portuguese sailor whose namesake is a representative traveling liar.

Like other suggestions that connect the name Mendez with mendaciousness, this reading threatens to be reductionist. Is the character of Mendez, so generative of interpretations of the *Travels*, to become a mere joke on Gulliver as Gulliver's reference to Sinon is often understood? Poor Gulliver reaching for a classical quotation on honesty happens upon the words of Sinon. Relating his first success in convincing a European of the truth of his fantastic adventure, Gulliver finds an "honest Portuguese" named Mendez. Here again, the clue is in the quotation from Virgil. For Sinon is not merely a spectacular liar; he is the instrument of wily Odysseus. The action of the lying may belong to Sinon, but the text of the lie belongs to the man responsible for the fall of Troy. Swift has positioned himself as the Odysseus to Gulliver's Sinon, suggesting that the Trojan Horse is not, as some commentators have suggested, the false gospel of Houyhnhnm rational philosophy, but the *Travels* itself. What Troy does Swift hope to bring down?

The Sinon quotation leads us back to a consideration of that lying Portuguese sailor, Mendez Pinto. The first thing a reader with Gulliver's Don Pedro de Mendez in mind notices on looking at the text available in the Purchas collection in Swift's library is that the first page includes, separately, both the name Don Pedro (Don Pedro de Sylva) and the name Mendez (Fernam Mendez Pinto), suggesting the possibility that Swift created Gulliver's Mendez by conflating these names. But even this abridged version of Mendez Pinto's account takes us beyond such speculation to an initial recognition of the Portuguese traveler's literary achievement. Not merely a travel account spiced with improbable wonders, Mendez Pinto's account is a sophisticated narrative. Episodes that at first appear to be descriptions of difficulties encountered by Mendez Pinto and his fellow travelers turn into elaborately structured stories with pointed moral observations that almost always reflect on the rapaciousness, violence, and even religious hypocrisy of the European sailors. In one wholly fictitious account, Mendez Pinto and his compatriots are evaluated in a meeting with the king of Tartary:

> He asked, What doe you seeke with so farre travels and great troubles? wee gave as good reason as we could; whereat he shaking his head, said to the King of Benan, an old man, that it seemed that our Countrey had much Covetousnesse, and little Justice; so, said the other, it appeares; for those men which flie on the top of all waters, by wit and industrie to get that which God hath not given them, either poverty forceth to foresake their Countrey, or vanitie and blindnesse caused by covetousnesse, makes them forget God and their Fathers. (*Observations*, 135)

Mendez Pinto here finds a heathen spokesman—the king of the most warlike people on earth no less—to condemn the Portuguese, and by implication, all European voyagers, on religious grounds. Like Gulliver at the end of the *Travels*, Mendez Pinto makes greed and covetousness the defining characteristics of a foreign view of Modern Europe, mocking the hypocritical righteousness of individuals and states who conquer, rape, and pillage in the name of

God. As Sinon's lie must be read within the context of the heroic exploits of wily Odysseus, so the lies of Mendez Pinto's first person narrator can only be understood within the context of Mendez Pinto's long-suffering condemnation of the evils of Europe's incipient colonial adventures.

In an essay published posthumously in *PMLA*, Richard Rodino explored the implication of the reference to Gulliver as "Splendide Mendax" on the 1735 title page of volume 3 of Swift's works. Rodino read Gulliver's reference to Sinon through the lens of Nietzsche's will to power, which makes lying a necessity in a world of terrifying cruelty. The lie here is not the mundane lie of the knave, but the nearly universal lie of the fool that allows us to persevere amidst the ambiguities of existence and the pain of experience. Arguing for "humility about the manifold errors and lies of human knowledge" (1067), especially in the critical enterprise, Rodino suggested that the multiplication of mirrored images in the *Travels* between author and character, character and reader, reader and author, and so on, pit the kind of determinate meanings critics usually draw from the text against Swift's "deliberate autocorruptions of his texts and his blurring of fictional levels" (1057). Rodino's argument against critical presumption would seem to be borne out in the established reading of Mendez. We critics have made Mendez, the first judge of Gulliver's veracity after leaving Houyhnhnmland, the *vir bonus* who restores a modicum of moderation and balance to a badly deranged Gulliver. Here we have merely found our own desired images of ourselves—benevolent critics who suffer Swift's insults as Mendez suffers Gulliver's. Like Mendez with Gulliver, we make it our work to retrieve Swift, particularly the Swift of Book 4, from the critical charge of lunacy, nursing him, critically, back to the moral equilibrium most clearly represented by his character Mendez. We send Swift back to the canon of the eighteenth century as Mendez sends Gulliver back to the common forms of Redriff.

But the fact that critics discover only their own reflections in the nemesistic mirror of Swift's satire is cause for little satisfaction to one who seriously considers Rodino's essay. The uncovering of one layer of a splendid lie only promises that more levels exist. Taking Mendez from Good Samaritan to splendid liar suggests that Mendez is Gulliver's own reflection, a fictional travel narrator insisting on literal truth. At the same time, as Rodino notices, the splendid lie is Swift's and so the reflection is from Swift to Mendez Pinto, wily authors, like Odysseus—yet another level of reflection—who send their lying creations on ultimately heroic missions of misdirection. The very multiplicity of reflections serves to undermine any critical project that claims to have found the tain of the Swiftian mirror.

If the search backward through successive mirrors is, as Rodino suggested, both necessary and ultimately futile, my backward reading makes me curious about the forward reflections of the work. Sinon is the instrument that opens the way to the destruction of Troy. Mendez Pinto, perhaps the greatest traveler of the European Age of Discovery, creates a first person narrator whose fictions seek to undermine the enterprise that is the bedrock of the Modern West. Their three-way reflection with Gulliver suggests the *Travels* is the work of a wily author who can make a Good Samaritan a splendid liar and a *vir bonus* all within an apocalyptic challenge, not merely to criticism, but to the powers criticism has served. Rodino's conservative deconstructive reading of the *Travels* may mark an epic beginning at the end of the Modern. As the story of the Trojan horse negotiates discourses from the nursery to the postgraduate seminar and out into the cultures that the *Odyssey* and the *Aeneid* help define, so the *Travels into Several Remote Nations* may be on the verge of being understood as the epic, at once ridiculous and horrific, of Modernity itself. Gulliver reaches Mendez, from a land where reason governs, on a boat he covers in, and with sails he fashions from, the skins of human beings. His literally productive use of human beings informs *A Modest Proposal*'s still more terrifying image of systematized human productivity in Dublin, an image, now attached to the names of death camps in other towns and cities, that defines the inhuman rational power of the Modern period. It is not, however, in figuring the horrors of Modernity that Swift's work may lay claim to the Modern epic, but in the telling of the story of a *Margit*, a story that draws the enormous reductive power of the critical *via moderna* into the irreducible ridicule of its satiric Nemesis.

AFTERWORD

Dear Frank,

You have often said that I am the most prompt of all your readers, and I have usually replied that it is no wonder: being far from the academy in my line of work and as one whose inclinations might have taken him there, I have found my small role in the margins of your academic work a pleasurable one. I recall this here, not because of my promptness this time, but as part of an explanation for my extraordinary delay. I know you were delighted when I told you that I wanted to reply more formally in writing this time. But I have misled you. I had hoped writing would allow me to find a voice to temper my unexpectedly harsh critique of *Swift as Nemesis*. But it has not. I take no pleasure in what follows.

I know that you cannot be expecting a negative critique when I have praised various parts of this work over the years you have been working on it. But this work is like a slave ship that collects a great group of vital individual parts and forces them on a deadening journey for the profit of a (critical) master. You know how much I enjoyed your work on Swift and Cowley. Though narrative skills have never been your strong suit, the power of the story you uncovered came through even your prose: the great friend of the new philosophers and great poet Cowley is answered by the upstart poet, Swift, under the painfully bad intellectual guidance of the great man Sir William Temple. And for all the embarrassing missteps of Swift's poem, it reveals the foundations of the intellectual path Swift would build his whole fabulous career upon. As I recall, this "foundational" chapter was to be at or very near the beginning of your book. Now I find it *after* your Gulliver chapters? Several years ago I could be confident that you would deny that you had made such an editorial decision in order to lead your book with a discussion of masturbation. But the tenure process has changed you, and I am afraid that if I were to ask for an explanation (which I will not), I would be served with a lecture on the realpolitik of academic publishing at the turn of the century.

Something very similar can be said about your work on Swift and Newton. I was infected with your enthusiasm when you made your "discovery" that Swift is specifically attacking Newton's *Principia* in *A Tale of a Tub*. But as with the Cowley chapter, your Newton chapter, which was to be literally central in this work, has been moved back. And it now occupies an odd position as the substantive end (though the work goes on) of your book. I also notice that you have backed away from the specificity of your "discovery." Now Swift is aiming at the entire seventeenth-century debate on air, in which the *Principia* can be read as one particularly important document. Growing up together you never gave me reason to suspect your courage. But the academy has done some terrible things to you. You show that the *Principia* was a work of vital importance to Bentley and Wotton, Swift's most immediate enemies. You show that a theory of ether is barely suppressed throughout the *Principia*. Is the risk really so great of saying what you believe?—that Swift took direct aim at Newton's greatest work?

What I have said so far was meant to be the positive part of my assessment. And indeed these things I have mentioned might be addressed in a thoroughgoing editorial process. But the problem with this work is, I'm afraid, something that—I here borrow the phrase you are so fond of from the *Tale*—"*aliqou modo essentiae adhaerere*."

Unlike those who will read the completed book, I know that you came upon—or you came to believe in—the Nemesis rubric well along the way of your work here. I was impressed early on with the way you drew references to Nemesis out of what are (symbolically at least) the satirist's first and last words. Your argument from Aristotle that Nemesis and satire were related in Swift's time, seemed plausible. But my initial enthusiasm was fueled by the expectation that, having identified this rubric, you would find Nemesis—not just Narcissus and Echo—throughout Swift's works. Even where you do find Nemesis, as in *The Lady's Dressing Room*, you use it along the way as if there were no need after your "theoretical" chapter to convince your readers that Swift identified with Nemesis.

Still I find I am avoiding the harsh thing I feel I must say. Throughout your previous writing on Swift you have presumed, as I suppose all critics do, to explain what Swift is saying, or doing, or not saying, or not doing in particular passages. In your own articulation of your Nemesis theory of satire, however, you take that authority away from critics: Swift's satiric texts mirror those who look upon them, including critics. You are at pains to make this point with respect to other critics in your last chapter. But what are you doing between your first and last chapters but revealing what Swift is "really" saying? When you find Temple or Cowley or Wotton or Newton's face in the satiric glass, aren't you recognizing every face but your own?

I have heard too many times how much you despise the biographical rehabilitation of Swift that has, in your view, attempted to tame a dangerously original mind. Your last chapter fairly seethes at the idea that a critic would attempt to make Swift acceptable in the pantheon of Leavis's "great tradition." For you, Nemesis is unattainable and indomitable. One cannot get around her in the same way one cannot get around the mirror that she and, in your theory, the satirist hold. Nemesis is ethically destructive. Her indignation is by definition righteous. Most importantly Nemesis is dangerous. You are at pains to point out that she has no interest in reform, only vengeance. The idea that destruction is a supremely ethical enterprise, is one you find in Nemesis and appropriate for the discipline you "profess," literary satire. It seems to me that in this work you create a Swift who, not unlike those Swifts of critics you call narcissistic, appears to your readers as a reflection of your own idealized image of yourself: the righteous professor of dangerous, antimodern truths.

It may be ungenerous to go on, but I cannot prevent myself from making one final and no doubt unfair point. One night over more than a few drinks, you told me that when you triumphantly presented your completed doctoral dissertation on Swift to your parents, your mother produced a story you had written when you were twelve or thirteen years old: it was a fifth book of *Gulliver's Travels*, and you had no recollection whatsoever of having written it. I made very little of the story at the time, but I became curious about it when I mentioned it on a later occasion and you angrily denied knowledge of our conversation and of the story. By your own account the story was juvenile and trite, but there is a connection, I am afraid, to your current work on Swift. Your early work was an attempt to finish Swift's work, to give some explanation to his impossible and improbable account. I think you said your Book 5 landed Gulliver in an insane asylum. In *Swift as Nemesis* you are still trying to complete Swift, your claims about the "openness" of satiric form notwithstanding. While in your juvenile eyes the world was sane and the man (Swift or Gulliver) was mad, you now know the world is mad and you hope for (and profess) the sanity of one who first pronounced it so. Perhaps the hope itself is noble. I wouldn't know. But your book has convinced me that Swift left a legacy for more than one asylum, and all these words after, in fiction or criticism, are so many footnotes scrawled on the walls of an institution you and your kind continue to call by his name.

Your friend, ——

REFERENCE MATTER

NOTES

PREFACE

1. See Toulmin's brief discussion of Gulliver in Lilliput as a critique of the impotence of the technically powerful. *Cosmopolis*, 197–98.

2. Miriam Starkman's *Swift's Satire on Learning in* A Tale of a Tub goes on to honor Swift's scientific targets as our noble progenitors (85–86). Herbert Davis says it was "necessary to admit that Swift did not realize that he was privileged to be living in the bright dawn of the scientific era." See Davis, *Jonathan Swift*, 207. More recently, the cultural historian Charles Olson claims *A Tale* and *Gulliver's Travels* "contain classic statements of conservative anti-scientific sentiment." See Olson, "Tory High-Church Opposition," 185.

On the other hand, studies of Swift's sources (including Starkman's) demonstrate that Swift was conversant in the scientific discourse of his day. Marjorie Nicolson investigated Swift's use of the *Philosophical Transaction of the Royal Society* for the *Travels* and considered at length Swift's knowledge of the work of Boyle and Newton, but she seems not to have connected these sources with *A Tale of a Tub*. See Nicolson, *Science and Imagination*, and Mohler, "The Scientific Background," 110–54. Frederik N. Smith has significantly expanded upon Nicolson's work with the *Travels*, suggesting Swift has Gulliver speak in the language of the Royal Society to show the limits of the literalist vocabulary. See Smith, "Scientific Discourse," 139–62.

Kenneth Craven's 1992 study, *Jonathan Swift and the Millennium of Madness*, argues that Swift understood the New Philosophy at a profound level. Craven's revisionary study calls for the kind of reconsideration of Swift that I attempt in this essay.

3. See Rhodes, *The Making*, 452.

CHAPTER 1, *Nemesistic Satire*

1. (*Metamorphoses* 3: ll. 389–90). A detailed treatment of Ovid's version of the myth including a discussion of the sexual nature of Echo's responses to Narcissus may be found in Kenneth Knoespel's *Narcissus and the Invention of Personal History*.

2. For a discussion of the flower in the Greek and Roman context, see Knoespel, 2–3.

3. The claim that Swift's work entraps and destroys readers is far from new. F. R. Leavis's reading of Swift as a destructive writer is perhaps the best-known instance of a critical position first articulated by Samuel Clarke in 1705. So-called "hard school" readings of *Gulliver's Travels* are often variations on the critical view that Swift was a dangerous, even evil writer. This book endorses such readings as largely accurate while uncovering an artistic context that illustrates the efficacy of Swift's vengeful satiric corpus. Leavis, Clarke, and certain other critics are discussed in the context of the relationship of criticism to the Nemesis myth in Chapter 7, below. For an interesting discussion of Swift's entrapping texts from the perspective of reader-response theory, see Richard Nash's "Entrapment and Ironic Mode."

4. This translation is taken from the *Oxford Authors Swift*, 694.

5. This reference to Swift's concern with self-love is more than rhetorical. The idea that self-love, as Swift says in *Cadenus and Vanessa*, "attends us first, and leaves us last," informs the premise of the *Verses on the Death of Dr. Swift* and appears as well in private correspondence. Narcissism is not something we can choose to avoid, for even such a decision would be an affirmation of it. Swift's satiric (nemesistic) temperament would seem to arise from this acute awareness of the motivating power of narcissism, including its power in his own actions and his own grief. As an artist deals in universals, Swift strives to identify with Nemesis. As an individual he seems acutely aware that he is no better able to evade narcissism than anyone else. This point is elaborated in the opening sections of Chapter 2, below.

Frederick M. Keener's important essay, "The Rub of Self-Love" in *The Chain of Becoming* shows that the problem of the distinction between self-love and self-interest was a major concern of a number of eighteenth-century thinkers, including Swift. Though my emphasis is different, I extend, in the chapters following on Gulliver, Keener's insight that Swift is acutely aware of and commenting on the "new" philosophical thinking about the self.

6. See "The Lady's Dressing Room"—

> But Vengeance, goddess never sleeping
> Soon punished Strephon for his peeping.
> (*Poems*, 451, ll. 119–20).

With reference to Alecto, one of the Erinyes who minister just punishment, Herbert Davis sees Swift "calling down vengeance from the skies," thinking "of himself as the scourge of the gods," and positioning himself as one who awards "those punishments the law demands" (*Essays*, 252–54). Davis links Swift to Greek and Roman notions of just punishment and draws the important conclusion that Swift as satirist "belongs ultimately to a wider world and an older tradition" (*Essays*, 259). His biographical focus, however, leads Davis to make the claim—for which I think there is little evidence in the satires—that Swift "was concerned rather to heal than to hurt." The older traditions of Nemesis and the Erinyes, and indeed of pre-Reform Christianity, recognized the ethical position of a righteous avenger.

7. A recent commentator on the *Poetics* has confirmed the reading that makes indignation (*nemesan*) the equivalent in comedy to pity in tragedy and links *nemesan* with *nemesis*. See Leon Golden's "Aristotle on the Pleasures of Comedy."

8. Discussing Swift in terms of eighteenth-century iconoclasm, Ronald Paulson describes Swift's work in a way that is entirely consistent with the Nemesis myth: Swift "reacts to an act of breaking"—the 'self-fragmenting of the Puritans'—with a more comprehensive one, in a characteristic Swiftean manner mimetic of their own ethos" (*Breaking*, 23). In other words, Swift "mirrors" his self-destructive subject in a manner that breaks or destroys comprehensively.

9. Later in this chapter, when discussing the works of Stephen Toulmin and Douglas Patey, I show how the Enlightenment is now coming to be understood as a reaction, not to scholasticism, but to Renaissance humanism.

10. There is probably no adequate way to define the term "contemporary criticism." In *The World, the Text, and the Critic*, Edward Said explores the question from a literary perspective, asking the reader to notice that today

> when professional students of literature now use words like "theory" and "criticism" it is not assumed that they must or should confine their interests to literary theory or literary criticism. The distinction between one discipline and another has been blurred precisely because fields like literature and literary study are no longer considered to be as all-encompassing or as synoptic as, until recently, they once were. (227)

It is no coincidence, as I argue below, that Said thinks Jonathan Swift, whose work is always both literary and worldly, serves as one of "the best critics" of "contemporary critical discourse" (28).

11. The discipline that is Freud's legacy has been revealingly concerned with the sociological manifestations of narcissism and the irony of psychiatry's role in promoting narcissistic behavior.

In 1982, Dr. Jarl Dyrud, professor of psychiatry at the University of Chicago, delivered the 25th Annual Frieda Fromm-Reichmann Memorial Lecture at the Clinical Center of the National Institute of Health in Washington. The text of his lecture on "Narcissus and Nemesis," published in *Psychiatry*, suggests that the occasion was one of nearly sublime satire. Addressing the elite of a profession whose founder wrote "On Narcissism," with a current literature replete with references to narcissism, the doctor defined his term in language suited to the uninitiated: "I chose 'Narcissus and Nemesis' as the title of this essay to remind us that 'Narcissistic' was originally a bad way to be and led to a bad end" (107). Like the speaker of Swift's *An Argument Against Abolishing Christianity*, Dyrud's disarming, contextually imbecilic observation gives way to a cunning attack on a trend he deems pernicious. His argument is interesting, not for whatever contribution it makes to his discipline's internecine struggles, but because the myth leads him to try to locate psychology in the context of its relation to modern culture. Dyrud does not doubt that *narcissistic* is the correct term for contemporary society, at least in the United States: "American society includes large numbers of people who exhibit self-absorption and shallow, unsatisfactory relationships with other people. To a sympathetic listener, they complain of feeling empty of purpose and of living meaningless lives. They seem to exist in a pallid world—not the dead world of the schizophrenic but one nonetheless insubstantial" (107). In sync with this cultural phenomenon, branches of modern psychology are working to normalize narcissism. Rather than helping people "to strip away illusion" in order to "find meaning and purpose in life," modern "self-psychologists" are suggesting "that a self, with itself in an envelope of mother as object, is the goal of all human activity" (112).

12. Spivak distinguishes her use of the story of Echo and Narcissus from the "modern Narcissus" in Freud, Lacan, and Lasch, which though distinct constructions of Narcissus, share a failure to examine "the frame" of the myth, and so ignore Echo. Her brief discussion of Lacan is, perhaps, most interesting in this context. Spivak argues that Lacan, in the "Mirror Stage" makes "the end of psychoanalysis . . . a rewriting of Narcissus's *iste ego sum* (I am that) into an ec-static "'*Thou art that*'" (22). Failing to see the

frame—particularly Echo's punishment by Juno—Lacan appropriates to the psychoanalyst the ability to reveal to the patient "the cipher of his mortal destiny." Spivak gives this revelation to Echo as the reward (that Echo is punished by Juno but not rewarded by Jupiter makes the myth "asymmetrical"), not as a positivist "ability," as in Lacanian psychoanalysis, but as "the instrument of the possibility of truth not dependent upon intention" (24).

13. In "Three-Part Inventions," a review of *The World, the Text, and the Critic*, Irvin Ehrenpreis attacked the details of Said's work on Swift. Even Ehrenpreis allowed, however, that Said's work on orientalism "sets fresh and important vistas before us" (37). My reading (particularly in Chapter 3, below) links Said's work on orientalism to his reading of Swift.

14. Consider, in particular, the conjunction Orwell—a writer celebrated for care and skill—uses in the following observations: "Swift ultimately blew everything to pieces in the only way that was feasible before the atomic bomb—that is, he went mad—but, as I have tried to show, his political aims were on the whole reactionary ones" (181). In spite of himself, Orwell ends up like a Laputan struck by his flapper. Here Orwell has seen, but refused to acknowledge, that the madness Swift portrays is modern madness, which finds its true emblem in the ultimately self-destructive machine.

15. The term is here quoted from Said (*World*, 35), but the concept belongs to Swift, as discussed in Chapter 5, below.

16. Another study that approaches Swift from a materialist point of view is Warren Montag's *The Unthinkable Swift*. Montag argues that in attempting to parody the philosophical works of his contemporaries, Swift has inadvertently extended the materialist implications of those works.

17. See Kelly's "After Eden" and *Swift and the English Language*.

18. See Smith's "Scientific Discourse and *The Philosophical Transactions*."

CHAPTER 2, *Gulliverian Narcissism*

1. When Bruno Bettelheim, in celebrated essays in the *New Yorker*, condemned the psychoanalytic profession for ignorance of the myths that are essential to reading Freud, he inadvertently diagnosed a critical problem that applies as well to reading Swift and any number of authors. As professional or amateur psychoanalysts—few now escape one category or the other—we regularly employ the formidable terms of psychology without conscious reference to the myths, rarely aware even of the narrative presence of Psyche herself. It is an irony worthy of Swift that the most sig-

nificant (though not the only) exception within the psychoanalytic discourse is Freud's work itself. Reading Swift's work in dialogue with the myth of Narcissus has the salutary effect of illustrating how much of what we now think of as revelations of psychoanalytic theory is actually available directly from the myths, at least to great readers like Swift and Freud.

2. This chapter owes a considerable debt to Fox's essays, "The Myth of Narcissus," and "Defining Eighteenth-Century Psychology." Both studies provide important correctives to anachronistic uses of psychological terms. The great accomplishment of Fox's work is that, rather than broadly dismissing psychological references as anachronisms, he uncovers a psychological vocabulary of the eighteenth century that has many later correspondences.

The current argument builds on Fox's work by recognizing the role of Nemesis in the myth of Narcissus and in Swift's understanding of the satiric mirror. Without Nemesis, Fox's reading looks for the significance of Gulliver's illness in the context of Swift's "Christian" and "moralist" identity. Seeing the satiric text in terms of the pool of Nemesis reveals that the myth of Narcissus in the *Travels* is not a general moralist statement against individual narcissism, but a detailed and devastating reflection of how individual narcissism is protected by, and fostered in, modern scientific culture.

3. I am working from the following approximate chronology culminating with the earliest date Gulliver mentions, May 4, 1699:

1660: Born in Nottinghamshire
1674: Enrolled Emmanuel College Cambridge at age fourteen, "resided three years"
1677: Bound Apprentice to Mr. James Bates for "four years"
1681: Studied Physick at Leiden "two Years seven Months"
1684: Surgeon to the *Swallow* continuing "three Years and a half"
1688: Settled in London until Master Bates dies "two Years after"
1690: Surgeon in two ships "for six Years"
1696: Stays home "three years"
1699: "Set sail from Bristol"

When Gulliver's children are born is not entirely clear. When he returns from his voyage to Lilliput in 1702 his son Johnny is in grammar school and his daughter Betty is "at her needle-work." Since he is married in about 1689, his oldest child would be twelve or thirteen years old.

4. In "Swift's Spirit Reconjured: das Dong-an-sich," Hugh Ormsby-Lennon reads *A Tale of a Tub* and other writings by Swift for evidence of Swift's own sexuality and its connection to Swift's writing. In attacking

theories that Swift suffered from "masturbatory insanity," Ormsby-Lennon argues that "Swift was privy to what people had always done with themselves," and suggests that he would more properly be termed mad if he had not occasionally "conjured his own spirit" (77). Whatever the case with respect to Swift's own sexual practices, there is evident sense in the argument that Swift would have known that people other than the insane masturbate. And of course the idea of "marrying rather than burning" was a scriptural commonplace, quoted here from Swift's earliest extant letter.

5. I am specifically recognizing that the period of change Gulliver's biography spans involves major changes in the economic order of Europe. I am in no sense suggesting that, because Swift attacks the emerging mercantile order, he is lamenting the loss of the former aristocratic order. The theory of satire I am working with precludes attempts to derive a satirist's affirmative position from what is represented as ridiculous.

6. Smith's work is very important to the general argument made here about the dehumanizing effects of the new science. Showing that Gulliver possesses a "Baconian notion of science founded not on rhetoric but on cautious, neutralized observation of phenomena," Smith speaks of the Royal Society's language as seeking a "new objectivity" (141). The vocabulary of the new science unwittingly masks inescapable links between observer and observed, locating what is true, and therefore valuable, beyond the corrupting influence of the human feeling. The vocabulary he brings with him on his voyages directly informs the misanthrope Gulliver becomes.

7. The relationship between Puritanism and the New Science is discussed in Chapters 5 and 6, below.

8. In *Patient's Progress*, Dorothy Porter and Roy Porter have examined the transformations of the medical profession in the eighteenth century, including the importance of the new science and the economic conditions of the new medicine.

9. In the "Digression on Madness" Swift's Hack offers two examples of how the vapors of madness work in the affairs of state. In one case Henry IV of France is said to have raised an invincible force sufficient to give rise to fears "he had laid a scheme for universal monarchy" because sexual arousal without emission caused a vapor to arise from his semen to his brain: "The very same principle that influences a *bully* to break the windows of a whore who has jilted him, naturally stirs up a great prince to raise mighty armies and dream of nothing but sieges, battles, and victories" (*OAS*, 140). In the second example, Louis XIV's violent national behavior is traced to his anus: "The same spirits which, in their superior progress, would conquer a kingdom, descending upon the *anus* conclude in a *fistula*" (*OAS*, 141).

In "The Excremental Vision," Norman O. Brown focuses on only the second example in arguing that Swift "anticipates the psychoanalytic theorem that an anal sublimation can be decomposed into simple anality." Swift, of course, gives the "theorem" to his Hack who understands that the "gentle, courteous, and candid reader" will not believe that he (the Hack) is mad though he attests to it. The insight that the sexual drive in the context of universal narcissism informs human behavior is less an anticipation of modern psychology than it is a confirmation of mythic sources of the works of Swift and Freud. The mad person is the one who, with the Hack, thinks the mythic insight can be used systematically.

10. In *Satire and Sentiment, 1660–1830*, Claude Rawson discusses the "revolutionary mass-murderousness" of the gunpowder episode, reading Swift's critique of modern warfare as fitting only uncomfortably within the Augustan imagination that informs Swift's satiric identity.

11. Though the terms *alienate* and *alienation* are not without potentially confusing resonances here, they seem appropriate nonetheless. Gulliver is an alien in *Laputa* in the most obvious sense of the word. His correspondence to those alienated (in a modernist sense) within Laputan society is striking and directly relevant to the work's representation of the effect of a scientific culture. Finally alienation carries from *alienatio* the sense of the madness, a consequence of Gulliver's own alien existence with respect to his home culture.

Robert Elliot refers to Gulliver's alienation in arguing that "a close reading of Gulliver's fourth voyage is such a shocking experience as to anesthetize the feeling for the ludicrous of even the most sensitive reader," "Satirist Satirized," 39.

12. In *Jonathan Swift and the Age of Compromise*, Kathleen Williams reads Swift's view of rationality in the context of Montaigne's *Apology*, 50–51; 87–88.

CHAPTER 3, *Traveling Metaphor*

1. Percy Adams makes the point, in each of his two great books on travel literature, that I am here drawing out of Van Den Abbeele's work. That is, Adams's literary historical approach traces movements of the idea of travel throughout this historical period, and Adams is of course especially important for exploring the way travel "truth" and travel "lies" exist in the same text. In *Travel Literature and the Evolution of the Novel*, Adams traces the relationship between travel-writing and the new science, particularly in the chapter entitled, "Language and Style."

2. For a discussion of the relationship between Cowley's *Proposition for the Advancement of Experimental Philosophy* and Bacon's *New Atlantis*, see Nethercot's *Abraham Cowley: The Muse's Hannibal*, 184–85.

3. See Merchant on the New Philosophy and the penetration of nature.

4. See Frank Boyle, *Heretic*; Gerald J. Pierre, "Gulliver's Voyage to China" and *The Influence of Sir William Temple*; Fumiko Takase, "The Houyhnhnms"; and Sutherland, "Satire and the Use of History" in *The Art of the Satirist.*

5. Valignano, "Admiranda Regini Sinensis."

6. Voltaire makes this observation in his *Lettres Chinoises*, 29: 471.

7. The story of China's role in European intellectual life in the late seventeenth and early eighteenth centuries has been extensively studied. See, for example, Virgile Pinot, *La Chine*; Basil Guy, *The French Image of China*; Arnold H. Rowbotham, "The Impact of Confucianism."

8. Swift, Alexander Pope, John Gay, John Arbuthnot, Thomas Parnell, and Robert Harley formed a literary club that they called the Scriblerians. For a detailed history, see Charles Kerby-Miller's introduction to the *Memoirs* of Martinus Scriblerus.

9. Charles Kerby-Miller, the modern editor of Scriblerus's *Memoirs*, has argued that the idea for *Gulliver's Travels* grew out of the Scriblerians' discussions of a satiric book of travels, though he is at pains to point out how completely Swift transformed the kernel of the idea he took from the club. Ehrenpreis follows Kerby-Miller in this reading, recognizing there is a "grain of truth" in tracing the origin of *Gulliver's Travels* to the Scriblerus Club, while at the same time recognizing that Swift fundamentally changed the plan for the satire itself. *Swift*, 3: 445–46.

10. In Brobdingnag the reference is to printing in China rather than specifically to the Chinese language. *PW*, 11: 136.

11. Wilkins's *An Essay Toward a Real Character and Philosophic Language* (1668), which is often pointed to as a source for the project of the "School of Languages," considers and rejects the real character of the Chinese, before advancing its own scheme (450–52).

12. In praising the Chinese, Pantoia was echoing the position his order had taken in the early days of their missionary effort. This effort began with Francis Xavier, whose experiences in Japan convinced him that if China were converted, the rest of the East would follow. But missionary efforts were unsuccessful until a Jesuit named Alessandro Valignano developed, beginning in 1577, what became known as the accommodation approach to the Chinese, a process of "becoming Chinese," which involved an educational saturation in the language and culture of the Chinese. Va-

lignano's justification for this most unorthodox approach to another culture was articulated in a work entitled "Admiranda Regni Sinensis," which speaks of the Chinese as civilized and virtuous to a degree Europeans had not imagined possible outside of Christendom. Indeed, Valignano suggests, in many moral virtues, the Chinese were superior to Europeans. Pantoia's positive statements about Chinese virtues are best understood in terms of the Jesuit approach, which was premised on the idea that the Chinese were a uniquely admirable people, while his negative views may be traced to his experience as one of two Europeans on the initial modern trip by Westerners to Beijing, the center of the Eastern world. For discussions of the Jesuit's China mission, see Spence's *The Memory Palace*; Trevor-Roper's "A Jesuit Adventure"; Rowbotham's *Missionary and Mandarin*; Dunne's *Generation of Giants.*

13. In the work by Wilkins on the real character, for example, his rejection of Chinese as a universal language is in part because of the difficulty of pronouncing a word "according to its various Accents" (452). In Trigault and Ricci's *Discourse of China*, in the Purchas collection of travels that Swift owned, the Jesuit writers observe that "no Word" is pronounced without the aid of one of five "Accents," 12: 422.

14. An interesting discussion of Swift's use of Temple's summary Confucianism occurs in W. O. S. Sutherland's *The Art of the Satirist* (116–22). Sutherland argues to a nearly opposite conclusion to that I set forth here.

CHAPTER 4, *Poetry and Science*

1. See Nicolson's reading of Donne and the New Philosophy in *Science and Imagination*, 53–57.

2. For an extremely detailed and often insightful study of Donne's knowledge and use of the New Philosophy, including an historical discussion of critical responses to the lines quoted, see Pamela Gossin's dissertation, *Poetic Resolutions of Scientific Revolutions*," chap. 1.

3. Swift used the phrase "studied in the world's disease" in his *Ode to the Athenian Society* (*Poems*, 138), which I discuss in the body of this essay. With this reference, however, I mean to refer more generally to his extended study of the ills of the human condition. George Ashe, Archbishop Marsh, and John Arbuthnot, each connected with the New Philosophy, are a few of those among Swift's friends and acquaintances who were very much involved with the New Philosophy: see Ehrenpreis's chapters on "Trinity College" and "The Dublin Philosophical Society" in vol. 1, *Mr. Swift and his Contemporaries*. Swift read and borrowed from the

Philosophical Transactions of the Royal Society: see Nicolson and Mohler on "The Scientific Background of Swift's 'Voyage to Laputa'" in *Science and Imagination.*

4. I am drawing a contrast between the beginning and end of the seventeenth century. Donne's *First Anniversarie* is a work of 1611, while Swift asks where one should search for fame in *Ode to the Athenian Society* of 1692, l. 175.

5. The Boyle lectures were delivered in large churches in or around London, and St. Paul's Cathedral (rebuilt since Donne was dean) was the primary site for many years. Samuel Clarke's important lectures, which relied heavily on Clarke's interpretation of Newton's thought, were delivered in St. Paul's. For a discussion of the social and political implications of these lectures see Margaret Jacob's *The Newtonians.*

6. Nethercot says Cowley's "position as a major English poet was considered by his contemporaries as secure as Shakespeare's own" (preface). Among his admirers was Swift himself: see the discussions in Ehrenpreis's *Mr. Swift,* 1: 112–14, and Nokes's *Jonathan Swift,* 20–21. The argument of the present essay works on the very conservative assumption that Swift might admire Cowley's poetic and yet revile Cowley's participation in the hagiography of the members of the Royal Society.

7. The Athenian Society was, in fact, the project of a bookseller, John Dunton, who employed a group of writers to publish a popular journal called the *Athenian Mercury.* See Joseph M. Levine's *Battle of the Books,* 29–30. Sir William Temple, in whose employ Swift was at the time, contributed to this journal. Therefore it is at least plausible that Swift might have thought the Athenian Society was in some way comparable to the Royal Society. See Ehrenpreis's discussion in *Mr. Swift,* 1: 109–31. On the other hand A. C. Elias Jr. raises the possibility that Swift was writing on more than one level: the surface level for Temple and Lady Giffard, his employers, with a satiric subtext in which he expresses his own disdain, or at least amusement, at the Athenian project. Elias points out that Dunton's work was a "grab bag of miscellaneous curiosities and advice to the lovelorn," and that Dunton is a satiric target in *A Tale of a Tub.* See *Swift at Moor Park* (7–94).

The reading of Swift's *Ode to the Athenian Society* that I advance does not depend on what Swift knew or did not know for certain about Dunton's Athenians, but the sophistication of Swift's treatment of Cowley supports Elias's suspicions that Swift was up to much more in this poem than a straightforward verse panegyric.

8. There have been a number of critical approaches to the poem in ad-

dition to the historical discussions referenced in the previous note. A common approach has been to consider the poem's music, structure, and use of poetic language unhistorically, and this has earned it the often repeated distinction of being Swift's "worst poem." Another approach reads Swift's work in terms of its stylistic debt to Cowley's English adaptation of the Pindaric form. See Peter J. Schakel's *The Poetry of Jonathan Swift*, 7–28. More recently critics have discovered in Swift's *Ode* certain incipient intellectual positions that inform Swift's attacks on the Modern in *A Tale of a Tub*, including thrusts at Hobbesian materialism and Greek atomism. See Roger Lund's "Strange Complicities."

9. Nora Crow Jaffe makes the claim that Swift's *Ode* is an obvious reply to Cowley's *Ode* in *The Poet Swift* (64). Ehrenpreis briefly looks into the relationship between the poems, finding that Swift's poem is "in some ways" a reply to Cowley. Ehrenpreis concludes that Cowley was "less conservative" in his assessment of science than was Swift, *Mr. Swift*, 1: 117.

10. In *Abraham Cowley*, James Taaffe says: "Cowley was a spokesman for the 'college,' and Sprat considered his prose essay, *A Proposition for the Advancement of Experimental Philosophy*, a crucial document in the formation of the society which Cowley had joined in 1662, its first year," 96.

11. See Dear's *Discipline and Experience*, especially pages 153–61.

12. The satire in the third book of *Gulliver's Travels* makes the journey to Laputa (*la puta*), a place where the new science offers the false and ultimately diseased promise of material deliverance.

13. William Wotton, in his *Reflections*, refers to Descartes as the forerunner of the Royal Society who "put the World in Hopes of a Masculine Off-spring," 348.

14. Feminist critics have argued that the new mechanical philosophy was defined in inherently misogynist terms. See, for example, the discussion of Bacon and other New Philosophers of the seventeenth century in Carolyn Merchant's *The Death of Nature*.

15. Swift is calling on an ancient poetic image of Echo as the painter's subject. See John Hollander's discussion of this tradition in *The Figure of Echo*.

16. In his *Proposition for the Advancement of Learning*, Cowley argued against assuming there is little new of use to be learned:

> If he conceives that all are already exhausted, let him consider that many lightly thought so hundred years ago, and yet nevertheless since that time whole Regions of Art have been discovered, which the Ancients as little dreamt of as they did of America. There is yet

> many a Terra Incognita behind, to exercise our diligence, and let us exercise it never so much, we shall leave work enough too for our Posterity. (2: 285)

Wotton, who lived to see the work of Boyle and Newton, had doubts about this last point.

17. The bee in *The Battle of the Books* describes his work as having "universal range, with long search, and much study," *OAS*, 9, and Aesop interprets this, with application to the Ancients, as representative of their "infinite labour, and search, and ranging through every corner of nature," *OAS*, 10. The modern spider, on the other hand, is ridiculed for his "lazy contemplation of four inches round," *OAS*, 9.

18. R. V. Sampson makes the important point that, while Descartes's "interpretation of the new scientific method was fundamentally scholastic in spirit," he largely succeeded in convincing his audience that he had made a complete break with a largely useless past, *Progress*, 20–38. In *The Battle of the Books*, Swift makes the assertion of present superiority—the Moderns begin the battle by demanding the Ancients vacate Parnassus—a basic characteristic of the Modern, and therefore sees Descartes as one in a line of "restless spirits" whose "books of controversy" find their true original in Duns Scotus.

For J. B. Bury "Cartesianism was equivalent to a declaration of the Independence of Man," 65. For Derrida, Descartes's cogito is the "zero point at which determined meaning and nonmeaning come together at their origin," *Writing*, 56.

19. It is interesting to contrast Nicolson's suggestion in *Science and Imagination* that science and poetry began to go separate ways during the seventeenth century with her argument in *Newton Demands the Muse* that "Poets, philosophers, scientists may visit each other's countries of the mind with pleasure and profit," but each ultimately remains a stranger in the other's lands, 132–33. She suggests, moreover, that it has always been this way, though she leaves open the question of where Lucretius should be entombed.

20. I do not mean to suggest that Locke follows or agrees with Descartes's views on language. Rather I am recognizing that since Locke himself termed "Descartes's principles . . . the most intelligible and most consistent with itself of any yet to be met with," it is appropriate to speak of his work as an extension of the Cartesian project. For a discussion of the close relationship between Locke's thought and Descartes's thought, with detailed distinctions, see John W. Yolton's *Perceptual Acquaintance*, 2–6, 88–94.

21. For a discussion of the history of the antipoetic sentiments of Newton and Locke, see Mordechai Feingold's "Newton and Locke," 302–4.

22. In *Descartes's Metaphysical Physics*, Daniel Garber argues that a general failure to recognize the interdependence of Descartes's metaphysical and natural philosophical work has led to distortions. Ironically, what Garber terms anachronistic—the attempt to distinguish Descartes's philosophic work from his scientific work—might also be termed Cartesian.

23. Aristotle and Descartes meet again in the *Travels* where Swift's treatment is less poetic but more immediately clear. When Gulliver has Descartes and Gassendi explain their systems to Aristotle, the

> great Philosopher freely acknowledged his own Mistakes in Natural Philosophy, because he proceeded in many things upon Conjecture, as all Men must do; and he found, that *Gassendi*, who had made the Doctrine of *Epicurus* as palatable as he could, and the *Vortices* of *Descartes*, were equally exploded. He predicted the same Fate for *Attraction*, whereof the present Learned are such zealous Asserters. He said, that new Systems of Nature were but new Fashions, which would vary in every Age; and even those who pretended to demonstrate them from Mathematical Principles would flourish but a short Period of Time, and be out of Vogue when that was determined. (*PW*, 11: 197–98)

Prior to Thomas Kuhn's *The Structure of Scientific Revolutions*, Swift's view here was easily dismissed. These issues are discussed in greater detail in Chapter 5, below.

24. Although many studies now trace the links between alchemy and the new science, Isaac Newton's career, which began and ended with a determined pursuit of the Philosopher's Stone, suggests that barriers Modern scientists were trying to erect between their disciplines and Modern science's alchemical past were less substantial than developmental histories of science suggest. For a discussion of Newton's view of alchemy, see Gale E. Christianson's *In the Presence of the Creator.*

25. The motto was adapted from Horace's *Epistles* (1: i) and was meant to signal an independence from authority, especially that of Aristotle. So among the ironies in the choice of this motto is that the idea is expressed "in the words of," and so by the authority of, the satiric poet. For a discussion of the context of the motto see Aarsleff's *From Locke to Saussure*, 267, n. 21.

CHAPTER 5, *Transubstantiation, Transmutation, and Critical Theory*

1. While trying to "counterbalance" the view that makes Scotus a "destructive critic," Copleston nevertheless highlights the features that comprise Swift's characterization. Acknowledging that Scotus "frequently criticizes Thomist positions," that he was "a subtle and sometimes a tortuous thinker and dialectician," 2: 484, Copleston sees Scotus as an important step to the later "radical and destructive criticism" characteristic of Ockham:

> When Scotus asserted that certain of the divine attributes cannot be proved by natural reason and when he denied the demonstrative character of the arguments adduced for the immortality of the human soul, he did not intend to undermine positive philosophy; but, looking at the matter from the purely historical viewpoint, his criticism obviously helped prepare the way for the much more radical criticism of Ockham. (2: 485)

The most important way in which Copleston affirms Swift's view of the history of the Modern is by linking Scotus with criticism (3: 10–12). Copleston's repeated assertion that Scotus had no intentions of contributing to this movement of the Modern serves to confirm Swift's assertion, however uncharitable or unscholarly it may be in spirit, that the Modern, and specifically modern criticism, can be traced to the original dunce.

2. The full text of the passage from *Areopagitica* suggests the extent to which Milton sees the problem of distinguishing good from evil as fundamental to the human condition:

> Good and evil we know in the field of this world grow up together almost inseparably; and the knowledge of good is so involved and interwoven with the knowledge of evil, and in so many cunning resemblances hardly to be discerned, that those confused seeds which were imposed on Psyche as an incessant labor to cull out and sort asunder, were not more intermixed. It was from out the rind of one apple tasted, that the knowledge of good and evil, as two twins cleaving together, leaped forth into the world. And perhaps this is that doom which Adam fell into of knowing good and evil, that is to say, of knowing good by evil. (728)

3. For a discussion of Swift and Milton, see chap. 4 of Craven's *Jonathan Swift and the Millennium of Madness*. Note in particular Craven's discussion of Swift's poem *A Dialogue Between an Eminent Lawyer and Dr. Swift*, in which Swift asks if he must . . .

sing like one of Milton's choir,
Where Devils to a vale retreat
And call the laws of wisdom fate.
(ll. 40–42)

4. See Walter Curry's *Milton's Ontology*; Dennis R. Danielson's *Milton's Good God*; John P. Rumrich's "Milton."

5. In referring here to the legacies of Aquinas and Scotus, I am distinguishing between what can be taken specifically from their work and what Swift sees as the historically verified implications of their work. Rather than questioning the faith or intentions of either theologian, I am arguing that Swift sees their controversy (Aquinas's synthesis inviting Scotus's attacks) as a prototype of Modern controversy generally, not simply because it can be called a controversy, but because it is a dispute that turns on an attempt to unify or harmonize material (natural) and spiritual (revealed) knowledge. Swift, I am arguing, sees the Thomistic synthesis as one that leads inadvertently to discussions of the spiritual that are mediated by an Aristotelian vocabulary inappropriate to and ultimately corrosive of a belief in "things invisible."

6. I make no claims in this discussion of transubstantiation to represent fairly the variety of opinions, ancient and modern, that are available on the subject, or to advance a true reading of the history of the Eucharist. I am, rather, attempting to understand the considerable significance Swift attaches to his understanding of this history.

The *New Catholic Encyclopedia* first locates the notion that the bread and wine are "transmuted" into the body and blood of Christ in the fourth century and then traces this idea through to the thirteenth century and Thomas Aquinas's summary of the "adequate formulation" of the doctrine: "The whole substance of the bread is changed into the whole substance of Christ's body, and the whole substance of the wine is changed into the whole substance of Christ's blood. Hence this conversion . . . may be designated by a name of its own, transubstantiation" (14: 259).

Some scholars have pointed out that earlier notions of substantial change can be distinguished from the thirteenth-century concepts that depended heavily on Aristotle's view of reality. For the Patristic theologian, Edward Schillebeeck argues: "The bread and wine were, after the consecration, to be sacramental *forms* in which the body of the Logos *appeared*. They had, in other words, lost their natural independence as things of nature—they had been dispossessed of themselves (*de-substantiatio*) and possessed by the Logos, received into the body of the Logos (*trans-substantiatio*)" (69). The same theologian argues that to understand what was meant by the pronouncement of the Council of Trent on the Eucharist, we have to perceive three levels of meaning in Aquinas's explication of the doctrine: "The level of *faith* (the special eucharistic presence), the *ontological* level (the change of being or *trans-entatio*) and the level of natural philosophy (*trans-substantiatio*)" (63).

For Swift, rightly or wrongly, it was not so complicated. By introducing the third level, and particularly by *naming* the doctrine with the term associated with natural philosophy, the Christian Logos was being traded for an older Greek *logos*, which was the beginning of the reduction of revealed religious truth to a system that, like other systems, might be exploded.

7. For a discussion of the problems with common modern images of alchemy, see chap. 1 of Nicholl's *The Chemical Theatre*.

8. Paracelsus, for example, claims that the "great virtues that lie hidden in nature would never have been revealed if alchemy had not uncovered them and made them visible," 144. One such discovery is of the "*Tinctura*, the last arcanum," which, "like the *rebis*—the bisexual creature—transmutes silver and other metals to gold . . . transforms the body, removing its harmful parts, its crudity, its incompleteness, and transforms everything into a pure, noble, and indestructible being," 148. For a discussion of the alchemists' contributions to experimental science, see Webster's *From Paracelsus to Newton*.

9. See Rosenheim, *Swift and the Satirist's Art*, 23. Reading Swift's work as a type of comedy other than satire is the unintentional effect of Phillip Harth's *Swift and Anglican Rationalism*. I agree with Harth that Swift was conversant with the works of the Anglican apologists Harth identifies as Anglican rationalists. But Harth's statement that Swift's religious satire in *A Tale of a Tub* "was already somewhat old-fashioned when Swift wrote it," 153, is premised on the idea that Swift can "hardly . . . be expected" to have been "completely *au courant* and aware of new trends in religious controversy," 163. This expectation evidently led Harth to overlook Swift's attack on the Newtonians.

10. Swift's contemporaries, of course, did not have the same narrow view of alchemy as a fraudulent discipline that develops as alchemy recedes into history. We might, however, be guided in the contemporary view by William Wotton who, in his *Reflections*, considers that alchemy may once have been a noble field of study but has declined to a point where it can not be countenanced by serious scholars:

> Whereas afterwards, every now and then, Footsteps of cheating Alchemists are to be met with in the *Byzantine* Historians. It was not

> possible to pretend to greater Secrecy in the Manner of their Operations, than is now to be found in all Writing of Modern *Adept Philosophers* (as they call themselves). And yet these Men, who will not reveal their Process would think themselves affronted, if any Man should question the real Existence of their Art, 118.

And it was not uncommon to link transubstantiation and transmutation as related frauds. Visiting Vienna in January 1717, Mary Wortley Montagu observed that

> There is indeed a prodigious number of alchymists at Vienna; the philosopher's stone is the great object of zeal and science; and those who have more reading and capacity than the vulgar, have transported their superstition (shall I call it?) or fanaticism from religion to chymistry; and they believe in a new kind of transubstantiation, which is designed to make the laity as rich as the other kind has made the priesthood. (1, 142)

CHAPTER 6, *A Critical Theory of Air*

1. See Kelly's "After Eden" and *Swift and the English Language*; Craven's *Jonathan Swift*; Smith's "Scientific Discourse."

2. Pamela Gossin, in her remarkable dissertation, *Poetic Resolutions*, traces with great detail many historical and intellectual links between Swift and Newton, though she reads the significance of her findings in ways that are often contrary to the conclusions I set forth here. Gossin and I agree, however, that in the "Apology" Swift was drawing a parallel between his *Tale* and Newton's *Principia*. Gossin, no doubt influenced by the critics who doubted Swift's interest and/or ability to read the great scientist's work, assumes Swift was pleading in a remarkably straightforward way for the kind of respect accorded the *Principia*. This deeply improbable assumption leaves Gossin searching for an explanation for the "striking" (234) change in Swift's attitude between the 1710 "Apology" and the 1726 *Travels*. The evidence in Gossin, particularly when combined with the additional details—Swift's use of Bentley's Boyle lectures; Clarke's "Newtonian" attack on *A Tale*—provided in the current chapter, make it far more than likely that Swift had a deeply ironic attitude toward the Newtonian enterprise throughout the period.

3. In the "Apology," Swift says the *Tale* was completed in 1696. While there is no reason to accept this claim whole—there would seem to be little doubt he at least reworked his text before publishing it in 1704—it

seems likely that some substantially complete form of the work existed at that time. *OAS*, 617, n. 62. Bentley's lectures were published in 1692 and 1693 and are explicitly referenced by Wotton in his 1694 *Reflections*, which directly precipitated the *Battle of the Books* controversy.

4. Clarke's attack on *A Tale* is discussed in Chapter 7, below. See also Boyle's "Profane and Debauched Deist."

5. The most influential proponent of this reading was Irvin Ehrenpreis. Suggesting that Swift mistreated Wotton and Bentley because they engaged in a controversy with Temple, Ehrenpreis finds that at "the heart of the digression on critics one finds little that Swift really stood for," 1: 209.

6. The controversy between Temple, Bentley, and Wotton, which eventually involved Swift, has been examined most recently in *The Battle of the Books* by Joseph M. Levine. This generally exhaustive study overlooks what I maintain (in the paragraphs that follow) is the central issue of the controversy: Wotton and Bentley's quasi-scientific basis for publicly charging Temple with contributing to the spread of atheism.

7. Bentley, *Eight Boyle Lectures on Atheism*, 7: 8. Subsequent references to this work are indicated by the sermon number and page.

8. Wotton says this explicitly in his preface: "But I had another, and a more powerful Reason, to move me to consider this Subject; and that was, that I did believe it might be some way subservient to Religion it self." *Reflections*, preface (unnumbered), 5–6. In this context it is important to point out that Bentley's scholarly demolition of Temple's claims for the *Epistles* of Phalaris—the usual focal point of critical discussions of this episode—was appended to the *second* edition of Wotton's *Reflections*. The controversy was fully engaged before Bentley was enlisted to call Temple's ancient learning into question.

9. Temple's modern biographers generally regard him a deist. See Marburg-Kirk's *Sir William Temple*, 18, 34–35; Faber, 133–36.

10. The Hack's "phenomenon of vapours" is an episode so richly allusive one is tempted, as with Swift's sartorial sect, to put aside claims for particular satiric targets in favor of illustrations of the kind of targets Swift aimed at. Hugh Ormsby-Lennon convincingly argues that "a veritable gallimaufry of sources informs Swift's account of cerebral function." Pointing out that Aristotle understood brain function by analogy to "steams" rising from the earth, Ormsby-Lennon shows how seventeenth-century commentators on the brain appropriated the imagery. Further, Ormsby-Lennon argues that Swift is interested in combining Aristotle's metaphor with atomist methodology. See "Swift's Spirit Reconjured," 31–37. Acknowledging the sources Ormsby-Lennon has identified, the current work argues

that Swift is satirizing the metaphor and methodology in their specifically new philosophical context. That is, with Boyle and Newton and other New Philosophers being heralded by Wotton and Bentley for revolutionizing our understanding of the world by rehabilitating atomist methodologies, Swift is most immediately connected to what is the most profound articulation of the circulating vapor motif.

11. Here in particular I am indebted to Steven Shapin and Simon Schaffer's discussion of the Boyle/Hobbes dispute in *Leviathan and the Air-Pump*.

12. *Eight Boyle Lectures*, 7, 9.

13. Ibid., 4, 6.

14. For a discussion of the ways Anglican churchmen came to see and employ Newtonian thought, see Margaret Jacob, *The Newtonians*.

15. (*Papers and Letters*, 179–80). Newton's "Hypothesis Touching on the Theory of Light and Colors," was read to and debated by the Royal Society over several sessions in late 1675 and early 1676, but was not published until 1744. I am using this paper, not because Swift's attack is based on it, but because it succinctly illustrates both the significance of a theory of air in Newton's intellectual framework and, most importantly, how Newton's view of air was conditioned by this seventeenth-century debate. I will also argue that this Newtonian framework was available to a reader approaching Newton's published works from the perspective of the debate on air.

The circulating vapors are fundamental to Newton's work. Consider this passage from a letter from Newton to Robert Boyle on the relationship of ether to gravity:

> If you consider, then, how by the continual fermentations made in the bowels of the earth there are aerial substances raised out of all kinds of bodies, all which together make the atmosphere, and that of all these the metallic are the most permanent. . . . Thus, I say, it ought to be with the metallic exhalations raised in the bowels of the earth by the action of acid menstruums, and thus it is with the true permanent air; for this, as in reason it ought to be esteemed the most ponderous part of the atmosphere, because the lowest, so it betrays its ponderosity, by making vapors ascend readily in it, by sustaining mists and clouds of snow, and by buoying up gross and ponderous smoke. (*Papers and Letters*, 253)

16. An attempt to explain how metaphor is at once essential to and undermining of the New Philosophical thought appears in Colin Murray Turbayne's discussion of Descartes and Newton in *The Myth of Metaphor*, 28–53. One might, with significant qualifications, argue that Swift and

Turbayne reach for related concepts in their readings of the metaphors of the New Philosophy, Swift representing mimetically what Turbayne tries to represent critically.

Recently Peter Dear has discussed this topic with great clarity, tracing the development of New Philosophical ideas about art and nature and the important metaphors these ideas engendered. See his chapter "Art, Nature, Metaphor" in *Discipline and Experience*.

17. In *The Janus Faces of Genius*, B. J. T. Dobbs illustrates how Newton's alchemical speculations are intrinsic to his New Philosophical discoveries, including his understanding of gravity. In *Force in Newton's Physics*, R. S. Westfall argues that aether as it had generally been understood in seventeenth-century mechanical thought was crucial in the development of Newton's thoughts on gravity. Westfall argues, however, that "force"—the central concept of Newtonian dynamics—replaced (it would not be wrong, perhaps, to say transmutated) aether in the years during which the *Principia* was produced; 395–400, and passim.

18. Historians of science argue with excellent reason that Newton had moved on from his interest in aether (at least as an explanation of gravity) by the time he wrote the *Principia*, though he returned to it later. See Westfall's *Force in Newton's Physics*, 424–67. Westfall's magisterial book in many respects confirms the reading of the *Principia* I am attributing to Swift. Aether was important to Newton early on, according to Westfall, because Newton was a mechanical philosopher working in the tradition of seventeenth-century mechanical philosophers who used aether to give mechanical rather than occult explanations to observed phenomena. In the *Principia*, Newton says he is concerned to give only mathematical representations of the laws of nature and will not speculate on fundamental mechanical causes. Westfall argues that a concept of "force," replaces aether in Newton's thinking, but Westfall also acknowledges that Newton eventually brings back aether "to provide a mechanical explanation of the forces which had appeared so occult to a generation raised on mechanical philosophy" (395). Westfall goes on to argue that this later aether was anything but a mechanical explanation. My point throughout this section is that Swift represented the *Principia* as a (failed) struggle between the desire for a universal mechanical system (of aether or vapors) and the occult. Although Westfall is certain Newton was not dealing in occult phenomena (how could he be? all modern science arises from Newtonian dynamics), Westfall and other historians of science are equally clear that Newton himself was at times tormented by his inability to give a mechanical explanation to the forces he had come to believe in.

19. Newton, *Mathematical Principles*, 18. All translations are taken from this edition. Unless otherwise indicated in the text, all quoted passages appear in the first edition, *Philosophiae naturalis principia mathematica* (London, 1687).

20. Westfall's *Force in Newton's Physics* offers the fullest explanation of the relationship between Newton's atomist philosophy and his concepts of force and aether. See note 18, above, for a discussion of how Westfall's reading of these issues relates to Swift's representation of Newton's work.

21. Aero duplo densior in duplo spatio quadruplus est. Idem intellige de Nive et Pulveribus per compressionem vel liquefactionem condensatis. Et par est ratio corporum omnium, quae per causas quascunq; diversimode condensantur. Medii interea, si quod fuerit, interstitia partium libere pervadentis, hic nullam rationem habeo. Hanc autem quantitatem sub nomine corporis vel Massae in sequentibus passim intelligo. Innotescit ea per corporis cujusq; pondus, nam ponderi proportionalem esse reperi per experimenta pendulorum accuratissime instituta, uti posthac docebitur.

Philosophiae naturalis principia mathematica, 1.

22. Westfall, whose authority in reading Newton I yield to completely, would, I think, ask me to make a number of distinctions here that I have not. My justification is that I am not attempting here, as Westfall does, to trace the subtle—and in the context of Newton's work, important—conceptual developments in Newton's thought. Rather, I am noticing that Swift's satire represents the anxiety Westfall traces in Newton's work, particularly in relation to Newton's concern that the "how" of his theory of attraction might be understood—given its seventeenth-century context—in terms of the occult. In fifteen particularly remarkable pages of *Force in Newton's Physics*, 386–400, Westfall moves from Newton's denial that "forces were equivalent to occult qualities" (386), through the good reasons—all relating to seventeenth-century mechanical philosophy—that Newton "was undoubtedly wise to conceal his full philosophy of nature when he published the *Principia*" (388), to Newton's reintroduction of aether later in his career to avoid being seen as endorsing occult qualities (395). Westfall is intent on showing that Newton moved definitively from the aether of older mechanical philosophy to the concept of "force" on which Newtonian dynamics rest. The satirist, however, is intent on representing the hubris inherent in the anxiety itself. That is, mechanical philosophy is not for Swift any defense from occult theory, but ultimately a species of it. Every claim to universal or totalizing knowledge must have at bottom an occult or "revealed" point of origin. Seeing aether in the *Principia* is not to deny Westfall's (and those of others') distinctions, but to recognize with Westfall that

Newton in the *Principia* is acutely aware of and troubled by the explanation at least some of his readers will see as lacking in his great work. Swift would have the *Principia* understood as being of a piece with other "mad" visions—a theory of near perfect rational integrity so long as one allows or overlooks certain "airy" assumptions.

23. See Andries Sarlemijn's "Newton's Pendulum Experiment," 113–31. Sarlemijn emphasizes that "the result of the experiment was not the rejection of the existence of aether . . . but only of it having a mechanical force," 117. In *Never at Rest*, Westfall traces Newton's thought on a nonmaterial form of ether to the alchemical agent, 377; subsequently B. J. T. Dobbs argues that Newton's understanding of Stoicism and other classical sources informed Newton's concept of the force that acts on bodies over a distance. See "Newton's Alchemy," 55–80.

24. Though it may appear that I am challenging recent Newtonian scholarship on Newton's concept of aether, my reading is indebted to that scholarship and substantially in accord with it. This may be illustrated by looking at comments of I. Bernard Cohen, who is, relative to B. J. T. Dobbs, cautious in assigning scientific significance to Newton's alchemical or theological concepts. In his introduction to Newton's *Papers and Letters*, Cohen says the *Principia* is "relatively free of references to aether," 11. But it becomes clear that what Cohen means is that relative to the frequency and importance of discussions of ether in Newton's work, aether is seldom mentioned in the *Principia*. Cohen notes, 11, n. 22, that aether figures large in Newton's discussion of comets in the *Principia* despite the pendulum experiments, which were directly concerned with aether. Elsewhere Cohen claims that the concept Newton tried to explain by way of aether "deeply troubled" him from the time of the *Principia* until his death, and all attempts to explain it "failed." Cohen characterizes Newton's return to aether in the General Scholium "a confession of failure." See Cohen's "Newton's Third Law," 40, 44.

25. Keynes's "Newton the Man" was published in 1947. For a discussion of the history of Newton's manuscripts on theological and alchemical issues, see Westfall's *Never at Rest*, 875–77.

26. See Popkin's "Newton's Biblical Theology," 81–97.

27. Indeed recent scholarship emphasizes the important connections between Newton's physics and modern chemistry. See W. Hornix's "Chemical Affinity," 201–15.

28. See John L. McMullan's *The Canting Crew*, 60.

29. See Westfall's *Life*, chap. 10; Christianson's *In the Presence of the Creator*, chap. 15.

30. Quoted from the documentary film, *The Day After Trinity*.

31. Margaret Jacob suggests Newton had precisely the kind of influence Swift feared he would have:

> On the basis of Newton's interest in the Boyle lectures, we must conclude that this foremost English scientist was, in a social and ideological sense, a Newtonian. He condoned the social vision articulated by Bentley, Clarke, and others; he lent the prestige of his achievements to what became in their hands an enlightened philosophy, in support of sober self-interest, of man's domination over nature, and of the pursuit of practical, material interests—in short, an ideology that could justify commercial capitalism and empire. (*Radical Enlightenment*, 90–91)

Translating from postcolonial to Swiftian terms, one might say that once the Anglican pulpit was used to articulate the gospel as a system that "after the fate of other systems" would be exploded, the cultural morality of a *Modest Proposal* was just ahead.

32. The lampoon of transubstantiation (bread changed to mutton) in section 4 of *A Tale* turns on the scholastic attempt to apply an Aristotelian natural philosophy to religious mysteries. The alchemist's transmutation in *A Tale* is the mirror image of transubstantiation, working from the material to spiritual.

33. *The World*, 28.

34. Dobbs, *The Janus Faces*, 8.

CHAPTER 7, *Critical Nemesis*

1. One particularly perceptive discussion of the change that did take place appears in Brian A. Connery's "Persona" in *Cutting Edges*.

2. For a discussion of Clarke's attack on *A Tale*, see Boyle's "Profane and Debauched Deist."

3. Bentley's Newtonian theology is discussed at length in Chapter 6, above.

4. Here I am specifically arguing that the paths are identical—narcissistic pursuits of happiness being manifested in individual and culture madness. Freud and Swift clearly have some different ideas about where the cultural madness manifests itself. Freud sees it in the religion that Swift publicly professed; Swift sees it in the modern scientific discourse of which, at least at times, Freud hoped his work would be taken as a fundamental part. Swift and Freud's respective readings of the myth of Narcissus are also discussed in Chapter 2, above.

5. Leavis is using D. H. Lawrence's phrase in positioning Lawrence's work in opposition to the negative influences of Joyce.

6. Here I am assuming rather than countering the more obvious interpretation of the allegory that sees the English Church escaping the combined forces of Roman Catholicism and Puritanism in the reign of James II. The fate of Martin in *A Tale* after the revolution is perceived through his representatives in *A Tale*, Wotton and Bentley chief among them, and the description of his pulpit being used to adumbrate "the writings of our *modern saints* in Great Britain."

7. Sure that Swift would have liked to "communicate his love for the Established Church," Ehrenpreis concludes "Swift would have accomplished his aim best by leaving Martin out," 1: 188.

8. See Boyle's "Ehrenpreis's *Swift*."

9. This is discussed in detail in Chapter 5, above.

10. See Maurice J. O'Sullivan's "Swift's Pedro de Mendez," (1984) and "'How Now?'" (1986).

11. The critical consensus on Mendez extended only so far as his characterization itself. Why a good man appears so near the end of the *Travels* was a central, much disputed question of the so-called "hard" and "soft" schools of Swift criticism.

WORKS CITED

Aarsleff, Hans. *From Locke to Saussure: Essays on the Study of Language and Intellectual History*. Minneapolis: University of Minnesota Press, 1982.

Adams, Percy G. *Travelers and Travel Liars, 1660–1800*. 1962. Reprint, New York: Dover, 1980.

———. *Travel Literature and the Evolution of the Novel*. Lexington: University Press of Kentucky, 1983.

Appleton, William W. *A Cycle of Cathay: The Chinese Vogue in England During the Seventeenth and Eighteenth Centuries*. New York: Columbia University Press, 1957.

Aristotle. *The Complete Works of Aristotle*. Ed. Jonathan Barnes. 2 vols. Princeton: Princeton University Press, 1984.

Asimov, Isaac. *The Annotated Gulliver's Travels*. New York: Clarkson N. Potter, 1980.

Bacon, Francis. *Advancement of Learning*. Ed. Arthur Johnson. Oxford: Oxford University Press, 1974.

———. *The Works of Francis Bacon*. Ed. James Spedding, Robert Leslie Ellis, and Douglas Denon Heath. 14 vols. London, 1857–74.

Bakhtin, M. M. *The Dialogic Imagination*. Trans. Caryl Emerson and Michael Holquist. Ed. Michael Holquist. Austin: University of Texas Press, 1981.

———. *Problems of Dostoevsky's Poetics*. Trans. and ed. Caryl Emerson. Minneapolis: University of Minnesota Press, 1984.

Barnett, Louise K. "Deconstructing *Gulliver's Travels*: Modern Readers and the Problematic of Genre." In *The Genres of Gulliver's Travels*, edited by Frederik N. Smith. Newark: University of Delaware Press, 1990. 230–45.

Bentley, Richard. *Eight Boyle Lectures on Atheism.* Facsimile reprint of sermons published 1692–93. New York: Garland Publishing, 1976.

Berman, Jeffrey. *Narcissism and the Novel.* New York: New York University Press, 1990.

Bernstein, Michael André. *Bitter Carnival: Ressentiment and the Abject Hero.* Princeton: Princeton University Press, 1992.

Bettelheim, Bruno. *Freud and Man's Soul.* New York: Vintage Books, 1984.

Blanchard, W. Scott. *Scholar's Bedlam: Menippean Satire in the Renaissance.* Lewisburg, Penn.: Bucknell University Press, 1995.

Boyle, Frank T. "Ehrenpreis's *Swift* and the Date of the *Sentiments of a Church-of-England Man.*" *Swift Studies* 6 (1991): 30–37.

———. "Heretic in the Modern 'Empire of Reason': Swift, Deism and Sir William Temple's Chinese Utopia." Ph.D. diss., Trinity College, Dublin, 1989.

———. "Profane and Debauched Deist: Swift in the Contemporary Response to *A Tale of a Tub.*" *Eighteenth-Century Ireland* 3 (1988): 25–38.

Boyle, Robert. *A Defence of the Doctrine Touching the Spring and Weight of Air.* Oxford, 1682.

———. *New Experiments Physico-Mechanical, Touching the Air.* 3d ed. Oxford, 1682.

Brown, Norman O. "The Excremental Vision." In *Swift: A Collection of Essays*, edited by Ernest Tuveson, 31–54. Englewood Cliffs, N.J.: Prentice-Hall, 1964.

Bury, J. B. *The Idea of Progress.* 1932. Reprint, New York: Dover, 1987.

Christianson, Gale E. *In the Presence of the Creator: Isaac Newton and His Time.* New York: The Free Press (Macmillan), 1984.

Clarke, Samuel. *A Demonstration of the Being and Attributes of God: More Particularly in Answer to Mr. Hobbs, Spinoza, and Their Followers.* London, 1705.

———. *A Discourse Concerning the Unchangeable Obligation of Natural Religion.* 2d ed. London, 1708.

———. *The Works of Samuel Clarke.* 4 vols. London, 1738.

Cohen, I. B. "Newton's Third Law and Universal Gravity." In *Newton's Scientific and Philosophical Legacy*, edited by P. B. Scheurer and G. Debrock, 25–54. Dordrecht: Kluwer Academic, 1988.

Congreve, William. *The Complete Plays of William Congreve.* Ed. Herbert Davis. Chicago: University of Chicago Press, 1967.

Connery, Brian A. "Persona As Pretender and Reader As Subject." In

Cutting Edges: Postmodern Critical Essays on Eighteenth-Century Satire, edited by James E. Gill. Knoxville: University of Tennessee Press, 1995.

Copleston, Frederick, S.J. *A History of Philosophy*. 6 vols. New York: Doubleday, 1946–60.

Cornelius, Paul. *Languages in Seventeenth- and Early Eighteenth-Century Imaginary Voyages*. Geneva: Libraire Droz, 1965.

Cowley, Abraham. *The Complete Works in Verse and Prose*. Ed. A. B. Grosart. 2 vols. Edinburgh: T. & A. Constable; Chertsey Worthies' Library, 1881. Reprint, New York: AMS, 1967.

Craven, Kenneth. *Jonathan Swift and the Millennium of Madness*. Leiden: Brill, 1992.

Curry, Walter Clyde. *Milton's Ontology, Cosmogony and Physics*. Lexington: University of Kentucky Press, 1957.

Danielson, Dennis Richard. *Milton's Good God: A Study in Literary Theodicy*. New York: Cambridge University Press, 1982.

Davis, Herbert. *Jonathan Swift: Essays on His Satire and Other Studies*. New York: Oxford University Press, 1964.

The Day After Trinity: J. Robert Oppenheimer and the Atomic Bomb. Jon Else (producer), Pyramid Films, 1980.

Dear, Peter. *Discipline and Experience: The Mathematical Way in the Scientific Revolution*. Chicago: University of Chicago Press, 1995.

De Porte, Michael. "Night Thoughts in Swift." *The Sewanee Review* 98 (fall 1990): 646–63.

Derrida, Jacques. *The Post Card: From Socrates to Freud and Beyond*. Trans. Alan Bass. Chicago: University of Chicago Press, 1987.

———. *Writing and Difference*. Trans. Alan Bass. Chicago: University of Chicago Press, 1978.

Descartes, René. *The Philosophical Works of Descartes*. Trans. E. S. Haldane and G. R. T. Ross. 2 vols. (1911). Reprint, Cambridge, Eng.: Cambridge University Press, 1973.

Dobbs, B. J. T. *The Janus Faces of Genius: The Role of Alchemy in Newton's Thought*. Cambridge, Eng.: Cambridge University Press, 1991.

———. "Newton's Alchemy and His 'Active Principle' of Gravitation." In *Newton's Scientific and Philosophical Legacy*, edited by P. B. Scheurer and G. Debrock, 55–80. Dordrecht: Kluwer Academics, 1988.

Donne, John. *Poetical Works*. Ed. Sir Herbert Grierson. Oxford: Oxford University Press, 1977.

Dunne, George H., S.J. *Generation of Giants: The Story of the Jesuits in China in the Last Decades of the Ming Dynasty*. Notre Dame, Ind.: University of Notre Dame Press, 1962.

Dyrud, Jarl. "Narcissus and Nemesis." *Psychiatry* 46, no. 2 (May 1983): 106–12.

Ehrenpreis, Irvin. "The Origins of *Gulliver's Travels*." In *Fair Liberty Was All His Cry*, edited by A. Norman Jeffares, 200–225. New York: St. Martin's Press, 1967.

———. *Swift: The Man, His Work, and the Age*. 3 vols. Cambridge, Mass.: Harvard University Press, 1962–83.

———. "Three Parts Invention." *New York Review* 30 (19 Jan. 1984): 37–39.

Elias, A. C., Jr. *Swift at Moor Park*. Philadelphia: University of Pennsylvania Press, 1982.

Elliott, Robert C. *The Power of Satire*. Princeton: Princeton University Press, 1960.

———. "The Satirist Satirized." In *Modern Critical Views of Jonathan Swift*, edited by Harold Bloom, 23–45. New York: Chelsea House, 1986.

Faber, Richard. *The Brave Courtier*. London: Faber & Faber, 1983.

Feingold, Mordechai. "Newton and Locke." In *Newton's Scientific and Philosophical Legacy*, edited by P. B. Scheurer and G. Debrock, 291–308. Dordrecht: Kluwer Academic, 1987.

Fielding, Henry. *Joseph Andrews with* Shamela *and Related Writings*. Ed. Homer Goldberg. New York: W. W. Norton, 1987.

Flynn, Carol Houlihan. *The Body in Swift and Defoe*. Cambridge, Eng.: Cambridge University Press, 1990.

Fox, Christopher. "The Myth of Narcissus in Swift's *Travels*." *Eighteenth-Century Studies* 20 (fall 1986): 17–33.

———. "Defining Eighteenth-Century Psychology: Some Problems and Perspectives." In *Psychology and Literature in the Eighteenth Century*, edited by Christopher Fox. New York: AMS, 1987.

Franke, Wolfgang. *China and the West: The Cultural Encounter, 13th to 20th Centuries*. Trans. R. A. Wilson. Oxford: Basil Blackwell, 1967.

Freud, Sigmund. *Beyond the Pleasure Principle*. Trans. James Strachey. New York: W. W. Norton, 1961.

———. *Civilization and Its Discontents*. Trans. James Strachey. New York: W. W. Norton, 1961.

———. "On Narcissism." In *The Standard Edition of the Complete Psychological Works of Sigmund Freud*, translated by James Strachey. London: Hogarth, 1957.

Garber, Daniel. *Descartes' Metaphysical Physics*. Chicago: University of Chicago Press, 1992.

Gasché, Rodolphe. *The Tain of the Mirror.* Cambridge, Mass.: Harvard University Press, 1986.

Gill, James E., ed. *Cutting Edges: Postmodern Critical Essays on Eighteenth-Century Satire.* Knoxville: University of Tennessee Press, 1995.

Gilson, Étienne. *Jean Duns Scot: Introduction a ses Positions Fondamentales.* Paris: Libraire Philosophique J. Vrin, 1952.

Golden, Leon. "Aristotle on the Pleasures of Comedy." In *Essays on Aristotle's Poetics*, edited by Amélie Oksenberg Rorty. Princeton: Princeton University Press, 1992.

Gossin, Pamela. "Poetic Resolutions of Scientific Revolutions: Astronomy and the Literary Imagination of Donne, Swift, and Hardy." Ph.D. diss., University of Wisconsin, 1989. Abstract in *Dissertation Abstracts International* 51–01A (1989): 273.

Griffin, Dustin. *Satire: A Critical Reintroduction.* Lexington: University Press of Kentucky, 1994.

Guy, Basil. *The French Image of China Before and After Voltaire.* Vol. 21 of *Studies of Voltaire and the Eighteenth Century.* Ed. Theodore Besterman. Geneva: Institute et Musée Voltaire, 1963.

Harth, Phillip. *Swift and Anglican Rationalism: The Religious Background of* A Tale of a Tub. Chicago: University of Chicago Press, 1961.

Hollander, John. *The Figure of Echo: A Mode of Allusion in Milton and After.* Berkeley: University of California Press, 1981.

Hornix, W. "Chemical Affinity in the 19th Century and Newtonianism." In *Newton's Scientific and Philosophical Legacy*, edited by P. B. Scheurer and G. Debrock, 201–15. Dordrecht: Kluwer Academic, 1987.

Jacob, Margaret C. *The Cultural Meaning of the Scientific Revolution.* Philadelphia: Temple University Press, 1988.

———. *The Newtonians and the English Revolution, 1689–1700.* New York: Cornell University Press, 1976.

———. *The Radical Enlightenment: Pantheists, Freemasons and Republicans.* London: George Allen & Unwin, 1981.

Jaffe, Nora Crow. *The Poet Swift.* Hanover, N.H.: University Press of New England, 1977.

Jarrell, Mackie L. "The Handwriting of the Lilliputians." *Philological Quarterly* 38, no. 1 (Jan. 1958).

"Jesuits in the Far East." Vol. 12 of *Hakluytus Posthumus or Purchas His Pilgrims*, edited by Samuel Purchas, 239–331. Glasgow: J. MacLehose and Sons, 1905–7.

Johnson, Cyraina E. "The Echo of Narcissus." *International Studies in Philosophy* 22, no. 1 (1990): 37–50.

Keener, Frederick M. *The Chain of Becoming: The Philosophical Tale, the Novel, and a Neglected Realism of the Enlightenment: Swift, Montesquieu, Voltaire, Johnson, and Austen*. New York: Columbia University Press, 1983.

Kelly, Ann Cline. "After Eden: Gulliver's (Linguistic) Travels." *ELH* 45, no. 1 (spring 1978): 33–54.

———. *Swift and the English Language*. Philadelphia: University of Pennsylvania Press, 1988.

Keynes, John Maynard. "Newton, the Man." In *The Royal Society Tercentenary Celebrations*. Cambridge, Eng.: Cambridge University Press, 1947.

Knoespel, Kenneth J. *Narcissus and the Invention of Personal History*. New York: Garland, 1985.

Kristeva, Julia. *Powers of Horror: An Essay on Abjection*. Trans. Leon S. Roudiez. New York: Columbia University Press, 1982.

Kuhn, Thomas K. *The Structure of Scientific Revolutions*. 2d ed., enl. Chicago: University of Chicago Press, 1970.

Landa, Louis A. *Swift and the Church of Ireland*. 1954. Reprint, Oxford: Oxford University Press, 1965.

———. "Swift, the Mysteries, and Deism." *Texas Studies in English* 23 (1944): 239–56.

La Mothe le Vayer, François de. *Oeuvres*. 7 vols. Dresde, 1756–59.

Leavis, F. R. *The Great Tradition*. New York: Doubleday, 1954.

Leibniz, Gottfried Wilhelm. *Discourse on the Natural Theology of the Chinese*. Trans. Henry Rosemont, Jr. and Daniel J. Cook. Monograph No. 4 of the Society for Asian Comparative Philosophy. Honolulu: University Press Hawaii, 1977.

———. *The Preface to Novissima Sinica*. Trans. Donald F. Lach. Honolulu: University Press Hawaii, 1957.

Levine, Joseph M. *The Battle of the Books: History and Literature in the Augustan Age*. Ithaca, N. Y.: Cornell University Press, 1991.

Locke, John. *An Essay Concerning Human Understanding*. Oxford: Clarendon, 1975.

Lucreti. *De Rerum Natura*. Ed. Cyrillus Bailey (1900). Reprint, Oxford: Clarendon, 1938.

Lund, Roger. "Strange Complicities: Atheism and Conspiracy in *A Tale of a Tub*." *Eighteenth Century Life* 13, no. 3 (Nov. 1989): 34–58.

Marburg-Kirk, Clara. *Sir William Temple: A Seventeenth-Century Libertine*. New Haven, Conn.: Yale University Press, 1932.

McMullan, John L. *The Canting Crew: London's Criminal Underworld, 1550–1700*. New Brunswick, N.J.: Rutgers University Press, 1989.

Merchant, Carolyn. *The Death of Nature*. San Francisco: Harper & Row, 1980.

Milton, John. *Complete Poems and Major Prose*. Ed. Merritt Y. Hughes. New York: Odyssey Press, 1957.

Montag, Warren. *The Unthinkable Swift: The Spontaneous Philosophy of a Church of England Man*. New York: Verso, 1994.

Montagu, Mary Wortley. *The Complete Letters of Lady Mary Wortley Montagu*. Ed. Robert Halsband. Oxford: Clarendon Press, 1966–67.

Montaigne, Michel Eyquem de. *Essais*. Paris: Garnier-Flammarion, 1979.

Nash, Richard. "Entrapment and Ironic Mode in *Tale of a Tub*." *Eighteenth-Century Studies* 24, no. 4 (summer 1991): 415–31.

Nethercot, Arthur H. *Abraham Cowley: The Muse's Hannibal*. 1931. Reissued with expanded notes, New York: Russell & Russell, 1967.

New Catholic Encyclopedia. 17 vols. New York: McGraw Hill, 1967–79.

New, Melvyn. *Telling New Lies*. Gainesville: University Press of Florida, 1992.

Newton, Isaac. *Mathematical Principles of Natural Philosophy*. 2 vols. Trans. Andrew Mott (1729). Ed. Florian Cajori. Berkeley: University of California Press, 1934.

———. *Papers & Letters On Natural Philosophy and Related Documents*. Ed. I. Bernard Cohen. Cambridge, Mass.: Harvard University Press, 1978.

Nicholl, Charles. *The Chemical Theatre*. London: Routledge & Kegan Paul, 1980.

Nicolson, Marjorie Hope. *Newton Demands the Muse*. Princeton: Princeton University Press, 1946.

———, ed. *Science and Imagination*. Ithaca, N.Y.: Cornell University Press, 1956.

———, and Nora M. Mohler. "The Scientific Background of Swift's Voyage to Laputa." In *Science and Imagination*, edited by Marjorie Hope Nicolson. Ithaca, N.Y.: Cornell University Press, 1956.

Nokes, David. *Jonathan Swift, A Hypocrite Reversed: A Critical Biography*. Oxford: Oxford University Press, 1985.

Olson, Richard. "Tory High-Church Opposition to Science and Scientism in the Eighteenth Century: The Works of John Arbuthnot, Jonathan Swift, and Samuel Johnson." In *The Uses of Science in the Age of Newton*, edited by John G. Burke. Berkeley: University of California Press, 1983.

Ormsby-Lennon, Hugh. "Swift's Spirit Reconjured: das Dong-an-sich." *Swift Studies* (1988): 9–78.

Orwell, George, "Politics vs. Literature: An Examination of *Gulliver's Travels*." In *Fair Liberty Was All His Cry*, edited by A. Norman Jeffares. New York: St. Martin's Press, 1967.

Osborne, Dorothy. *The Letters of Dorothy Osborne to Sir William Temple*, edited by G. C. Moore Smith. Oxford: Clarendon, 1928.

O'Sullivan, Maurice J. "'How Now? What Means the Passion at His Name?'" *AN&Q* 24 (May/June 1986): 140–42.

———. "Swift's Pedro de Mendez." *AN&Q* 22 (May/June 1984): 131–33.

Ovid. *Metamorphoses*. Trans. Rolfe Humphries. Bloomington: Indiana University Press, 1983.

Pantoia, Diego de. "Letter of Father Diego De Pantoia, One of the Company of Jesus, to Father Luys De Guzman, Provinciall in the Province of Toledo." Vol. 12 of *Hakluytus Posthumus or Purchas His Pilgrims*, edited by Samuel Purchas, 331–410. Glasgow: J. MacLehose and Sons, 1905–7.

Paracelsus. *Selected Writings*. Ed. Jolande Jacobi. Princeton: Princeton University Press, 1951.

Patey, Douglas Lane. "Swift's Satire on 'Science' and the Structure of *Gulliver's Travels*." *ELH* 58, no. 4 (winter 1991): 809–39.

Paulson, Ronald. *Breaking and Remaking: Aesthetic Practice in England, 1700–1820*. New Brunswick, N.J.: Rutgers University Press, 1989.

———. *Theme and Structure in Swift's* Tale of a Tub. New Haven, Conn.: Yale University Press, 1960.

Pierre, Gerald J. "Gulliver's Voyage to China and Moor Park: The Influence of Sir William Temple upon *Gulliver's Travels*." *Texas Studies in Literature and Language* 17, no. 2 (summer 1975): 427–37.

———. "*The Influence of Sir William Temple upon the Mind and Art of Jonathan Swift*." Ph.D. diss., University of Minnesota, 1970. Abstract in *Dissertation Abstracts International* 32–03A (1970): 1484.

Pinot, Virgile. *La Chine et la formation de l'esprit philosophique en France (1640–1740)*. Geneve: Slatkine Reprints, 1971.

Pinto, Fernam Mendez. "Observations of China, Tartaria, and Other Easterne Parts of the World, Taken out of Fernam Mendez Pinto his Peregrination." Vol. 12 of *Hakluytus Posthumus or Purchas His Pilgrims*, edited by Samuel Purchas, 54–141. Glasgow: J. MacLehose and Sons, 1905–7.

Pocock, J. G. A. *Virtue, Commerce, and History*. Cambridge, Eng.: Cambridge University Press, 1985.

Popkin, Richard H. "Newton's Biblical Theology and His Theological Physics." In *Newton's Scientific and Philosophical Legacy*. Dordrecht: Kluwer Academic, 1988, 81–97.

Porter, Dorothy, and Roy Porter. *Patient's Progress: Doctors and Doctoring in Eighteenth-Century England*. Stanford: Stanford University Press, 1989.

Purchas, Samuel, ed. *Hakluytus Posthumus or Purchas His Pilgrims*. 20 vols. Glasgow: J. MacLehose and Sons, 1905–7.

Rawson, Claude. *Gulliver and the Gentle Reader: Studies in Swift and Our Time*. London: Routledge & Kegan Paul, 1973.

———. *Order from Confusion Sprung: Studies in Eighteenth-Century Literature from Swift to Cowper*. London: George Allen & Unwin, 1985.

———. *Satire and Sentiment, 1660–1830*. Cambridge, Eng.: Cambridge University Press, 1994.

Real, Hermann J., and Heinz J. Vienken. "What's in a Name: Pedro De Mendez Again." *AN&Q* 24 (May/June 1986), 136–40.

Rhodes, Richard. *The Making of the Atomic Bomb*. New York: Simon & Schuster, 1986.

Rodino, Richard. "Splendide Mendax." *PMLA* 106 (Oct. 1991): 1054–70.

Rorty, Amélie Oksenberg, ed. *Essays on Aristotle's Poetics*. Princeton: Princeton University Press, 1992.

Rosenheim, Edward W. *Swift and the Satirist's Art*. Chicago: University of Chicago Press, 1963.

Rousseau, G. S. "Science and Medicine at Leiden." In *The Age of William III and Mary II: Power, Politics and Patronage, 1688–1702*, edited by Robert Maccubbin and Martha Hamilton-Phillips, 195–201. Williamsburg, Vir.: The College of William and Mary, 1989.

Rowbotham, Arnold H. "The Impact of Confucianism on Seventeenth-Century Europe." *The Far Eastern Quarterly* 4, no. 3 (May 1945): 224–42.

———. *Missionary and Mandarin: The Jesuits at the Court of China*. Berkeley: University of California Press, 1942.

———. "Voltaire, Sinophile." *PMLA* 4 (Dec. 1932), 1050–65.

Rumrich, John Peter. "Milton, Duns Scotus, and the Fall of Satan." *Journal of the History of Ideas* (Jan. 1985): 33–49.

Said, Edward W. "Opponents, Audiences, Constituencies and Community." In *Postmodern Culture*, edited by H. Foster. London: Pluto Press, 1985.

———. *Orientalism*. New York: Vintage Books, 1979.
———. *The World, the Text, and the Critic*. Cambridge, Mass.: Harvard University Press, 1983.
Sampson, R. V. *Progress in the Age of Reason*. Cambridge, Mass.: Harvard University Press, 1956.
Sarlemijn, Andries. "Newton's Pendulum Experiment and Specific Characteristics of His Scientific Method in Physics." In *Newton's Scientific and Philosophical Legacy*. Ed. P. B. Scheurer and G. Debrock, 113–31. Dordrecht: Kluwer Academic, 1988.
Schakel, Peter J. *The Poetry of Jonathan Swift: Allusion and the Development of a Poetic Style*. Madison: University of Wisconsin Press, 1978.
Schiebinger, Londa. *The Mind Has No Sex? Women in the Origins of Modern Science*. Cambridge, Mass.: Harvard University Press, 1989.
Schillebeeck, Edward. *The Eucharist*. London: Sheed and Ward, 1968.
Scriblerus, Martinus. *Memoirs of the Extraordinary Life, Work, and Discoveries of Martinus Scriblerus*. Ed. Charles Kerby-Miller. Oxford: Oxford University Press, 1988.
Seidel, Michael. *Satiric Inheritance: Rabelais to Sterne*. Princeton: Princeton University Press, 1979.
Shapin, Steven, and Simon Schaffer. *Leviathan and the Air-Pump: Hobbes, Boyle, and the Experimental Life*, including a translation by Simon Schaffer of Thomas Hobbes's, *Dialogus physicus de natura*. Princeton: Princeton University Press, 1985.
Smith, Frederik N. "Scientific Discourse: *Gulliver's Travels* and *The Philosophical Transactions*." In *The Genres of Gulliver's Travels*, edited by Frederik N. Smith, 139–62. Newark: University of Delaware Press, 1990.
Spence, Jonathan. *The Memory Palace of Matteo Ricci*. New York: Viking, 1984.
Spivak, Gayatri Chakravorty. "Echo." *New Literary History* 24, no. 1 (winter 1993): 17–43.
Sprat, Thomas. *History of the Royal Society*. London, 1667.
Starkman, Miriam Kosh. *Swift's Satire on Learning in* A Tale of a Tub. Princeton: Princeton University Press, 1950.
Sutherland, W. O. S., Jr. *The Art of the Satirist: Essays on the Satire of Augustan England*. Austin: The University of Texas Press, 1965.
Swift, Jonathan. *The Complete Poems*. Ed. Pat Rogers. New York: Penguin Books, 1983.
———. *The Correspondence of Jonathan Swift*. Ed. Harold Williams. 5 vols. Oxford: Clarendon, 1963–65.

———. *The Prose Works of Jonathan Swift*. Ed. Herbert Davis, et al. 16 vols. Oxford: Basil Blackwell, 1939–69.
———. *The Oxford Authors Swift*. Ed. Angus Ross and David Woolley. Oxford: Oxford University Press, 1984.
Taaffe, James G. *Abraham Cowley*. New York: Twayne Publishers, 1972.
Takase, Fumiko. "The Houyhnhnms and the Eighteenth-Century *Goût Chinois*." *English Studies* 61 (Oct. 1980): 408–17.
Tatler, The. Ed. Donald F. Bond. 3 vols. Oxford: Clarendon Press, 1987.
Temple, Sir William. *The Works of Sir William Temple*. 4 vols. New York: Greenwood Press, 1968.
Toulmin, Stephen. *Cosmopolis: The Hidden Agenda of Modernity*. Chicago: University of Chicago Press, 1990.
Trevor-Roper, Hugh. "The Paracelsian Movement." In *Renaissance Essays*. Chicago: University of Chicago Press, 1985.
———. "A Jesuit Adventure." *New York Review* 32 (13 June 1985): 12–15.
Trigault, Nicolas, and Matteo Ricci. "A Discourse of the Kingdom of China." Vol. 12 of *Hakluytus Posthumus or Purchas His Pilgrims*, edited by Samuel Purchas (411–69). Glasgow: J. MacLehose and Sons, 1905–7.
Turbayne, Colin Murray. *The Myth of Metaphor*. Rev. ed. Columbia: University of South Carolina Press, 1970.
Valignano, Alessandro. "Admiranda Regini Sinensis." In *De Rebus Japonicis, Indicis, et Pervanis Epistolae Recentiores*, edited by J. Hayus. Antwerp, 1605.
Van Den Abbeele, Georges. *Travel as Metaphor from Montaigne to Rousseau*. Minneapolis: University of Minnesota Press, 1992.
Vaughn, Thomas. *The Works of Thomas Vaughn*. Ed. Alan Rudrum. Oxford: Clarendon, 1984.
Voigt, Milton. *Swift and the Twentieth Century*. Detroit: Wayne State University Press, 1964.
Voltaire. *Lettres Chinoises, Oeuvres*. Vol. 29. Ed. L. Moland, 471. Paris, 1879.
Vossius, Isaac. *De Septuaginta Interpretibus eorumque Translatione et Chronologia Dissertationes*. The Hague, 1661.
———. *Dissertatio de vera aetate mundi qua ostenditur natale mundi tempus annis minimun 1440 vulgarem ram anticipare*. The Hague, 1659.
———. *Variarum Observationum Liber*. London, 1685.
Webster, Charles. *From Paracelsus to Newton: Magic in the Making of Modern Science*. Cambridge, Eng.: Cambridge University Press, 1982.
Weinsheimer, Joel C. *Eighteenth-Century Hermeneutics*. New Haven, Conn.: Yale University Press, 1993.

Westfall, Richard S. *Force in Newton's Physics: The Science of Dynamics in the Seventeenth Century*. New York: American Elsevier, 1971.
———. *Never at Rest*. Cambridge, Eng.: Cambridge University Press, 1980.
Wilkins, John. *An Essay Toward a Real Character and Philosophic Language*. London, 1668.
Williams, Kathleen. *Jonathan Swift and the Age of Compromise*. Lawrence: University of Kansas Press, 1958.
Wotton, William. *Reflections upon Ancient and Modern Learning*. London, 1694.
———. *A Defense [of the Reflections upon Ancient and Modern Learning] . . . With Observations upon* A Tale of a Tub. London, 1705.
Yolton, John W. *Perceptual Acquaintance from Descartes to Reid*. Oxford: Basil Blackwell, 1984
Young, B. W. "'See *Mystery* to *Mathematics* Fly!': Pope's *Dunciad* and the Critique of Religious Rationalism." *Eighteenth-Century Studies* 26 (spring 1993): 435–48.

INDEX

In this index an "f" after a number indicates a separate reference on the next page, and an "ff" indicates separate references on the next two pages. A continuous discussion over two or more pages is indicated by a span of page numbers, e.g., "57–59," and *passim* is used for a cluster of references in close but not consecutive sequence. Character names are entered in quotation marks followed by the title of the work in which they appear, e.g., "Martin" in *A Tale of a Tub*.

Library of Congress Cataloging-in-Publication Data

Boyle, Frank
Swift as nemesis : modernity and its satirist / Frank Boyle.
p. cm.
Includes bibliographical references (p.) and index.
ISBN 0-8047-3436-4 (cloth : alk. paper)
1. Swift, Jonathan, 1667–1745—Criticism and interpretation.
2. Satire, English—Ireland—History and criticism.
3. Civilization, Modern, in literature. I. Title.
PR3728.S2 B69 2000
828'.509—dc21 99-087972

∞ This book is printed on acid-free, archival-quality paper.

Original printing 2000

Last figure below indicates the year of this printing:
09 08 07 06 05 04 03 02 01 00

Designed by James P. Brommer
Typeset in 10.5/13 Bembo and Carpenter display